STUDIES IN HISTORICAL

Rural Settlement
in
Britain

STUDIES IN HISTORICAL GEOGRAPHY

Also published in this series

Southern Africa
A. J. CHRISTOPHER

Finland
MICHAEL JONES

STUDIES IN HISTORICAL GEOGRAPHY

RURAL SETTLEMENT
in
BRITAIN

by

BRIAN K ROBERTS

DAWSON · ARCHON BOOKS

First published in 1977

Wm Dawson & Sons Ltd, Cannon House
Folkestone, Kent, England

Archon Books, The Shoe String Press, Inc
995 Sherman Avenue, Hamden, Connecticut 06514 USA

British Library Cataloguing in Publication Data

Roberts, Brian K
    Rural settlement in Britain. – (Studies
in historical geography.)
    Bibl. – Index
    ISBN 0–7129–0701–7
    ISBN 0–208–01621–X (Archon Books)
    ISSN 0308–6607
    301.35'0941   GF127   LC76–030000
    Rural geography
    Anthropo-geography – Great Britain

Printed in Great Britain
by W & J Mackay Limited, Chatham
by photo-litho

To my wife

In succession

Houses rise and fall, crumble, are extended,
Are removed, destroyed, restored, or in their place
Is an open field, or a factory, or a by-pass.
Old stone to new building, old timber to new fires,
Old fires to ashes, and ashes to the earth
Which is already flesh, fur and faeces,
Bone of man and beast, cornstalk and leaf.

T. S. Eliot, *East Coker*

Contents

Illustrations

Preface

THE BRITISH ISLES are notable for the rich variety of rural landscapes found within their boundaries, and this diversity provides an essential background for numerous works of literature, a framework for countless planning problems and, more importantly, a setting for the lives of the people who live, work and play amid the varied scenes. This volume is an exploration of the rural roots of Britain, and it examines some of the forces creating and remaking the distinctive landscapes of rural settlement. The approach adopted is partly chronological, partly systematic, and the aim has been to discuss a series of generalized situations within which particular cases can be studied. The material selected has been conditioned in part by the need to achieve a measure of balance, and in part by the author's own interests. Many of the patterns and models discussed in Chapters 4 and 5 have proved useful when examining specific areas or questions in the field, and it is in this real world context that the distinction between site and situation, the effects of village expansion or contraction, or the breaking down of an individual settlement into its component plan elements become more than mere academic exercises. The simple models used in this volume form a framework within which questions can be asked, problems defined and explanations attempted. The study has been written in a way that it is hoped will be useful for undergraduates, sixth-form students, teachers and indeed all those with an interest in the countryside. It briefly covers such basic ground as settlement contrasts in Britain, some of the problems of prehistoric and Roman settlement, the evidence of Domesday Book and population trends, while within three key systematic chapters the book examines aspects of the practical manifestations of man-land relationships in the study of settlement patterns, village and farmstead forms, and the difficult but fundamental question of settlement continuity. Above all, the role of time is emphasized, or more properly the operation of various processes through time in the creation of our existing heritage of rural settlement patterns and forms.

B. K. Roberts

1

Man, Land and Time in Britain

THE BRITISH ISLES are notable for the diverse landscapes found within their relatively small area, and there is no doubt that long before the traumatic events of the Industrial Revolution of the late-eighteenth century strong regional contrasts in rural life were already present. These contrasts, still visible in spite of industrialization, are deep-seated and are broadly the result of two factors. First, within relatively short distances, usually little more than a dozen or so miles, there are marked changes in the physical geography. This involves variations in the nature of the land, the terrain, soils, climate, and hence in the scenery which develops from them. Furthermore, the intricately indented outline — there being some four hundred islands within the British Isles of which more than two hundred are inhabited by man — the latitudinal extent, and the variable weather conditions, involving exposure to both marine and continental influences, ensure the presence of a striking variety of habitats, each of which presents differing opportunities, challenges and rewards. Secondly, this diversity extends to the people, and through the last four millenia successive movements of folk — conquerors and refugees, traders and missionaries, peasants and aristocrats — have created a complex network of communities living on and off the land. In the centuries before large-scale industrialization most of these groups were bound to the soil, relying directly upon the successful succession of sowings and reapings in what has been aptly termed the 'everlasting circle' of birth, procreation and death. The Industrial Revolution, however it be defined, in essence involved a fundamental break with this past, and saw the application of inanimate energy in the form of fossil fuels to certain tasks of production, making possible increased levels of output,

13

product standardization, and extended consumption. This has, throughout the more 'developed' nations of the world, severed the ancient bonds between man and land, and created a world-wide superstructure of trade and financial life, although it is worth noting that even today no more than 25 per cent of the total world population is living in urban clusters in excess of 20,000 folk. This volume is an exploration of our own rural roots in Britain prior to industrialization.

The British Isles reveal a remarkable variety of forms and patterns of settlement, and although over 80 per cent of the population now lives in urban areas it is increasingly important to appreciate that these are superimposed on former rural landscapes and that, particularly during the last two centuries and at an ever-accelerating pace, the growing towns have engulfed old villages, hamlets, farmsteads, woods and fields. Improved transport facilities, particularly motor cars, are encouraging town workers to move out into the countryside in ever-increasing numbers, and this leads directly to the further dissolution of those rural landscapes which we have inherited. This volume attempts to explain the factors underlying the development of the diverse rural landscapes of Britain, and stresses the importance of the time element. Britain is an old country, in spite of the fact that it long remained marginal to the important developments of the ancient and classical worlds, and it is necessary to think in terms of at least six thousand years of occupation, beginning with the incursions of the first farmers about 4,000 years before the birth of Christ. This is no more than eighty-five lifetimes if we reckon in terms of three-score years and ten; put this way it sounds shorter, but it is a long, long time, and most people, until comparatively recently, have failed to live their allotted life span. In dealing with such a lengthy period, with all that this means in terms of human life and cultural advance, it is inevitable that the character of the evidence changes substantially, and for this reason it has been decided that the period between the end of Roman Britain and the mid-eighteenth century warrants particular attention. The selection of this phase sidesteps the thorny problem of treating in detail a settlement landscape which has to be reconstructed entirely from archaeological sources, and it carries the story forward to a time when the rural landscapes familiar today were established but had yet to suffer the complex changes wrought by industrialization and the transport revolution of the twentieth century.

Contrasts in Settlement

The modern motorist speeding along one of the new motorways is too often hardly aware of the countryside except as a setting for the continuing sweep of the road. But let him leave the highway and the main roads and he is at once sharply conscious of more difficult driving conditions as the road twists and turns for no apparent purpose, let alone a logical reason, and he cannot fail to become aware of the presence of distinctive places which force themselves on his attention as the road passes through market towns and villages, and villages and hamlets. The great routeways since Roman times, the north-south route to the east of the Pennines, the route to the North West and Wales via Shrewsbury and Chester, and the route west from London to Bristol have always had a tendency to run directly, but most main roads following traditional routes tend to be less direct, for they developed to serve local communities rather than the long-distance traveller. The motorist on the by-ways soon becomes aware of certain fundamental contrasts: in some regions the dwellings are concentrated into villages with farmhouses, cottages and outbuildings clustering tightly around a church, a road junction or the gates of a great house, while such single farms as do occur lie thinly scattered in the intervening fields. In contrast, a dozen or so miles further on, villages are scarce, and farms, cottages and even churches seem scattered, sometimes in isolation, sometimes in small clusters. Within Britain four zones can in fact be recognized, each characterized by differing settlement patterns (Fig 1). Three of these are dominated by nucleated rural settlements, with the individual farms, houses and cottages forming clusters of varying sizes. Differences in cluster-size and differences in the extent to which the pattern is made up of single dwellings or clusters serve to differentiate between the zones. Thus, the southeast and east of the country are dominated by small clusters, hamlets, interspersed with many scattered homesteads, while occasional larger villages and market towns give texture to the scene. To the west, extending from the Channel northwards, through Dorset, Somerset, Gloucestershire, Oxfordshire, the Midland counties, Yorkshire, Durham and Northumberland, is a second zone, dominated by villages, although scattered farms and hamlets do appear. In the third zone, the West Midlands and much of Cheshire and Lancashire, the emphasis is again on hamlet settlements, smaller clusters, which extend westwards to the Welsh Border country and as a long tongue along the south coast of Wales, while in the West

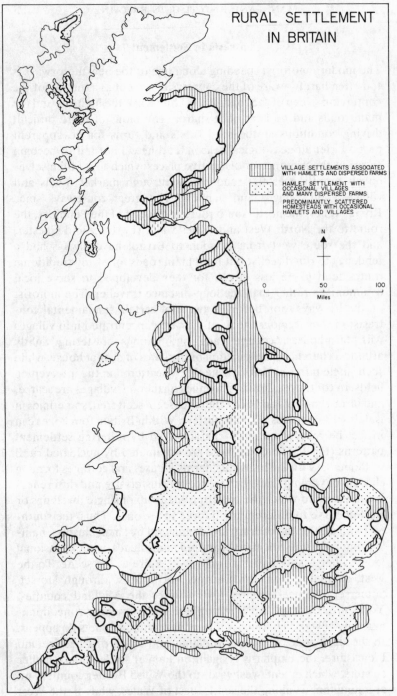

RURAL SETTLEMENT
IN BRITAIN

VILLAGE SETTLEMENTS ASSOCIATED
WITH HAMLETS AND DISPERSED FARMS

HAMLET SETTLEMENT WITH
OCCASIONAL VILLAGES
AND MANY DISPERSED FARMS

PREDOMINANTLY SCATTERED
HOMESTEADS WITH OCCASIONAL
HAMLETS AND VILLAGES

N

0   50   100
        Miles

Fig 1   Rural Settlement in Britain, after Thorpe, in Watson and Sissons (1964), 360

Country the lower lands are yet another region of hamlets, with the occasional larger cluster. Finally, and with certain notable exceptions in eastern and central Scotland, the emphasis in the remainder of Britain is upon dispersion, a scattering of farms and dwellings, with occasional clusters. These zones are very generalized: in detail there are many small-scale, intensely localized variations, but even at the generalized scale of Fig 1 it is fair to ask why these variations occur. What caused them?

At this stage Fig 2 may be introduced, for it permits some basic terms concerning settlement to be simply defined. The term 'settlement pattern' is applied to the distribution of units of settlement, be these farms, hamlets, villages or indeed towns, over the face of the land, and a map of settlement patterns tells of presence or absence, regular or irregular spacing, in lines or in clusters. Each pattern is, furthermore, made up of individual forms, and these may be large enough to be termed villages, small enough to warrant the term hamlet, or they may be single farms or cottages. In practice each pattern, if towns are wholly excluded, is made up of varying proportions of these basic ingredients, and it is reasonable to ask why this should be so. It is, of course, possible to focus more closely and to examine particular forms in greater detail, to consider the different shapes of villages and hamlets: indeed, to look at the structure of the individual farm, house or cottage. The generalized pictures presented in Fig 2 are all derived from real situations, and the differences are such as to demand explanation.

This must be sought in the interaction between three groups of factors, physical, economic and cultural — terms in themselves no more than shorthand headings for large groups of forces which, in combination, produce the response of a particular kind of settlement pattern or form. They operate over the whole range of scales shown in Fig 2 and to them must be added a final element, time.

Physical Factors

Attention has already been drawn to the varieties of landscape found within Britain, and to the fact that these are linked with equally varied climatic zones and biological regions. Figs 3A and B classify the basic relief of the British Isles, and a comparison between these and Fig 1 quickly demonstrates a broad correlation between uplands and dispersed settlement. Quite clearly, the presence of high ground has tended in some way to discourage clustered

Fig 2   Rural Settlement Patterns and
Forms including material derived from
Beresford and Hurst (1971) and Evans, as
indicated in note 3 to Ch. 4 *supra*

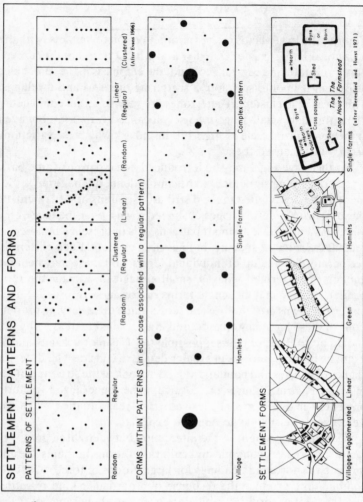

SETTLEMENT PATTERNS AND FORMS

PATTERNS OF SETTLEMENT

Random   Regular   (Random)   Clustered (Regular)   (Linear)   Linear (Regular)   (Clustered) (After Evans 1966)

FORMS WITHIN PATTERNS (in each case associated with a regular pattern)

Village   Hamlets   Single-farms   Complex pattern

SETTLEMENT FORMS

Villages-Agglomerated   Linear   Green   Hamlets   Single-farms   The Long House   The Farmstead (after Beresford and Hurst 1971) settlements, but it is important to appreciate that the link need not be a direct one. The variations in altitude, latitude and longitude involved, as Fig 3C demonstrates, result in a distinctive pattern of regional climatic differences, and it is these, in combination with the relief patterns, which underlie the broad contrast between areas of nucleated and areas of dispersed settlement. A dense scatter of nucleated agricultural settlements can only develop where relief, soils and climate combine to permit intensive agriculture sufficient to support the folk involved, and in fact the lowland-upland contrast demarcated by the 200m (700 ft) contour is broadly a division between intensive land use, producing grain crops and grass, and a more extensive pattern of pastoral farming using the restricted potentialities of the uplands. Today, diversity is the outstanding characteristic of agriculture in these islands, a diversity made possible by the immensely varied character of the relief, rocks and soils, and by the climatic differences resulting from variations in altitude, exposure and location. Undoubtedly former patterns of exploitation were simpler, less specialized, for all communities were striving to support themselves, but, then as now, each economy operated within the constraints imposed by physical and climatic conditions, which directly affected the types of habitat available and the nature of the crops which could be produced, and also imposed limitations on the character of the farming.

It is well to appreciate the extent to which physical factors can operate indirectly on settlement patterns through the intermediary of economic activity. Nevertheless, the physical landscape, the disposition of hills, valleys, marshes and mountain masses, does in fact 'influence' settlement in another way; it conditions lines of movement and accessibility, and the presence of river crossings, fords and bridge-points has had a powerful effect in elevating certain settlements above their neighbours, making them more important. In detail, of course, physical factors operate at several scales, and while the comments above apply to the location of settlement in the broadest sense, there is at the level of the individual settlement the situation, the character of the immediate surroundings, the hills and the valleys, steep lands and flat lands, dry lands and wet lands, all of which bear on the economic viability of the individual unit, while, in an even more restricted sense, there is the site, the area covered by houses and gardens. Site and situation will be examined more fully in later chapters.

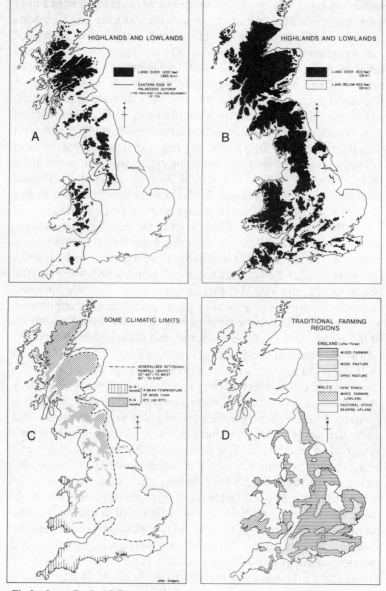

Fig 3   Some Regional Contrasts in Britain, after Gregory, in Watson and Sissons (1964), 59 and Thirsk, (1967), 4 and 128

Economic and Cultural Factors

Physical factors cannot be disassociated from economic factors. In former centuries the basic necessities of water, arable and grazing land were integrated within a farming system, which could vary in character according to the particular emphasis adopted, whether arable or pastoral farming; the emphasis adopted and the crops grown depended in turn upon the nature of the physical environments available. A farming system involves both the establishment of a certain yearly cycle of events — land-preparation, sowing, weeding and harvest, for instance — and a spatial expression in the form of cropping units and grazing areas. The sophistication of the arrangements can reflect the degree to which the economy is geared to purely subsistence or market production, while technical factors such as the nature of the ploughs and other tools used and the extent of manuring, as well as the complexity and character of the rotations, will be echoed in the structural frame within which the system operates, namely the field system. Improving husbandry practices, better rotations and better crops can cause change in the pattern both of fields and settlement, a classic example being the enclosure of the English open fields in the eighteenth century. Because it destroyed the necessity for village-based farming, enclosure encouraged the dispersal of new farmsteads out to the newly created ring-fenced farm units.

Thirsk, working from sixteenth-century sources, recognized three farming types within England, and as these provide a particularly useful framework for discussion her map is reproduced as Fig 3D. A number of broad correlations can be made between this and Figs 1 and 3 A-C, although in detail each region is complex and many exceptional situations are present. In lowland England mixed farming predominated, with slight regional variations in emphasis: sheep and corn husbandry on the chalk downs and limestone wolds; corn and stock in various combinations in the clay vales; corn and stock-fattening on the marshlands of the east coast. A careful comparison with Thorpe's map shows that almost without exception these are areas dominated by village settlements. The remaining portions of lowland England are given over to pasture-farming types; in the south-east, east, and parts of the Midlands and south are found 'wood-pasture' regions, early-enclosed and, as will be shown, late-settled areas, generally, but by no means invariably, associated with hamlet and single-farm settlement. In the remaining portions of England — the grass-growing lands of the north and west, many of them of considerable elevation — several varieties of open pasture-farming were found, rearing and fattening sheep and cattle, and sometimes concentrating upon dairy produce. The lands of the fen country form a notable exception to the upland open-pasture link. In general, open-pasture regions are characterized by dispersed settlements, although a notable exception emerges in the West Midlands and Cheshire, where Thirsk's rearing and fattening region corresponds remarkably closely with the West Midland zone of hamlet settlement mapped by Thorpe. The explanation lies, of course, in the crudity of the generalization, for the region in question may be viewed as a zone of wood pasture rather than open pasture, producing a more predictable linkage with a hamlet-dominated settlement pattern. As Thirsk stresses, her map is 'very tentative', but it is nevertheless important, for it is a picture of England at a time when the character of farming was undergoing substantial changes and specialist regional production was becoming more marked; it draws attention to the antecedents of the complex farming patterns of the present while at the same time acting as a reminder that earlier farming systems may have already possessed a regional diversity which is all too often concealed beneath the need to generalize, or lost because of deficient or partly analysed evidence.

Work by Emery provides a basis for carrying these generalizations concerning seventeenth-century farming patterns into Wales (Fig 3D), and once again the relationship to the settlement regions mapped by Thorpe is clear-cut in broad outline, although complex in detail. A comparison of Fig 1 with Fig 3 shows that a strong measure of physical control is involved. Unfortunately it is impossible to generalize in this way for Scotland, although it is very tempting to make a projection on the basis of Fig 1. Without doubt, a strong contrast must have existed between the lowlands of central, eastern and south-western Scotland, the upland core of the Highlands proper, and the dissected and fragmented island chains and peninsulas of the west and north.

Finally, it must be emphasized that a way of life is more than its economic or social components; it is a habit, inherited from one's father and grandfather, and in former centuries patterns of living changed relatively slowly. Estyn Evans has demonstrated the way in which within Atlantic Europe cultural threads can be traced for thousands of years; fishing techniques still used and recorded in the last two centuries have roots in the cultures of Middle Stone Age hunters and gatherers, while a turf cabin, standing in the earlier part

of the present century, would have left archaeological traces virtually identical with those found in the Neolithic house at Knocka-
doon, Lough Gur, Co. Limerick. These are tantalizing and elusive
threads but they are an integral part of settlement history.[1]

At any one period of time, settlement of the land, and all that this
implies in terms of economic and social organization, constitutes a
complex system made up of a series of interacting components, and
the historical geographer is concerned with the sometimes gradual,
sometimes cataclysmic, replacement of one system by another. No
single theme can ever be an adequate medium for discussing all the
variables present, but in examining Thorpe's map the scale of the
problem can be appreciated if it is realized that this complex pattern
is but a single transient stage in several thousand years of development: not, it must be emphasized, a final stage, but a stage as
ephemeral as that present in 1086, mapped as Fig 16.

The history of settlement may in fact be seen in two ways: either
as a state of continuous change, or as periods of rapid innovation
separated by phases of relative stability. In practical terms, at any
one time there is always a delicate adjustment between the character of the environment, both physical and biological; the population; the extent of the cultivated area; the nature of farming systems; the administrative framework, and the patterns and forms of
settlement present, to specify only the salient variables. In explaining detailed local contrasts, it is the unique combination of these
variables at a particular time within a particular region which
determines the character of the settlement to be found. In a sense,
changes involve competition between two opposing forces; on the
one hand are pressures towards innovation, the creation of new
orders of society, new economic systems, new landscapes, while on
the other hand the process of inertia tends to inhibit change and
encourage the adaptation to new uses of existing orders, systems
and patterns. The end-product is a complex blend of old and new,
and it is a period of between two and six thousand years of such
interblending that gives to British landscapes and institutions their
distinctive character.

The Beginnings of Settlement in Britain

The beginnings of settlement in Britain are rooted deeply in the
past, and this chapter must briefly carry the story back ten or twelve
thousand years to the period when Mesolithic folk first began to
leave archaeologically detectable remains. The treatment of this

immense time span, with all that it necessarily implies in terms of superficiality and generalization, cannot be undertaken lightly, and there are two practical reasons for covering the ground at all. First, man's impact on the range of environments found within Britain has been variable in intensity both from area to area and from millennium to millennium, but cumulative in total effect; no incoming cultural group can ever have totally ignored the previous inhabitants: indeed the environments available for their exploitation were, in part at least, invariably the product of man-induced changes.

Any generalized statements concerning settlement within the prehistoric period must take account of three developments currently taking place within archaeology: on one hand is the tendency to extend and adjust the chronologies involved; on the other hand two critical re-evaluations of the evidence are occurring under the impact of new attitudes and new discoveries. Much of our knowledge of absolute chronology during the prehistoric period depends upon the use of radio-carbon dating.

During the lifetime of living organisms a small portion of the carbon in their tissues is converted, by means of cosmic radiation, into radio-active carbon. On death this radio-activity is gradually lost, and after about five and a half thousand years the original proportion of radio-carbon is reduced by one half. This constant can be used as the basis for calculating the absolute age of stratified organic remains from archaeological sites. Recent work, however, is suggesting that dates so far accepted are not in fact entirely accurate, and that discrepancies occur, particularly in the third millennium BC. In practice this means that the dates would be some 500 years older than was calculated. This has important practical repercussions — the Neolithic period is now considered to begin in Britain between 4000 and 3500 BC while the Beaker invasions of the Early Bronze Age are now seen to fall between 2500 and 1700 BC. This fact, in combination with certain re-evaluations of the provenance of much Bronze Age material, makes an acceptable general chronology particularly difficult to establish. It means that prehistoric farmers were affecting the landscape for many more centuries than was formerly thought to be the case.[2]

A second tendency is equally important. The prehistory of Britain has hitherto been viewed in terms of a series of invasions, with immigrations of folk from the Continent imposing new cultures upon the lowlands, cultures absorbed only gradually within the more difficult terrain of the highlands. This is admittedly a gross oversimplification of such views, but current thought is questioning

Fig 4 Cockfield Fell, County Durham. This remarkable air photograph reveals a bewildering variety of earthworks, ranging in date from oval enclosures of possibly Iron Age or Romano-British provenance to nineteenth-century quarries and waggonways. The village of Cockfield is a fine example of a two-row green village with long tofts, a type established before 1250. Photo: Durham County Council and BKS Surveys Ltd

the basic premise, namely the influx of new folk with fresh and distinctive ways of life. Many of the so-called 'new' cultures can be seen as indigenous developments in which many lines of continuity can be observed between the Neolithic period and the Bronze Age, and between the Bronze Age and the Early pre-Roman Iron Age. Furthermore, as has long been recognized, when dealing with the rural settlements of Roman Britain, particularly north Britain, it is important to realize that many native settlements remained essentially Iron Age in habit and economy, while even in the case of characteristically Roman institutions, notably the villa, it is often possible to postulate a measure of continuity. Moreover, recent excavations on the sites of deserted medieval villages are producing evidence for Saxon, Roman and even Iron Age sites beneath the later remains. Continuity of life is an important theme in settlement evolution.[3]

A third trend involves the nature of the evidence. The advent of air photography has, in the last twenty years, revealed sites in hitherto unimagined numbers, not only along the great river valleys of southern and midland England but also in the Fens and, increasingly, on the clay tracts of the Midlands and the boulder clays of the North East. Fig 4 is an informative case: twelve or so miles south west of Durham there is an area of open fell, somewhat under a thousand acres of rough grazing, which is used by the local people for hanging out washing, siting pigeon 'crees' (*huts*), or garages, and grazing a selection of beasts. On this fell lie at least four, possibly more, ancient earthworks, of Iron Age, Romano-British or possibly even Dark Age date (if shape affords any clues at all!). The fell is a survivor from thousands of acres of such rough grazings enclosed on the lower Pennine spurs in west Durham during the late-eighteenth or early-nineteenth centures. This tract of open fell in the landscape of today affords a 'window' through which it is possible to look backwards to the lowland fells of 1750 and to the complex of coalpits, waggonways and ancient earthworks which would then have been visible. Confirmation of this conclusion is found on air photographs, which reveal the ploughed-out remains of similar assemblages, and these, in west Durham at least, occur almost without exception where open fell was present in 1750. They are visible on air photographs (Fig 5) because, at the maximum, only about 200 years of ploughing are involved, frequently much fewer. Such archaeological sites are exceedingly difficult to detect beneath the much-cultivated townfields and several closes of earlier centuries, where tillage has extended over hundreds of years in cumulative total.[4]

Fig 5   Braun's Den, near Brancepeth, County Durham. This site has been ploughed away and only appears as a slight crop-mark. There appear to be traces of two round huts within the enclosure, and a Roman or pre-Roman date is possible. The site is overlain by the geometric hedgerows of late eighteenth-century enclosure and a contemporary farmstead lies nearby. Photo: NCB and Fairey Surveys Ltd

It follows that such visible evidence need bear little or no relationship to the earlier or 'original' patterns of occupation; a distribution map of surviving features from earlier landscapes, be these Bronze Age farm sites or medieval moated manors, reflects both the character of the original distribution and the presence of such 'windows', areas within which earlier landscapes have been preserved. There is, of course, the additional factor of the assiduity, skill or indeed the presence of an observer capable of collecting the basic field data. This makes the final map very difficult to interpret, and nice judgment is needed before basing any conclusions upon distribution maps, particularly demonstrably incomplete ones. These arguments have long been familiar, and recent discoveries have brought the point sharply home, for careful work along motorway lines in south-west England, in advance of the bulldozers, has revealed the presence of sites in unsuspected densities. According to one estimate, the past lies beneath our feet at a density of one site per quarter of a square mile. The future is at once frightening and challenging, and rescue work is increasingly being planned with these densities in mind. But one thing is certain: our view of the past will change and expand.[5]

Vegetation Change: a Measure of Cumulative Impact

The millenia between the Mesolithic period and the Iron Age saw a gradual transition from ephemeral settlements of a few days' or temporary settlements of a few weeks' duration through to seasonal and permanent settlements taking advantage of the rational exploitation of localized economic resources. The surviving remains indicate a transition from an economy based entirely on collecting, hunting and fishing to one based on the exploitation of arable and grazing lands whose productivity was maintained by means of a scheme of manuring or management which is reflected in the character of the settlements found. One critical break was undoubtedly occasioned by the advent of a new food-producing economy with the gradual arrival, around 4000 BC, of Neolithic colonists and the establishment of ecologically potent farming groups. The impact of these folk on the natural environment, notably soils and vegetation, is of vital importance to our overall theme, for they occupied a range of habitats and initiated the process of cumulative change.

At this point it is necessary to digress into the field of palaeobotany, for vegetation change provides a useful index of man's activities. The history of post-glacial vegetation change in Britain is complex, but by about 5500 BC the onset of the Atlantic period saw the establishment of a continuous forest cover over all the dry land, extending to altitudes of at least $762 \cdot 20$m (2500 feet). This woodland was made up of oak forests with an admixture of other trees, and can be visualized as pure oakwood in some localities; in others as a mosaic of oak, elm and lime (where elm and lime would tend to occupy the better soils); and in places, on poorer soils in the lowlands and including most of the north and west of Britain, containing much birch. In Ireland and most of Scotland there would have been no lime — indeed, in the Scottish Highlands pine and possibly birch forests provided an alternative type of climax forest. Alder was predominantly a tree of wet places, in both uplands and lowlands. The only remaining open habitats were likely to have been along the sea-coasts and on the tops of the highest mountains, apart from a few areas where local topography was absolutely unfavourable to tree growth, because of either gradient or drainage conditions. The impact of Mesolithic folk on these environments has been examined by Simmons,[6] who argued that in upland areas such as Dartmoor, the Pennines and the North York Moors, their hunting procedures and their possible use of fire caused the enlargement of natural forest glades, particularly around springheads or at stream-side sites; the more open habitat so created permitted the spread of light-demanding species, while the better grazing in turn attracted more game. The desertion of the clearing occurred when human activity caused game to avoid the area, but in these upland environments the exposure of the soil would, by this stage, have already resulted in some leaching and deterioration, thus preventing the regrowth of high forest to its former condition.

The vegetational history of prehistoric Britain has been reconstructed by counting the almost indestructible pollen grains preserved at various levels in the peat deposits which have been accumulating over thousands of years. Many of our native plants are wind pollinated, so that a large bog tends to provide a regional picture, and a count of the grains in a series of samples taken at varying depths in the bog gives a clear cross-section of the vegetation at the stage when that particular peat lay at the bog surface. The distinctive phase of bog growth known as the Atlantic phase terminates at the end of the fourth millennium BC and is characterized in pollen diagrams by a sharp decline in the amounts of elm pollen present. An increasing volume of evidence suggests that man was the cause of this change: a new technique of keeping stalled domestic animals was introduced into Europe on a very wide scale at the opening of the Neolithic period, and it is probable that these animals were fed by repeated gathering of leafy branches from those trees known to be nutritious, in particular the elms. Associated with the decline of elm in pollen diagrams, the evidence of certain vegetation phases frequently suggests a deliberate clearance of forest by Neolithic agriculturalists, no doubt using the effective polished stone axes so characteristic of these cultures. A detailed study of the pollen curves linked with such changes suggests the clearance of all the trees in a limited area by felling and burning (sometimes revealed in the bogs by charcoal layers), followed by a primitive form of cereal cultivation in the cleared patches. On good lowland soils the regeneration of the forest followed quite quickly, with colonization by pioneer trees such as birch leading towards the re-establishment of high forest. Turner has shown that such 'small temporary clearances' are characteristic of pollen diagrams from Somerset to Durham during what may be broadly termed the Neolithic and Bronze Ages, and that furthermore in England and Wales the period between 400 BC and 350 BC saw the onset of more or less permanent disforestation on a large scale. Significantly, evidence from Ayrshire and Perthshire shows that this clearing phase was deferred until AD 100-500. The details of the main gradual destruction of the natural vegetation need not concern us further, but this is a theme which necessarily runs parallel to the development of settlement, having a direct bearing upon the all-important transition from ephemeral to permanent occupation and the emergence of distinctive regional settlement.[7]

Paradoxically it is easier to summarize the principal vegetation changes of the prehistoric period than to carry the story into the Roman period and beyond, and it is quite clear that, after the major and persistent decline in the woodlands, individual sites often reflect very complex local histories. Fig 6 shows two generalized pollen diagrams from Co. Durham, one from a lowland site, the other from the uplands at 381·1m (1250 feet) above sea level. Both diagrams show the trends in the proportions of tree pollen (oak, pine, birch, ash, elm and lime), shrub pollen (willow and hazel), and grass pollen (all the herbaceous species). At both sites drastic clearance occurs during the Iron Age and Romano-British periods (conclusions based upon radio-carbon dates) when the tree pollen drops to a level comparable with that of today (at the top of each diagram). However these diagrams are interpreted, and there are

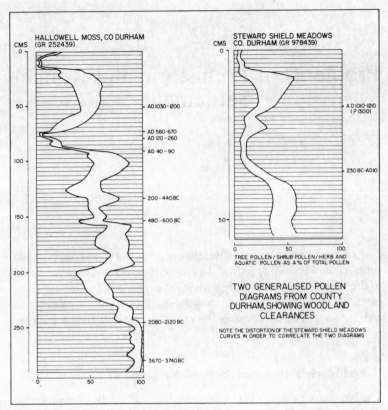

Fig 6   Two Generalized Pollen Diagrams from County Durham

indeed problems, extensive clearance obviously took place. At Hallowell Moss, woodland reappeared during the Dark Ages to be finally cleared in the Middle Ages, but at the second site, Steward Shield, the moorlands, for such they were, remained open until the early decades of the fourteenth century, when increasing wetness, Scottish raids and a general economic recession encouraged a retreat from the margin and led to the local resurgence of scrub-woodland, finally cleared in the seventeenth century. The creation of tillage and pasture, fuel cutting and timber extraction resulted in the depletion of the woodlands, and it is only at the top of each diagram that a slight upswing of pine pollen indicates the presence of plantations. Well might the Anglo-Saxon riddle refer to the ploughman as the 'enemy of the hoar-wood', for the development of rural settlement has been inevitably and directly linked with the destruction of our woodlands.[8]

2

Problems of Prehistoric and Roman Settlement

THE CUMULATIVE CHANGES described in the previous chapter have roots in the Mesolithic period, but there is no doubt that the arrival of the first colonists, bringing with them exotic cereals and domesticated animals, marks a particularly significant development and represents a true invasion in the cultural rather than the military sense.

Prehistoric Settlement: the Neolithic period and Bronze Age

The Neolithic period must begin in about 4000 BC, but it is probable that the earliest farmers arrived several centuries before this, for the earliest remains may not yet have been discovered. The initial crossing, for Britain had been an island since the beginning of Atlantic times, must have been a hazardous affair, with intrepid colonists bringing small numbers of cattle, sheep and other domesticated animals, as well as the vital seed-corn, in fragile skin boats or on rafts. Centuries must have passed before these folk were present in sufficient numbers to leave traces in the archaeological record. The reasons underlying this expansion are difficult to ascertain — perhaps the ability to produce a food supply, when first introduced into south-eastern Europe, resulted in localized but chronic over-population. The fertility of virgin soils was being tapped, giving high yields per unit of sowing seed, but these yields would decline, probably fairly rapidly, leaving behind relatively infertile fields and a crop of healthy babies. The clearance of fresh fields, involving population movement, solved the immediate problem of food supply, but the maintenance of a constant supply of grain would be

Fig 7 The Village of Faulking, Sussex. The village is sited upon a bench of Upper Greensand and shows signs of being a planned two-row settlement. It is located so as to be central to a territory extending from the Chalk downs to the Weald Clay. Photo: Aerofilms Ltd

dependent upon repeated migrations as each clearing was exhausted. In short, while they were on the move Neolithic populations could both sustain their numbers and grow, and in this we may perhaps see the reason for the hazardous colonization of a remote group of islands off the north-western coast of Europe. No doubt a stage would be reached when increasing populations within those woodland areas, and by implication on those soils suitable for Neolithic settlement, would lead to a stable situation, with the establishment of semi-permanent sedentary groups moving within restricted territories and practising some variant of shifting agriculture. Less bounteous yields, resulting from the cropping of rested soils instead of virgin land, would eventually stabilize population levels, and within each territory the settlement would be periodically moved. In Czechoslovakia, Soudsky has drawn a graphic picture of twenty-five families of Danubian Neolithic peasants moving every fifteen or sixteen years, and has postulated the presence of up to six periodically occupied village sites within a total territory of about 200 hectares (500 acres).[1] Once established in Britain, such farming communities developed continuous traditions extending over hundreds of years, and a multitude of local variations are detectable in the archaeological record.

It is increasingly clear that the same cultural traditions, with infusions of some new traits, continued into the Bronze Age; thus Piggott is of the opinion that, although the great chambered long barrow at West Kennet (Wilts.) was built in the middle of the third millennium BC, it continued in use as a communal tomb until the seventeenth century BC, when the chambers were finally sealed, and has produced pottery and other artifacts ranging in character from Early Neolithic to Early Bronze Age.[2] Our knowledge of these early farming communities is largely derived from the great earthen and stone tombs they constructed, and these demonstrate three important points. Firstly, they are found widely distributed throughout Britain, from Dorset to the Orkneys and from Kent to the western coasts. It is clear that these folk penetrated, occupied and farmed a wide range of local environments, from the relatively kindly chalklands to the windy Atlantic coasts. Jones has argued that in Anglesey the distribution of tombs shows a fine adjustment to the well-drained good agricultural soils, and it is probable that these farmers, guided perhaps by local vegetation contrasts, already possessed a sound fund of practical knowledge concerning soil variations. Secondly, the assemblages of artifacts, tomb types, flint and bone work, stone axes and pottery which are used to identify these people, show considerable local diversity, those of the Medway valley of Kent differing from those of the Severn-Cotswold region, and those of Wiltshire being different from those of the lands around the northern Irish Sea. In practical terms this probably indicates the emergence of local communities, to some extent interacting and possessing trade channels, but sufficiently isolated to develop and preserve their own particular variant of the basic Neolithic economy. Thirdly, the dimensions of these tombs should be appreciated; the most usual length of the mound is 30·5 m (100 ft) and widths of between 9 and 15 m (30 and 50 ft) are common. A mound of these dimensions merely one foot high implies the movement of between 85·0 and 140·0 cubic metres (3000 and 5000 cubic feet) of soil, and the tapering mounds, resembling half a pear, must often have reached a height of 3 or 4 metres (10–13 ft). While it is now recognized that these barrows represent the culmination of centuries of effort on a particular site, they bear witness to enormous investments of time and labour. Furthermore, a second category of visible Neolithic site, the sacred sites of which Stonehenge and Avebury (Wilts.) are the best-known examples, surely represents the surplus time and labour of more than mere local communities and betrays a degree of organization which is remarkable. Actual Neolithic settlements have so far proved remarkably elusive, probably being destroyed by subsequent soil changes and agricultural activity. Even the so-called 'causewayed camps', banked and ditched enclosures formerly interpreted as cattle corrals, are now seen in terms of ritual enclosures.[3] Only from the Orkneys, at Scara Brae, has a late Neolithic settlement been preserved in a striking and visible way, as a result of being swamped by shifting sands and because these semi-subterranean huts, lying beneath their own midden or rubbish heap, were constructed of drystone walling.

The Bronze Age is in many ways the Dark Age of British prehistory; the large numbers of surviving round barrows imply a substantial population, while the frequent and widely dispersed finds of bronze weapons and tools of the highest quality suggest that Bronze Age dwellings should often be found: in fact they have so far been very elusive, and the singular rarity of house sites found in the Neolithic period extends into the Early Bronze Age, possibly because of the continued employment, in wooded environments, of constructional techniques which depended upon sill-beams, which leave very few traces in the ground. An early Bronze Age settlement of Beaker Folk, at Belle Tout, Sussex, is producing traces of a variety of huts, three circular and three rectangular or trapeze-

shaped. The whole question of Bronze Age settlements is complicated, however, by recent chronological adjustments, in that the
establishment of permanent cultivation as opposed to shifting
agriculture has, in archaeological terms, been associated with a
cultural invasion linked with the Deverel Rimbury folk of southern
England and placed within the Late Bronze Age, between the
twelfth and the tenth centuries BC. The position of this culture in the
Late Bronze Age is now far from clear; indeed, Burgess has gone so
far as to indicate that much nominally Iron Age material may prove
to be Late Bronze Age. These conclusions have important repercussions concerning our view of the Iron Age, traditionally seen as
the result of successive invasions from the Continent. It is now
realized that many of the cultural traits characteristic of the Iron
Age do in fact represent indigenous developments and are
decidedly foreign to the Continent. Such classic 'Iron Age' features
as round timber houses, storage pits, 'Celtic fields' and bone 'weaving' combs were already in existence in the Bronze Age, in particular in the Deverel Rimbury culture of southern England. Farmsteads with round houses set amongst small embanked 'Celtic' fields
and droveways were indeed an established feature of the Late
Middle Bronze Age in southern England, from the Sussex Downs to
Dorset and Dartmoor, and excavations at Gwithian have shown
that small lynchetted fields were being cultivated by cross-
ploughing in Cornwall already at the transition from the Early to the
Middle Bronze Age. The cultivation of individual fields over a
considerable period of time is implied by the development of lyn-
chets, and if the semi-permanent settlements of Neolithic and Early
Bronze Age folk leave but few traces, we are on firmer ground by
the Middle Bronze Age, for the survival of actual fields implies the
presence of permanent settlements lasting for several generations.
An important series of sites such as Shearplace Hill (Dorset),
Plumpton Plain (Sussex) and Itford Hill (Sussex) shows the presence of Middle Bronze Age farming communities firmly stabilized
in southern England, and in these round compounds, containing
round huts and associated with small rectangular fields, we see the
antecedents of the more developed farms and clusters of the Iron
Age. The Middle and Late Bronze Ages, however, pose many
questions, and current views are susceptible to rapid revision as
excavations of such sites as Mam Tor (Derbyshire), Grimthorpe
(East Riding), and Norton Fitzwarren (Somerset) progress. One
point, however, does emerge clearly: by the Middle Bronze Age the
accumulated experience of the previous two millenia was bearing

fruit, and stable farming communities based upon permanent settlements and fixed fields were emerging. The Iron Age, in part indigenous, in part the result of immigration, saw the establishment of these communities throughout Britain.[4]

Prehistoric Settlement: The Iron Age

Perhaps the most obvious manifestation of Iron Age settlement is to be found in a series of major defended sites — the almost indestructible hill-forts, which are very general throughout most parts of Britain where there were sufficient folk to construct and maintain them. The Iron Age hill-fortress is indeed one of the commonest and most striking types of prehistoric monuments, abundant on the southern chalklands and limestone country and amongst the hills of the west and north. Usually sited upon eminences, they afford striking and commanding views and their great ramparts and complex defended entrances emphasize both their military function and the care lavished upon their construction. Most hill-forts show few obvious signs of permanent occupation, but excavation rarely fails to reveal at least some traces of dwellings and, ignoring for the moment certain problems of chronology, it is clear that some sites, notably Maiden Castle and Hod Hill in Dorset, Tre'r Ceiri in North Wales and Traprain Law in East Lothian, all containing numerous huts, must have housed fair-sized populations, even if all were not occupied contemporaneously. At the other end of the scale the small fort of Dane's Camp on Bredon Hill, Gloucestershire, contained enough huts to warrant the term 'village', while the grain-storage arrangements, wicker-lined and slab-roofed pits, attest permanent occupation. Nevertheless, hill-forts are not uniformly distributed (Fig 8), and are known to be absent from large areas of northern England where other evidence suggests the presence of Iron Age folk.

Hill-forts probably range in date from the Late Bronze Age to the Roman Conquest, but in Scotland and parts of Wales occupation continued throughout the Roman period and into the Dark Ages; indeed, there is an increasing body of evidence for the re-use of hill-forts in post-Roman contexts even within southern Britain. Their names, Cissbury and Cadbury, Caesar's Camp and Dane's Camp, Almondbury, Merlin's Hill and the Barmkin of Echt reflect their place in the folklife of the past, and represent concrete evidence for a complex web of relationships and beliefs between these almost indestructible structures and later populations — primitive

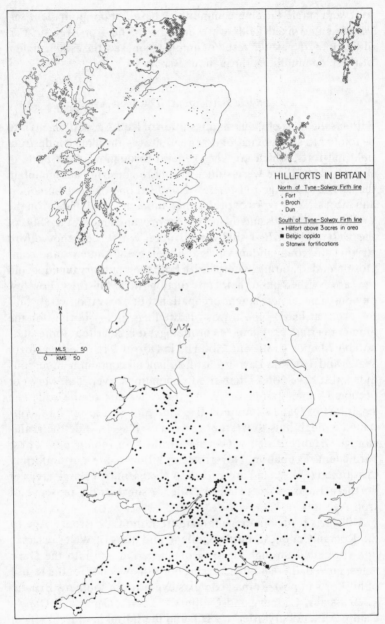

Fig 8   Hill forts in Britain, after Ordnance Survey (1962) and Rivet (1966)

attempts to explain that which was half-remembered or unknowable. In this sense hill-forts are a class of artifact on a par with the great stone tombs and ritual sites of the third millennium before Christ. Intangible as these threads are, they cannot be ignored, for they reflect a condition of cohabitation and continuity which is an essential theme of this volume. Nevertheless, hill-forts must not be viewed in isolation: they form no more than one element in the total Iron Age settlement pattern, and to see them in isolation would be comparable to discussing the castles of feudal England while ignoring the villages of the peasant cultivators. Their size, numbers and distribution pose questions of both a social and an economic nature.[5]

It is clear that hill-forts must represent important focal points, essentially, but not completely, military in nature, the foci of local power: the analogy with the feudal castle may not be wholly inappropriate. In some cases, for example near Dorchester, Winchester, Ilchester and Wroxeter, it is significant that they appear to have been superseded by Roman towns: indeed the fortified lowland sites or *oppida* of the most advanced Iron Age group, the Belgae, who imposed their rule over much of south-eastern England, appear to have possessed quasi-urban functions. Fig 5 maps only those hill-forts in excess of 1·2 ha (those below 1·2 ha (3 acres) being included in Fig 9) and it can well be imagined that they reflect, at least to some degree, the distribution of Iron Age folk and were intended to hold both people and herds from the surrounding district in times of trouble. Literary sources emphasize the social stratification of Celtic society, and Caesar describes how in Gaul the *equites* or warrior aristocrats were followed into battle by large numbers of their retainers; the hill-forts may be seen as the castles of this aristocracy. No doubt their followers provided the labour needed to construct and maintain the fortifications, and Rivet sees the hill-forts as surrounded by unfortified farms, the occupants of which would have to bear their part in construction work.[6] This is an arrangement remarkably like that to be described, in Chapter 3, in medieval Wales, where the lord had a *llys* or palace, in some cases actually sited in a hill-fort, maintained by a network of dependent farms and hamlets; indeed Glanville Jones has argued for the survival of Iron Age practice in such cases. Seen in a wider context, hill-forts represent a specialized but universal need in a society in which the acts of war were an essential attribute of manhood and in which, judging by Irish sources, cattle-rieving and feuding were integral parts of the life of the aristocratic members of the com-

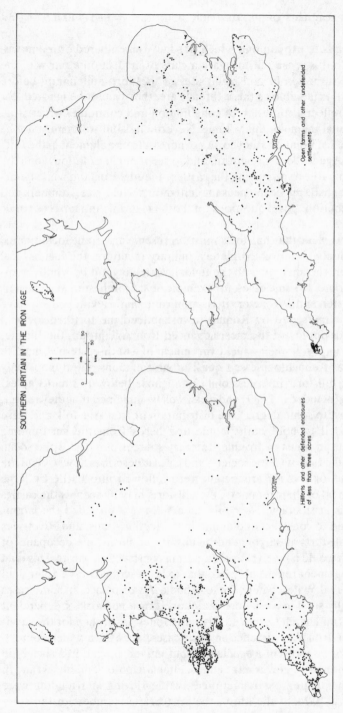

SOUTHERN BRITAIN IN THE IRON AGE

Hillforts and other defended enclosures of less than three acres

Open farms and other undefended settlements

Fig 9 Enclosed and Open Farms in Southern Britain in the Iron Age, after Ordnance Survey (1962) and Rivet (1969), 193

munity. Hill-forts cannot be viewed in isolation; they were part of a system of settlement in which they formed no more than one constituent element.

At levels below the scale of the hill-forts, Iron Age rural settlements reveal great local diversity: in general, within the lowlands of England 'open' undefended homesteads and clusters tend to be the rule, while in the uplands such sites tend to be enclosed (Fig 6), but this division is by no means hard and fast, and a classic lowland site at Little Woodbury (Wilts.) was enclosed, at first with a palisade and eventually with an earthen bank and ditch.[7] A single large round house, some 13 m (45 ft) in diameter lay in the middle of the enclosure, which was about four acres in extent, sufficient, as Bowen emphasizes, to take about thirty modern houses. This type of site is generally regarded as a superior dwelling, perhaps having the status of a lord's hall, and may itself have been the focus of dependent settlements and the recipient of services. Such farms were found throughout south-eastern England and occur as far north as coastal Northumberland. If the hypothesis concerning their status is indeed correct, then other forms of settlement, appropriate to lower social groups, may be expected.

Bowen documents a number of these, ranging from the three huts in an enclosure of 0·8 ha (one-fifth of an acre) from Draughton, Northamptonshire, to the extensive Boscombe Down settlement, Wiltshire, which extends over 32·4 ha (seventy-six acres) and chronologically spans the whole Iron Age and part of the Roman period. The volume of evidence for the presence of Iron Age cluster settlements of varying size appears to be increasing steadily. The realization by Fowler and Bowen that the surviving traces of Celtic fields on the Marlborough Downs represent the upper limits of systems which extended upwards from the lower lands, with the evidence downslope and on the lowlands being largely obliterated by open-field agriculture in the Middle Ages and later, is particularly important, emphasizing that many Iron Age settlement sites may have been wholly destroyed by open-field agriculture during the Middle Ages: indeed Little Woodbury itself was heavily scarred by the furrow lines of former ploughing.[8] The next decade will probably see the evidence for extensive clearance during the Iron Age on a wide range of soil types. These lowland sites are normally considered to be based upon mixed farming, involving corn production on fields maintained by manuring (suggested by pottery scatters) and grazing beasts on the remaining lands. As in the Middle Ages the feeding of stock during the winter months was probably a major problem and it may be that the forest clearances visible in the pollen diagrams are in part the result of depredations by hungry stock and possibly of the cutting of leafy branches for winter fodder. In western and northern Britain the stone-built huts, generally enclosed but sometimes open, sometimes set singly, at other times forming 'village'-sized groups, are considered to be the homesteads of folk whose economy contained a substantial pastoral component, although, as at Grassington in Wharfedale, great field systems attest the presence of tillage. In the far north there is an inevitable blurring of the chronological relationships found further south, particularly in Scotland, where the relative absence of Roman influence means that no clear-cut line is drawn across time, and settlements established in the Bronze Age could be continuously occupied right through to the Middle Ages; or perhaps it would be truer to say that evidence of such continuity of occupation (necessarily not without some gaps) has been disclosed at sites such as Jarlshof and Clickhimin.

It is difficult within the scope of the present volume and in the present unequal state of knowledge to produce a brief coherent overview of Iron Age rural settlement. Nevertheless, the period is of vital importance and certain basic trends are clear. First, despite the uneven quality of the evidence, we glimpse substantial regional contrasts, contrasts in the density of the population and perhaps in man's use of the land. Population densities had clearly reached such levels that man was no longer chipping at a wilderness, and there are grounds for postulating the existence of substantial areas of tamed, farmed land especially in the valleys and uplands of the chalk and limestone lands, but also, if recent air photography is a guide, in many of the great valleys of the inner Midlands, while in Northumberland the presence of over fifty enclosed farms on the boulder clays of the coastal lowlands provides much food for thought. Second, the evidence of pollen analysis attests increasingly to the impact of the period on our uplands and upland margins, although there is an inevitable bias in this evidence because of the physical controls over the location of suitable peat bogs. Third, the survival of evidence may well be a function of the marginality of land in later economic terms, and of the degree to which defensive features were present, for it is usually the enclosures rather than the pottery which reveal the presence of a site: in the spring of 1970 the author sherded a Durham site he suspected to be a homestead and found nothing, although subsequent air photography revealed a substantial surrounding enclosure. Furthermore, prosperous establishments have more chance of survival than the less substantial structures of lower social groups. On land in continuous occupation since the Anglo-Saxon period, subject to repeated ploughings, negative evidence may not imply an absence of occupation. Finally, in the better-recorded regions it is abundantly clear that we are dealing with a complex system of settlement in which hill-forts occupy a high place in a hierarchy which then descends through clusters of varied size and character to the level of the single farm which may be aristocratic or plebeian. In the labour demands and agricultural surpluses implied by hill-fort construction we glimpse something of the interactions between the component parts of the system; it is only a fleeting glimpse, but one which can be made more meaningful, as later chapters will show, in the light of other viewpoints. As a formative phase in the landscape of Britain, however, the contribution of the Iron Age should never be underestimated.

Romano-British Rural Settlement

The Roman occupation of Britain began in AD 43 with the invasion and conquest of the south-east and led to the emergence of a series of coherent town-centred states as opposed to a diffuse and loosely knit collection of tribes. It must be appreciated, however, that the 'conquest of Britain' was in fact never completed, for although after forty years of hard fighting Agricola had carried Roman arms deep into eastern Scotland, it proved impossible to consolidate these ephemeral gains, and the year AD 122 saw the establishment of the *limes*, stretching from the Tyne to the Solway Firth, known today as Hadrian's Wall. This massive and complicated system of frontier works and fortifications was superseded for a period of about sixty years from AD 143 to the end of the century by a slighter system of defences based upon the Antonine Wall between the Firth of Clyde and the Firth of Forth. The third century saw a return to a frontier based on Hadrian's Wall, but with defences in depth extending northwards into the southern uplands in the form of outposts. The establishment of this frontier is important to our theme in that it led to the emergence within Britain of three distinct zones, each associated with distinctive physical, cultural and economic features and each characterized by differing degrees of Romanization. The Lowlands, broadly east of the Tees-Exe line, were the most successfully penetrated by Roman culture and standards; the Highlands of the south-west, Wales and north Britain (south of the Wall) were frontier areas; Wales and the north carried heavy garrisons, while the final zone, what may be termed Atlantic Britain, remained largely un-Romanized, peopled by turbulent Celtic folk who, never subjugated by Roman arms, retained native culture in a vigorous form whilst enjoying some of the benefits of trading with the Roman world. It is against this background that we must view the rural settlement of Roman Britain.[9]

Two trends may be observed. On one hand we see the evolution of indigenous forms, on the other the introduction of exotic forms. Military needs stimulated the development of a complex pattern of communication and ports, while the rational exploitation of rural resources to a level unthinkable in the Iron Age (although in this assumption we must be cautious), linked with the demands of taxation, created pressures for change and rural re-organization. It is clear from the evidence available that even within the broad pattern of zonation indicated above there were sharp regional contrasts, and in reviewing the diversity of rural settlement found in Britain during the Roman period we are perhaps seeing the strengthening of regional contrasts which were already present by the Iron Age.

The patterns and forms of rural settlement in Roman Britain revealed by the archaeological record occur at two levels: there are the 'native' settlements in which peasant farmers carried on a way of life altered little by contact with Rome, and in sharp contrast, at a higher level of culture and comfort, we find Romanized buildings known as 'villas', and exotic farms, confined almost exclusively to the civil zone of lowland Britain. To describe the villa as exotic, however, may in some senses well be incorrect, for if one excludes the sumptuous early villa at Fishbourne, Hampshire (more a palace than a farm), then, as Collingwood indicated, the term *villa* is primarily economic in significance, implying a farm. The essential characteristics of these farms were, first, the acceptance of Roman standards of building construction and comfort, and, second, their integration into the social and economic life of the Roman world, a definition which only assumes full significance when we consider contemporary 'native' settlement forms such as the pastoral homesteads of the Cheviots. Nevertheless, it must be appreciated at the outset that there is a strong body of modern opinion which considers the bulk of the owners and occupiers of British villas (terms which were of course not necessarily synonymous) to have been of native Celtic stock. Indeed in several instances, at Park Street (Hertfordshire), Catsgore (Somerset) and Winterton (Lincolnshire), there are archaeological grounds for suggesting a transition from native farmstead to Romanized villa, although a similar transition at Lock-leys (Hertfordshire) has recently been challenged. Furthermore, in talking of villas we are compressing into one word some four hundred years of development, and lumping together such simple rectangular cottages as the earlier fourth-century building at Lock-leys or the late third-century dwelling with cowhouse attached found at Iwerne (Dorset) with complex residences and farmeries arranged around spacious courtyards such as those at Chedworth (Gloucestershire) or North Leigh (Oxfordshire), where it is often possible to demonstrate a long history of development and addition. The stone foundations and timber-frame construction of the earlier buildings are a long step from the well-built walls, multiplicity of rooms, hypocausts, tessellated pavements and mosaics of later vil-las, and we may see here social as well as temporal variations. Some six hundred and twenty structures which can be loosely termed villas are known in Britain, and although only a score or so have been scientifically excavated, the volume of evidence is greater than anything available for earlier times.

There is no clear-cut correlation between the degree of struc-tural complexity and the date. In practice, two principal parallel developments can be observed: on the one hand a process of increasing sophistication of the internal arrangements, with the multiplication of specialist rooms; on the other, increasingly sharp differences between the more luxurious structures of the third and fourth centuries, and the more numerous smaller establishments. The villas of the first and second centuries AD were generally simple structures based upon the elaboration of a long rectangular building to which subsidiary wings were added. The principal construction technique was probably half-timbering. During the third century, however, many excavated sites reveal a period of decay or general lack of maintenance and rebuilding, but in the late third and early fourth centuries new and remarkable developments appear, with elaborate reconstructions appearing on old sites, and large new mansions on fresh sites. These great country houses, with their multiplicity of rooms and sumptuous interior fittings, possessed elaborate standards of comfort not to be seen again until the eigh-teenth century. There is little doubt that, following a period of decline, linked perhaps with disturbed political conditions, the aris-tocracy, in addition to owning farms, took an interest in the country and, permanently or not, went to live there. The large luxury villas account for no more than one-eighth of the total number of known sites, indicating sharp social contrasts even amongst villa owners.

This diversity of form is complemented by distributional complexity and Fig 10 demonstrates some aspects of distribution. In general terms, villas are a phenomenon of the lowland zone, showing a distinct preference for regions with soils of light to medium

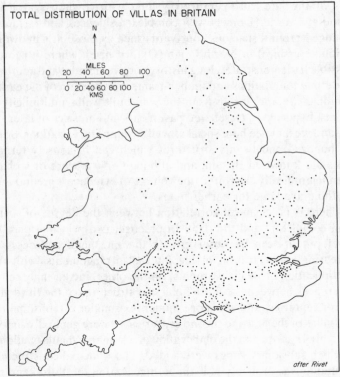

Fig 10   The Distribution of Roman Villas in Britain, after Rivet (1969), 211

texture, and a marked concentration occurs south of the Severn-Wash line. This distribution is clearly a reflection of three factors: the intrinsic suitability of the lowlands for farming, with either an arable or a stock emphasis; the military situation in the uplands, which were heavily garrisoned right through the Roman period; and finally the level of economic development achieved in pre-Roman times. It is perhaps worth stressing the variety of soil conditions associated with villas, ranging from the chalk and limestone of Wiltshire and the Cotswolds, and the sands and gravels of Hampshire, to the heavier lands of East Anglia and the clays of Somerset. It is abundantly clear that villas occur in those regions which succeeding centuries have shown to be suitable for mixed farming, with corn, stock and sheep variously combined, on soils which later assessments have viewed as good or medium quality.

In detail, the distribution of villas requires a consideration of their relationship to other components of the total pattern and some speculation concerning the tenurial units which were associated with them. It can be argued that there is a relationship between the distribution of villas and of towns, with the former seeming to cluster around the latter. The villa-groups around Ilchester (Fig 11) and Cirencester are cases in question, and Rivet has gone so far as to state that the two 'did indeed form connected parts of one economic system'. The precise nature of these links is not of course archaeologically detectable; the ties may be strongly economic, for it is in the villa that storage and processing facilities were to be found, the towns being markets for produce. On the other hand the links may be social, with the villas' owners wishing to possess town houses and to share in the offices and social recreations of urban life.

Two very large areas of southern Britain are notable because of the absence of villas: Salisbury Plain together with Cranbourne Chase, and the Fens (Fig 10). Significantly, both areas have produced evidence for Romano-British villages. In Dorset and Wiltshire, Fowler and Bowen have documented a series of settlements of sufficient size, having enough house-platforms to be fairly called 'villages', incorporating complexes of house-platforms, roadways and open spaces; indeed these plans are nearer to those of some medieval villages than anything found previously, although their associated fields are securely in the prehistoric tradition. The absence of normal development is striking, particularly as villas are to be found on the chalklands of Hampshire, and this has led to the suggestion that the Dorset and Wiltshire region was, at an early date, converted into an imperial domain. In a study of the Roman Fenland, Hallam has demonstrated that a scatter of single farms present during the first century AD had by the early third century developed into a series of small clusters, villages and hamlets, only to revert to single farms during the late third and fourth centuries. This development is a pointer to the difficulties of reconstructing complex patterns of spatial change from archaeological evidence. Only under exceptional conditions does the picture emerge with clarity.[10]

It would be wrong to see the villa/village dichotomy as entirely characteristic of Roman rural settlement in the lowland zone, for the gravel terraces which flank the great midland rivers have in

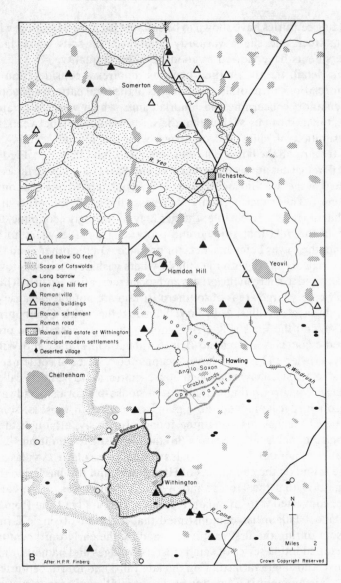

Fig 11   Settlement in the Neighbourhood of Yeovil, Somerset, and Chedworth, Gloucestershire, Crown Copyright Reserved, after O.S., 1 inch 7th ser., sheets 144, 177; Ordnance Survey (1956); H. P. R. Finberg, *Roman and Saxon Withington* (Leicester, 1959); H. P. R. Finberg, *Early Charters of the West Midlands* (Leicester, 1961)

recent years revealed extensive traces of settlements. The writer of the Ordnance Survey's notes entitled *Field Archaeology* makes two particularly significant points when he suggests that no area south of the Scottish border today undergoing successful intensive cultivation should be left out of account as a possible area of Roman-British farming, and that in Roman times rural settlement at peasant level seems in most respects to be only an intensification of the type which prevailed in the Late Iron Age.[11]

The Ordnance Survey map of Roman Britain, however, records two further categories of settlement which may be broadly 'rural' in character (Fig 12): those termed 'other major settlements' and those termed 'minor' settlements. A line from the Humber to the

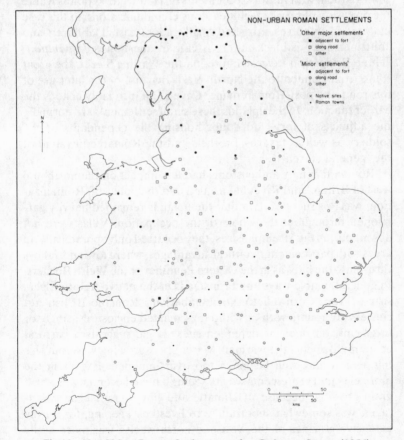

Fig 12   Non-Urban Roman Settlements, after Ordnance Survey (1956)

Dee and thence to the Bristol Channel at Newport separates these sites into two categories — those to the south and east, closely linked with the main Roman roads, and those to the north and west, linked primarily with forts, and therefore, by definition, with principal routeways. The number of such settlements is impressive and it may well be that some possessed local market functions, being the points where the surrounding peasantry could purchase such necessities as iron and salt, and luxuries from the wider Roman world, the most significant item possibly being pottery. Certainly the widespread diffusion of standardized products points to the presence of well-developed marketing chains. Very few of these sites have been satisfactorily explored, but they all possessed substantial buildings with stone foundations. It may not be inappropriate to compare some of them with railway settlements of a later age, at points where the provision of service facilities along communications, in this case inns and fresh horses, attracted small traders, casual labourers and craftsmen such as blacksmiths. A case in question is *Tripontium*, 'Three Bridges' in Leicestershire, on the Watling Street, the great route from London to the North West. Because of the later use of this road, the post-Roman name 'Cave's Inn' probably echoes the earlier function. In the uplands these small settlements are normally the adjuncts of forts, no doubt housing the dependants of the soldiery as well as taverns, brothels and the Roman equivalent of the 'general store'.

Roman manners and customs had less impact on the north and west of Britain, and Rivet has argued that the policy of 'Romanization' was less successful, in that the uplands remained heavily garrisoned throughout the whole of the occupation. Villas were not absent but, as Fig 10 emphasizes, they occurred only sporadically, in areas with particular agricultural advantages, where lowland valleys thrust into the hills, as in the eastern Pennines or the Welsh Borders. In general, native ways and farmsteads in the native tradition persisted. From Cornwall to Northumberland Romano-British hut clusters are found, with or without associated enclosures, singly or in groups, on open or defended sites. Logic suggests a pastoral economy, as befits the warmer, wetter grass-growing west, but this impression may well be much too oversimplified. Except in the more elevated settlements we are seeing a mixed economy in which grain-growing, because of climatic and physiographic disadvantages, was somewhat subordinate to livestock keeping, for on the extensive grazings of the west and north wealth was more easily amassed in cattle than in cornfields.

Throughout the north and west of England and Wales, round stone-built huts surrounded by oval, round or polygonal enclosure walls were a basic form for several centuries. These seem to be family settlements, single farms, but during the Roman period not only did their numbers multiply, but also homesteads which started as a single nucleus can be seen growing into hamlets or sizeable family settlements, made up of a series of such nuclear groups, as at Ewe Close, east of Shap in Westmorland.[12]

Almost all of these upland homesteads and settlements were surrounded by walls or ditches, but these clearly had no military significance, being designed to keep cattle, sheep and children in, and thieves, wolves, and perhaps rodents out. In Scotland several classes of defensive settlement appear; broadly there is a contrast between the south and east, dominated by forts defended by timber-laced ramparts and having cultural affinities with the great hill-forts of lowland Britain, and a group of defensive structures in the north and west in which relatively small areas are defended by massive enclosures and towers using drystone construction (Fig 8).

Summary

The Roman period lasted four centuries and during this time conditions were not static. This account, uneven in treatment, necessarily telescopes the evidence, but two general points emerge: first, the increased diversity both between the regions and within regions; second, although concrete evidence is all too rare, one can speculate concerning increasing interaction between the varied elements of two major settlement systems, lowland and upland. Whatever the precise effects of the Dark Ages which follow, it is clear that, because of the decay of centralized control, this interaction declined and local economic self-sufficiency became more usual. A key problem is how much of the Roman order survived, and to what extent the imported Anglo-Saxon institutions and settlements were influenced by what had gone before. This question will be tackled in the chapter to follow, but a different approach must be adopted. Instead of presenting a largely chronological account, the chapter will begin with the relatively firm ground provided by Domesday Book in 1086 and move retrogressively to the 'dark age' of the post-Roman period.

3

Domesday Book and Beyond

'DOMESDAY BOOK tells us more about the human geography of England in the eleventh century than will ever be known about the condition of any other part of the world at that early period.' These words by Lennard underline the pre-eminent place of the surveys known as Domesday Book in an account of the historical geography of rural settlement in Britain. However, because of the way in which the evidence has survived the hazards of nine hundred years, the Domesday survey does not give us a uniformly detailed picture. It deals most fully with the highly developed areas of the lowland zone, which possessed a relatively dense population, intensive agriculture and high land values; East Anglia, the south-east, the south-west and much of the Midlands are comparatively rich in detail. The survey extends northwards to the Tees and the Lune and westwards to the Welsh border to embrace portions of the less prosperous north and west, but these areas are more hastily dispatched, while the more northerly counties of Durham, Westmorland, Cumberland and Northumberland are completely ignored. The absence of such a comprehensive survey for the remainder of the British Isles is apt to create a quite erroneous impression of an outer darkness, and it is significant that these peripheral regions, old in terms of land, landscape and culture and all falling within the 'Highland Zone' of Fox soon attracted the cupidity of the Norman conquerors and, although the discussion which follows must needs lean heavily on Domesday Book, some attempt will be made to redress the balance.[1]

We have no clear understanding of why the Domesday survey was compiled, but probably the most satisfactory brief explanation is to be found in the Anglo-Saxon Chronicle when it states that:[2]

> at midwinter (1085) the King (William) was at Gloucester with his
> counsellors . . . and afterwards held a great council and very deep speech
> with his wise men about this land, how it was held and with what men.

He then sent the commissioners all over England into every shire to
collect the information now preserved in the two manuscript volumes known as Domesday Book. This evidence provides us with a
remarkable picture, and shows that, in 1086, villages, farms and
hamlets were to be found scattered throughout the length and
breadth of the land. Some measure of the comprehensiveness of the
survey is to be seen in the fact that a large proportion of the villages
which appear in the later records were already present in 1086,
while in England south of the Tees and east of the Wye today's
motorist is rarely more than five miles from a village 'mentioned in
Domesday Book', a phrase which, popular with local guides and
estate agents, has become a hallmark of respectable antiquity. For
many thousands of settlements Domesday Book provides us with
reasonably consistent information which varies in character, quantity and detail, and as H. C. Darby and his co-workers have demonstrated, is particularly suitable for conversion into maps. The
Domesday survey constitutes a datum line across both space and
time; it forms a base from which it is possible to look both backward
'beyond Domesday' to the patterns of settlement evolving in the
darker centuries before 1086, and forward to the mature patterns of
the Middle Ages, but such studies must be securely based on a third
vital level of interpretation: an understanding of the contemporary
scene in 1086. Although the question of what Domesday Book tells
us has long been the subject of scholarly dispute and cannot be
easily resolved, a brief statement must needs be attempted.

The Evidence of Domesday Book

There is no single entry characteristic of the rich regional and local
diversity demonstrated by the Domesday record: indeed every page
of the account raises particular problems of interpretation, for the
Norman scribes and commissioners tended to impose their own
preconceptions and terminology on the reality of Saxon and Scandinavian England. The scope of the survey may be summarized as
follows: for each settlement it was intended to record the name and
extent of the manor or estate; the owner in the time of Edward the
Confessor and in 1085–6; the number of tenants, their status and

the size of their holdings; the size of the lord's demesne or home farm; the quantity of woodland, meadow, pasture and arable ground; the number of mills, quarries, mines and fisheries; and finally the value of the estate in the time of King Edward, in 1066 and in 1085–6. Unfortunately, not many of the reports answer all of these requirements, but the following extract indicates the form in which a normal entry is cast:[3]

Tysoe (Warwickshire, folio 242b): The same Robert (de Statford) holds Tysoe. There, are 23 hides. There, is land for 32 ploughs. In demesne are 11 (ploughs), and 9 serfs, and 53 villans, with a priest and 23 bordars, have 23 ploughs. There, 16 acres of meadow; and in Warwick 3 houses pay 13d. It was worth £20. Now, £30. Waga held it freely.

This sets out the five recurring items found for most villages: a statement of the numbers of hides or other taxable units such as *carucates* or *sulungs*, an indication of the extent of arable land available to the settlement expressed in terms of plough lands; the number of eight-ox plough-teams the *vill* could muster to till the arable lands; some data on population, subdivided into various categories according to status; finally a figure expressing the value of the settlement, probably the income which could normally be expected from its rents and other renders. In addition, amounts of woodland and meadowland do tend to appear regularly.

Domesday statistics such as these permit several scales of analysis. Professor H. C. Darby adopted the county as the most useful frame of reference, because inconsistencies tend to arise as county boundaries are crossed, reflecting no doubt the idiosyncrasies of different groups of commissioners, but at one end of the scale it is possible to consider settlement in England while at the other we are faced with the individual entry, and the problem of relating the Norman clerk's thumbnail sketch to the reality of houses, village, fields and woods in 1086. In this chapter our concern must be largely with the broader patterns, for the forms of settlement present in 1086 must be considered more fully in Chapter 5. It is, however, important at this juncture to note that the size of a *vill*, the basic unit of settlement described by Domesday Book, could vary greatly, ranging from a few hundred folk to a mere hamlet with no more than two or three households. Average sizes mean little, but the table below is derived from a series of figures cited by Maitland and gives some impressions of size ranges for settlements in central and southern England:[4]

| | Recorded | | | Calculated | | |
	Number of *vills*	Total recorded non-servile population	Average per *vill*	X4	Actual range	X4
Cambridge (Armingford Hundred)	14 vills	457 folk	*32*	*128*	*12–62*	*48–248*
Staffordshire (Random)	14 vills	200 folk	*14*	*56*	*3–43*	*12–180*
Somerset (Bishop of Contenances estates)	14 vills	153 folk	*11*	*44*	*3–23*	*12–92*

(the italicized figures are calculated)

These figures exclude serfs or slaves, and as the recorded population represents, in all probability, heads of households, the totals must be multiplied by a factor — say 3, 4, or 5 — depending on one's view of the size of the medieval family. Within the groups of *vills* selected, the population is seen to have varied from 3 to 62 families, say 10 to 250 souls.

These variations must be kept in mind when examining Fig 13 showing the location of all recorded Domesday settlements. This map reinforces a point strongly made by Lennard that, by 1066, England was already an 'old country', and although, judged by modern standards, the population was no doubt very scanty (in all about 1·5 to 2 million in England, as compared with over 50 million today) and the area of wood, waste and marsh was very large, Anglo-Saxon farmers were not nibbling at the edges of a wilderness that was still unsubdued. It must be appreciated, however, that such a map cannot give a truly accurate picture of settlement in the eleventh century for, in addition to the omission of unidentified *vills*, supplementary evidence from Kent, Lindsey and Leicestershire emphasizes that there were many settlements which must have gone unmentioned because their resources were included with those of their parent villages; indeed Maitland went so far as to state that 'when more than five and twenty team-lands or thereabouts are ascribed to a single place, we shall generally find reason to believe that what is being described is not a single vill.' Be this as it may, while not conveying correctly every nuance of the distribution and intensity of settlement in the late eleventh century, Fig 10 probably gives a fair general picture, and it is evidence that the framework of rural England as we know it was already laid out: although *Chenesitun, Chelched, Lanchel, Sudwerca, Stibenhede* and *Grenviz* may have been far from the present Kensington, Chelsea, Lambeth, Southwick, Stepney and Greenwich, these locations had already been settled and at least partially tamed. Throughout most of the more hospitable portions of the lowland zone below 244 m (800 ft), a scatter of communities living in grouped settlements or *vills* were to be found; indeed it was only the less hospitable upland areas — the Pennines and Dartmoor, for instance; extensive tracts of marsh and fen; the Somerset levels; the Fens and the alluvial area at the head of the Humber, together with areas of particularly heavy or

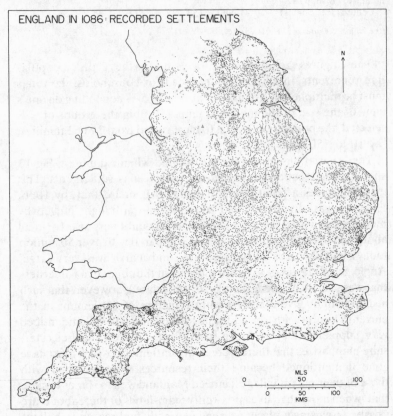

ENGLAND IN 1086 : RECORDED SETTLEMENTS

Fig 13   The Distribution of Settlements in England Recorded in Domesday Book in 1086, after Darby, (1952-67)

particularly infertile soils, notably the Weald clays, the Bunter Sandstones of Nottinghamshire, the Norfolk Brecklands and the London clays and Bagshot beds — which were wholly devoid of recorded settlements. In the mild south-west what seem to be small hamlets or single farms were to be found at altitudes in excess of 305 m (1,000 ft). At Radworthy in Devon, for example, four folk were working one and a half plough-teams at some 365 m (1,200 ft) above sea level. In general, however, occupation was extensive only below 244 m (800 ft), spreading out across the broad plains to thrust deeply into the valleys of the Pennine foothills, and through the Aire Gap to link Yorkshire with Lancashire. The highest densities of population, in excess of fifteen recorded folk per square mile, are only found in a few favoured localities, along the south coast of Sussex and Kent, and on the mixed loamy soils of the East Anglian plateau, although densities of between ten and fourteen were to be found along the Jurassic scarpland from Lincolnshire to Somerset. Elsewhere in the south, south-west and midlands, densities of between 2·5 and 9 recorded people per square mile were usual, while in the north densities rarely rise above 2·5. It is instructive to note that while these figures imply a total population averaging between about 10 and 60 folk per square mile, most of rural England today has densities of the order of 100 to 200 folk per square mile. As with people, so with plough-teams. The south and east of the country emerge as rich in terms of the teams which could be mustered, an essential condition if the larger population was to be fed. With regard to the state of tillage in 1086 and the extent of arable land, it is, as Lennard indicates, necessary to speak with some caution, but the evidence unmistakably suggests that the area under plough in England (exclusive of Middlesex and certain northern regions for which the evidence of Domesday is either wanting or misleading) was not much less, and may even have been somewhat greater, than the extent of arable in the early years of the twentieth century. One must remember, however, that the England of Domesday Book lacked the fine fields of permanent grass that are such an important element in modern farming, and that the pastures consisted mostly of very rough grazing grounds, maintained and gradually extended by grazing, fuel-cutting and accidental and deliberate firing. England in 1086 must be seen as a countryside rich in woodland, with substantial tracts of standing timber in the less accessible watershed areas within the lowland zone — Arden, Cannock, Delamere, Charnwood and the Weald for instance — but the picture is probably less one of vast tracts of extensive woodland than of each *vill* adjoining an area of woodland spared by that 'enemy of the hoar-wood', the ploughman;[5] it was only here and there that there were blocks of untouched woodland and marsh larger by far than anything to be found in modern England, apart from Dartmoor and Exmoor and the moors and fells of the north. In a few areas, notably the Feldon of south Warwickshire (Fig 18), the woodland was so depleted that few estates appear to have possessed any at all, and survivals were only to be found along the wooded scarpface of the lower Lias Limestone.

Even some twenty years after the Conquest an important element of the landscape of 1086 was 'waste', implying, not the natural waste of mountain, marsh or heath, but land that had gone out of cultivation. The southern counties bear the imprint of the Conquest, with wasted *vills* occurring spasmodically throughout the whole region, particularly to the north, west and south of London, attributable perhaps to William's campaigns of the invasion.[6] However, in 1086 waste formed an outstanding element in the human geography of the northern counties, and the devastated condition of the countryside is graphically illustrated by Fig 14. This devastation seems to have been the product of the 'harrying of the north' during the punitive campaigns of 1069–70, and was no ordinary reprisal. William deliberately took a terrible revenge and left the countryside in a condition in which it would give him no further trouble. The impact of this devastation on rural settlement has yet to be fully assessed, but it is clear that we are here dealing with something more deliberate, more lasting and more fundamental than the usual spasmodic wastings which were characteristic of medieval warfare and from which the relatively primitive agriculture of the period speedily recovered, unless population, plough-teams and livestock were actually destroyed in great numbers. Sporadic, local, and relatively ephemeral devastation was an essential ingredient in the life of medieval settlements, but the scars in the north persisted for decades rather than years, and it is sobering to appreciate that over one half of the *vills* in the North Riding of Yorkshire and one third of those of the East and West Ridings were wholly or partly waste, while almost the whole of north Lancashire was devastated. While it must be admitted that not all of this wasting can be laid on King William's conscience (for Norwegian armies, Irish pirates, and Norman lords, moving folk from remote hill villages to recolonize the plains, must all have added their tithe), there seems little doubt that his punitive campaign left deep scars. In some instances these persist in a disguised form until today. Furthermore, our knowledge of the devastation north of the Tees is deficient because of the absence of Domesday Book for that region, although William's armies certainly reached the Tyne.

In the light of these facts it can be appreciated that the picture given by the recorded details of the Domesday Survey bears no clear witness to the actual achievements of Anglo-Saxon and Scandinavian folk in the north, and Fig 13, showing all named localities, waste or populated, is at best a skeletal outline. England in 1086 was a land of villages, and although in many districts there was enough untamed waste and woodland to provide opportunities for generations of pioneering effort directed to the enlargement of the

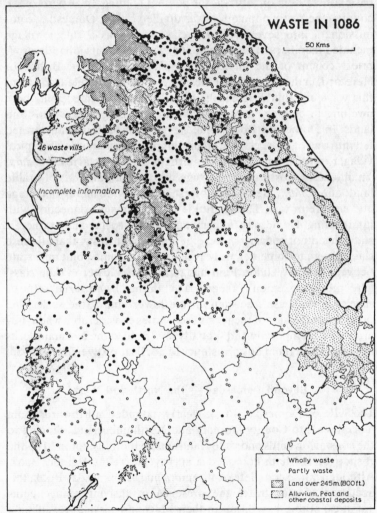

Fig 14   Recorded Waste in the North of England in 1086, after Darby, (1973), 60

cultivated area, these villages were, as Lennard points out, thick enough on the ground for nearly all to be within easy reach of other villages. The social implications of this fact are important; the 1½ to

2 million folk living in England in 1086 were not backwoodsmen; they lived in an old country, and they lived in communities, both local and regional.

England in 1086 was a land of villages and great estates, but the basic constitutent of both was the peasant holding. In all parts of the country the rustic population was divided by the Domesday commissioners into several distinct classes, and as a rule a village included members of more than one class among its inhabitants. A brief account of the inquest was written by Robert, Bishop of Hereford, in the very year Domesday Book was compiled, and from this we learn that England held both serfs and free men, those dwelling in cottages as well as those possessing homesteads and lands. In Domesday Book some 72 per cent of those enumerated fell into one of three classes: *villans*, implying apparently the typical villager, with a small farm of perhaps 25 to 35 acres; *bordars*, smallholders, possessing a cottage and a small amount of arable land; and *cottars*, men at the lowest level, having merely a cottage and an acre or two. The multitude of problems in connection with interpreting Domesday information about social and economic status need not concern us here; it is sufficient to say that all these classes were to some degree servile, falling at some point on a scale between what Welldon Finn has termed the 'lower middle class' ('freemen', 'sokemen', 'thegns' and 'drengs') and *servi*, serfs or slaves, in no sense free men, at the lower end of the scale. The precise significance of the terms used varies considerably when they are viewed temporally and spatially, and indeed the Norman clerks imposed upon them no consistency of application even in 1085–6.

Beyond Domesday — the North and West

The *vills* of Domesday Book clearly extended northwards from Yorkshire into County Durham and Northumberland, clinging to the coastal lowlands and valley lands in the foothills, for in 1183 the Bishop of Durham compiled a survey known as Boldon Book. Although not so complete or all-embracing as Domesday Book, this document demonstrates the presence of thriving village communities, arable-based, but in their rents and services revealing a pastoral sub-stratum which may well be of great antiquity. Furthermore, in Durham and Northumberland we read of *vills* being grouped into clusters for the purpose of rendering service to their lord, an arrangement which has close parallels in the *berewicks* or scattered members of large estates of Domesday Book. Two

renders in particular, *cornage,* and *metride* (*metreth* or *milchcow*),
seem to have Celtic antecedents, and in the ancient kingdom of
Northumbria, as Jolliffe indicated, our sources make us sharply
aware of a pre-Saxon sub-stratum of settlement and renders.[7] There
is no comprehensive documentation to reconstruct eleventh-
century settlement patterns 'beyond' Domesday in the spatial
sense, but fortunately the Gloucestershire folios contain some hints
in the form of an account of the country beyond the Wye, in Welsh
hands until 1065. Some of these entries seem to refer to territory on
which the Welsh land system had remained unaltered, and instead
of being divided into separate *vills* assessed in terms of hides,
ploughlands or plough-teams, the territory was divided on the basis
of groups of *vills*, each group recorded under the control of a bailiff,
reeve or *prepositus:*

> Under Waswic, the prepositus, are 13 vills; under Elmvi are 14 vills;
> under Blei 13 vills; and under Idhel are 14 vills. These render 47 sestars
> of honey, 40 pigs, 41 cows and 28s. for the hawks. Under the same
> prepositus are 4 vills wasted by King Caraduech.

The ancient laws of Wales indicate such a grouping of *vills (trefi)*,
each group being under the control of *prepositus* (bailiff or reeve) or
maer; they also show how each group of *vills* rendered certain
specified food rents to a central point on the estate. It seems probable that a reflection of these arrangements can be seen in the
groupings of northern English *vills* into shires, to the chief villages
of which labour services and rents were due. Glanville Jones has
argued cogently that the same arrangement is found in the multiple
estates of Domesday Book made up of *berewicks* and *sokelands,*
(detached members), many of which lie at great distances from the
caput or chief village. In the light of these indications, eleventh-
century Wales is best seen as a land of small clusters or hamlets,
normally taking advantage of the resources of arable land available
in the coastal lowlands and valleys, but often possessing extensive
grazing and hunting rights in the dominant mountain lands. These
trefi (*vills*, or townships) appear to have been grouped into larger
units termed *maenors* or *maenols*, and a contrast seems to have
existed between the more pastoral *maenors* of the uplands and the
agricultural *maenors* of the lowlands, for a Welsh law (of tenth-
century origin?) states that 'there are to be seven townships in a
lowland maenor; thirteen townships in an upland maenor'. These
groupings were specifically related to the rendering of *gwestfa* or
food rent, support for the lord and his entourage. In the case of bond

settlements, servile *vills*, inhabited by bondsmen, a particular township normally stood out because it was the focus around which the
life of the neighbouring settlements revolved and, as this was often
the settlement near which the local lord had a hall, it was over-
looked by an official — a *maer* or reeve — and hence was termed the
maerdref. On any one estate individual *trefi* may have possessed a
specialist function, some being based on the arable resources (*hen-
dref*), others taking advantage of the pastoral resources in the hills
(*hafod*). Some were inhabited by free tenants, others by servile
tenants. Some contained a lordly palace (*llys*), others contained a
church or place of worship (*llan*), while others served as hunting
resorts. Fig 15 illustrates the distribution of settlement nuclei in
north-west Wales in the late-thirteenth and fourteenth centuries,
emphasizing the social and tenurial diversity at that stage. If the
trends in Wales did indeed follow those of the rest of Europe, then

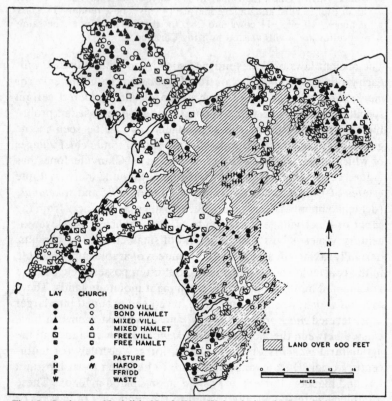

Fig 15   Settlement Nucleii in North-West Wales during the Late Thirteenth and
Early Fourteenth Centuries, after Jones (1964), 22

about 1300 might represent a population peak, and settlement in the eleventh century may have been less intense, so that comparisons between Figs 10 and 12 are dangerous. Unfortunately no detailed survey of such a *vill* in the eleventh century survives, but a tenth-century law records 'This is the complement of a lawful hamlet: nine buildings, and one plough, and one kiln, and one churn and one cat, and one cock, and one bull and one herdsman.' This is a settlement corresponding in size to some of the smallest *vills* recorded in Domesday Book, if we are to take one plough as a measure of the capacity to support the inhabitants.[8]

Scotland does not yield, as Welsh records do, an abundance of medieval evidence, but the small cluster is a settlement type which in some form or other would appear to have been a common feature of Celtic lands. In Ireland, for instance, there is some evidence to suggest that clustered settlements were found during the Middle Ages and the facts that the Irish word *baile* replaces the English *ton* and the Latin *villa*, and that all are found combined with Irish terms in place-names, suggest that some at least of these clusters must have been pre-Norman in origin. Proudfoot has pointed out that *bally* place-name elements in Co. Down have a complementary distribution with the large single farms of Dark Age origin known variously as *raths*, *cashels* or *ring forts*, clearly suggesting the presence of two social groups living side by side, although the precise functional and social relationships between the two has not been established.[9] A reasoned guess would suggest that in eleventh-century Scotland small hamlet settlements were found scattered over the better lowlands, becoming less and less subject to any centralized control in regions of more broken terrain, and tending increasingly to be in essence complex family farms. It would, however, be unwise to overemphasize the physical isolation of even such areas as the north-west Highlands, remote only to a land-based culture, for the sea offered, to those knowing its ways, an open network of routeways, and the Norse Kingdom of the Southern Isles, which persisted until 1266, embraced the island groups of the west coast of Scotland from Lewis and Skye to Islay and Man, and possessed a common parliament and diocesan organization. In this context it is well worth recalling Fraser Darling's comments on the Highland township:[10]

If the lie of the land allows a few acres to be made into cultivated ground, a township grows upon it . . . It is probable that these few acres will be isolated from other similar ground by moor on three sides and the sea on the fourth, and the size of the township depends on the acreage of ground cultivable. There was a lower limit to the size of a township in earlier days when the unit was fully functional, imposed by the number of men necessary for a work team or boat's crew. This number was generally four, and such larger townships made possible by a greater amount of cultivable land or by geographical accident of good anchorage tended to be composed of a number of work teams or crews of four . . . The system was one of essential co-operation by people living near the fringe of possible human existence.

This was written about twentieth-century conditions, but the points that it makes were probably equally valid in the tenth or even in the first century AD. The basic unit of settlement in these northern regions was the long-house type of farm (Fig 2) with an integrated subsistence dual economy based on land and sea, and as population increased there seems to have been a growth of small clusters of settlement or townships, for example at Jarlshof in the Shetlands and Westray in the Orkneys. At Jarlshof in the eleventh century (Fig 29) there was a cluster of three farms, and it must be remembered that one farm would house not only the established farmer but also his landless sons, making perhaps in all a community of between ten and twenty folk, men, women and children.

Beyond Domesday — the Antecedents of Norman England

The antecedents of the settlement patterns in eleventh-century England may be traced to two roots. They can be regarded as an expression of either subsequent expansion from Anglo-Saxon clusters or of Scandinavian pioneering during and after the ninth century, or as the indeterminate and shadowy patterns inherited from the Roman and Iron Age past. These two views were hotly debated in the late-nineteenth century, and within the last decade the question has been reopened. Turning first to the contribution of Anglo-Saxon and Scandinavian folk: the departure of the last regular units of the Roman army from these shores early in the fifth century was followed by a period of internal disorder and raids from outside, which encouraged a process of infiltration by Germanic folk. There are strong grounds for believing that this process had in fact begun *before* the end of the fourth century when Germanic troops, *foederati*, were introduced into parts of southern England, a process which seems to have been continued and extended by native British rulers in the early years of the fifth century, as is well demonstrated by the traditional account of Vortigern inviting Hengest and Horsa into Kent. Certainly by the mid-fifth century Germanic folk were establishing permanent settlements in Kent and East Anglia and

parts of Yorkshire, apparently taking advantage of the deep
estuaries and slow-moving rivers which 'invited' penetration.[11] In
these circumstances it is difficult to obtain a truly balanced view of
the Anglo-Saxon 'invasion' of the islands, but the following points
are important: firstly, what was involved was clearly a folk movement, with substantial numbers of people moving from homelands
in northern Europe, transferring the language and culture of these
regions to England; secondly, this event is not to be seen as a
planned invasion in the sense of the Spanish Armada or Operation
Sealion; it was rather a process of gradual infiltration which slowly
gathered momentum until it was possible for German field armies
seriously to challenge British authority and establish kingdoms of
their own. This naturally occurred first of all in the more easterly
portions of the lowland zone, where Saxon troops had probably
been established even before AD 410, and where it was possible to
receive sea-borne reinforcements. It is worth noting in this context
that the Sutton Hoo ship, dating at least 250 years after the initial
invasions, was a mere $26 \cdot 0$ m (85 feet) long with a greatest beam of
$4 \cdot 3$ m (14 feet), drawing a mere $0 \cdot 6$ m (2 feet) when laden. The
boat probably possessed 19 pairs of oars and could perhaps have
accommodated a maximum of 50 folk, leaving little room for gear.
This, in the context of the invasion period, may be regarded as a
large vessel, for two centuries or more earlier the shipwrights' craft
was less developed and smaller boats were more usual. Such large
open rowing-boats were not vessels in which to make a sea-borne
invasion, and a knowledge of local tides and friendly harbours must
have been of immense help.[12]

Thirdly, and perhaps more significantly, the Anglo-Saxon settlement of England was a protracted process, and some two centuries separate the initial arrivals from the occupation of the entire
lowland zone (Fig 16) — two centuries during which British resistance was slowly worn down by the increasing numbers and increasing organization of the new settlers, so that the initial footholds
were gradually extended and consolidated. The story of the thrusts
inland at first involves conflict between German and Briton, and in
recent years there has been much debate over the extent to which
British population, language and institutions were absorbed by the
invaders. The process of intermingling was complex, and was
admirably summarized by Bede when he wrote of Aethelfrith, King
of Northumbria in AD 603, 'he conquered more territories from the
Britons, either making them tributary or driving them clear out, and
planting English in their places, than any other King.' As British

political power waned, the picture was increasingly one of competition between the various incipient Germanic kingdoms whose boundaries often strongly reflected geographical factors. Sussex was hemmed in between the sea and the forest of the Weald; Kent was similarly placed on the southern side of the Thames estuary,

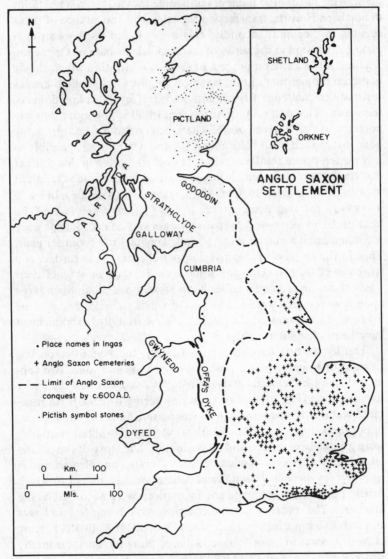

Fig 16   Anglo-Saxon Settlement and Celtic Kingdoms, after various sources, including Jones (1973) and the references cited therein

while East Anglia was bounded to the west by fen and wood except where a corridor of open chalk country gave access via the Gog Magog Hills, significantly strongly defended by a series of cross-dykes. It is no accident that the drive to the west was accomplished by three larger kingdoms with less clear-cut borders: Wessex, focusing on the downland node of southern England, the meeting place of numerous ancient trackways; Mercia, based on the rich valley lands of the Midlands, Avon, Trent and Severn, but inherently unstable because it was exposed to war on several fronts; and Northumbria, having secure footholds in both the north-eastern lowlands and the vale of York. These three kingdoms jostled for supremacy and stabilized boundaries, a process which carried Anglo-Saxon colonists to the borders of the Highland Zone by the middle years of the seventh century. Nevertheless, it is a measure of the complexity of the situation that during the early years of the seventh century Penda of Mercia was making war on Northumbrian Deira with the help of a powerful Welsh king, Cadwallon of Gwynedd![13]

Few well-travelled topics offer more pitfalls for the unwary than the creation of Saxon England: the Anglo-Saxon Chronicle presents what purports to be a traditional account; the evidence of graves, often clustered in cemeteries, provides tangible proof of the presence of simply equipped warriors and their brooch-bedecked wives; the language of the incomers was firmly implanted in the landscape in the form of place-names. In practice, however, the Chronicle is an interpretational quagmire whose political propaganda for the royal house of Wessex can only be utilized after particularly careful analysis and qualification; the archaeological evidence tells us of folk dead, not folk living, and is often difficult to date, even to the historically broad limits of a quarter of a century; the interpretation of place-names, as Morris points out, requires 'a nice attention to Old English spelling, grammar and usage' and modern scholarship is currently engaged in subtle re-evaluations of hitherto acceptable generalizations. Fig 16 incorporates two basic classes of evidence: cemeteries, probably indicative of the earlier phases of Saxon penetration, and place-names involving the termination-*ingas*, as in *Haestingas* — the modern Hastings — implying a place or a people belonging to the word preceding it — in this case 'Haesta's people' — which represent sixth-century colonization away from the fifth-century centres using the cemeteries. As Dodgson's work shows, however, the picture is in detail exceedingly complex and Fig 13 is, as it stands, the crudest of generalizations.

Nevertheless, it makes one point clear; the Saxons penetrated and colonized the lowlands of the south and east but failed to conquer the uplands. By about 600 AD the foothills of the Highland Zone (Fig 17) had been reached, and the year 613 saw Aethelfrith of Northumbria winning a victory over the Welsh near Chester; the eighth century saw the construction by Offa of the dyke, that still bears his name, between the Severn Sea and the Dee to separate unconquered British, later Welsh, lands from the Saxon kingdom of Mercia. In a sense British rulers were driven to the west, but humbler folk stayed on in England, surviving the change of masters, and their presence amid the dominant Saxon folk is well-attested by clauses in law-codes, the survival of certain art forms, and the presence of place-names incorporating the elements *walas*, *brettas* or *cumbran* widely scattered throughout the better-quality lands of the lowland zone. The complete destruction of the British population by the Saxons is now emerging as a scholarly myth which is not supported by the detailed evidence.[14]

To the west and north of the emerging Saxon kingdoms, British states survived; the Celtic traditions of Wales and Scotland are well known, but between the Celtic west and Saxon England there lay a fascinating, tantalizing twilight zone extending from Devon and Cornwall, through the Welsh border country, Lancashire, Westmorland, Cumberland, including Durham, Northumberland and the border counties, in which British traditions and life are variously interblended with Saxon and, at a later date, Scandinavian traditions and life-styles. The British kingdoms of southern Scotland appear to have originated in arrangements made by the Roman northern military command after the great barbarian 'conspiracy' of AD 367, when Hadrian's Wall was breached, and the dynasties of the border, the rulers of Strathclyde and Manaw Gododdin, traced their ancestry back to Roman antecedents (Fig 16). English influence penetrated northwards along the coastal corridor from southern Northumberland, and eventually extended as far as the Firth of Forth, until Egfrith was defeated by a Pictish army at Dunnichen Moss, near Forfar (Angus) in AD 685. The Picts occupied the eastern coastlands and glens to the north of the Clyde-Forth line — the Roman Antonine wall — and these barbarian peoples, never subdued by Rome, were instrumental in precipitating the Saxon 'takeover' of the lowlands, in that it was Pictish raids southwards in the fifth century which initially encouraged British rulers to employ Saxon mercenaries. Modern Scotland, ironically enough, owes its name to immigrants from Ireland; before the fifth century AD Scots,

from northern Ireland, began to colonize the girdle of islands and
headlands between the Clyde and Inverness, and in AD 843 the two
realms, Pictland and Scottish Dalriada, were united under Kenneth
MacAlpine; by the early eleventh century the medieval kingdom of
Scotland had come into being. The most dramatic monuments to
the Picts (Fig 13) are their enigmatic standing stones whose strange
symbols — lively, fantastically intertwined beasts, mysterious
cloaked horsemen and intricate decorative interlaces — tell of
mixed artistic traditions, skilled craftsmen and wealthy patrons;
they are, however, silent on settlement, and much awaits the spade.[15]

We can look back from Domesday and appreciate the centuries
of patient colonization represented by the dense scatter of settlements throughout the lowlands, in part no doubt the results of a
more ancient heritage of Celtic settlement, but bearing nevertheless
the heavy imprint of Anglo-Saxon folk in the form of place-names;
place-name studies is a field in which a little knowledge is particulary dangerous, but with this warning in mind it can be stated that in
general terms names terminating in -ing (ingas, a group of people),
-ham (a homestead or an estate), -ingham (-ingaham, -ingas and
-ham combined, usually preceded by a personal name), -tun (an
enclosure, farmstead or cottage) and -ingtun (-ingtun, -ing and -tun
combined) are all representative of stages of Anglo-Saxon settlement earlier than that characterized by names terminating in -ley
(-leah, forest, wood, glade, or clearing), -worth (an enclosure) and
field (cleared land); this fundamental distinction can often be used
to provide a general view of the progress of settlement (Fig 15). One
must regret that it may never be possible to study the differences of
settlement over a substantial area during this important formative
period for, as Beresford and St Joseph stressed, our evidence tells us
only of the *faits accomplis* rather than the actual steps in the progress of early settlement, and they have traced in detail the
emergence of the mother and daughter settlements of Great Gidding, Little Gidding and Steeple Gidding in Huntingdonshire. Little
Gidding appears to have been created as a separate unit soon after
the Conquest, but Steeple Gidding represented an earlier foundation. This question of village generations is one that must be
examined more fully in a later context.[16]

The development of Anglo-Saxon England was sharply arrested
in the ninth century by a series of pirate raids by Norse and Danish
vikings and the entries in the Anglo-Saxon Chronicle describe
graphically, if not entirely accurately, how sporadic raids, beginning
in the first two decades of the eighth century, gradually increased in

duration and intensity until by 855 'the heathen for the first time
wintered in Sheppey.' This wintering in fortified encampments
became more and more common, and some ten years later, in 865,
'a great heathen host came to England and took winter-quarters
from the East Anglians and were provided with horses.' The
decades which followed were a terrible period of raid and counter-
raid, with the predatory Danish war-host possessing both mobility
and initiative. Most of these Danes came in search of plunder, but
some stayed as settlers, and we learn from the Chronicle that 'In this
year (876) Halfdan (the Danish war-leader) shared out the lands of
Northumbria and they were engaged in ploughing and making a
living for themselves.' The story of Alfred's eventual victories need
not be recounted, save that in 886 he routed Guthrum and divided
England into two by treaty, the boundary between the English lands
and the Danelaw being 'on the Thames then up the Lea to its source,
then right to Bedford, then up on the Ouse to the Watling Street'. It
is ironic that England was finally unified in 1016 when a Dane,
Canute, succeeded to the throne.

   The impact of these Viking colonists on settlement in Britain
may conveniently be considered in two sections: first, their impact
on England, where the density of Danish settlement has recently
been seriously questioned, and second in north Britain, where
Norse sway persisted until the fifteenth century. The Scandinavian
names in eastern England and the east Midlands (Fig 17) are
certainly in general terms a reflection of the contribution of ninth-
century Danish colonists to English settlement history, and names
terminating in -by (a farm, village) and -thorpe (a secondary settlement or hamlet) are frequent throughout Yorkshire, Lincolnshire
and Norfolk, spreading westwards into Leicestershire and Northamptonshire. However, a note of caution must be entered, for many
such names were not formed until after the Norman Conquest, and
even the names recorded in Domesday Book are the result of two
centuries of expanding settlement, so that it is impossible to determine how many of these names represent the first phase of Danish
settlement. Without doubt a Danish aristrocracy, Danish settlers
and Danish language were introduced into eastern England, but
Sawyer has argued cogently that, as the Danish armies involved
hundreds rather than thousands of men, it would be an error of
judgment to see the new colonists utterly swamping the English,
and indeed in the process of development it is often possible to see
English names developing Scandinavian forms; thus Aldeby in
Norfolk was *Aldeburg* in Domesday Book but had become *Aldeby*

by the end of the twelfth century, and such 'Danish' names as Naseby, Thornaby and Kirby in Gretton (Northamptonshire) show a similar post-Domesday change. Throughout the whole of the area of 'Danish' settlement, Scandinavian place-names are intermixed with English and, more significantly, occur frequently on lands

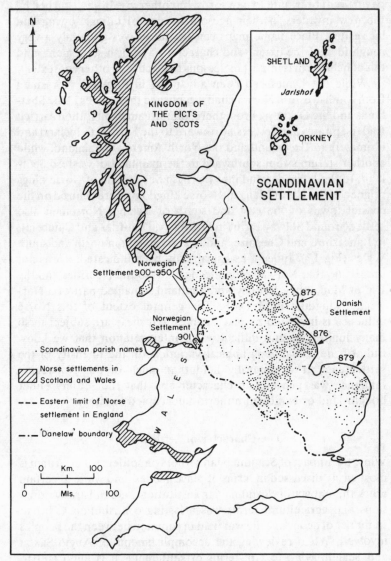

Fig 17   Scandinavian Settlements in Britain, after various sources, including Jones (1973) and the references cited therein

which the English had not yet occupied; this argues strongly against the wholesale occupation of native English settlements by the invaders, while the survival of English place-names for some of the most desirable settlement sites, even in heavily Scandinavianized areas, suggests that the English continued to live in their villages, paying rent or tribute to new lords, but otherwise little disturbed by the new invaders in their age-old routine of tilling, sowing and harvesting. Place-name maps can by themselves give only a very rough idea of the extent and character of Danish settlement, and this conclusion has important lessons to teach us in other contexts.[17]

While the Danes had been advancing in England, Norsemen from south-western Norway had established themselves in the Shetlands and the Orkneys. From there, one stream of migration carried traders, pirates and settlers northward to the Faroes, to Iceland and ultimately to Greenland and the North American mainland, while another stream swept southward to the mainland of western Scotland, to the Hebrides and into the Irish Sea. A line of Norse kings reigned in the Isle of Man, and Norse kingdoms were centred on the coastal towns of the east and south of Ireland. Norsemen also settled around Solway Firth (in Galloway, Dumfries and Cumbria), in Lancashire and Cheshire, and to some extent in north and south Wales (Fig 17). Indeed, as has already been indicated, it was not until 1266 that Norway renounced claims to the Hebrides and the Isle of Man, while Orkney and Shetland remained part of a Norwegian kingdom until 1468. The general extent of this Norse influence is indicated by place-names, but these are subject to so many limitations and difficulties of interpretation that we know little of the actual geographical variations in the intensity of the settlements. It is generally held that much of the Norwegian influence was peaceful in character and that the settlers either bought land or exploited hitherto unoccupied territory.[18]

The Character of Settlement

While the impact of Scandinavian settlers on settlement in Britain is most easily discussed in terms of place-names, and while in certain areas the impact of Scandinavian institutions, administrative divisions and agricultural terms was a lasting contribution, a broad similarity of economic life was held in common between the peoples involved. When reviewing the accomplishments of Anglo-Saxon and Scandinavian folk in terms of settlement, it is important to appreciate that the distribution maps seen in Figs 13, 16 and 17,

with all their inherent difficulties, are nevertheless a reflection of
two patterns superimposed by man on the land, two patterns which
may for convenience be separated but which in reality are in themselves complex and indivisible. First, there is a pattern of economic
exploitation, for around the clustered dwellings of each village lay
the fields, arable lands, meadows and pastures; these were integrated within a second pattern, which may broadly be termed
administrative, which reflected both the ownership of land and
estates, and the degree to which society was organized into groupings larger than the mere village. It is the study of the interaction
between these two cultural patterns and the value judgments, in
terms of the physical landscape which they represent, which forms
an important component of settlement geography. The importance
and antiquity of these cultural patterns in England was stressed by
Aston, who pointed out that in many places -*ingas* settlements,
implying a close link between a settlement and a personal, family or
'class' name, must have been unitary since estate and village, manor
and *vill*, were one, and he goes on to trace the emergence of more
complex forms found in 1086, seeing them as a predictable result of
the disintegration of the primitive estate. He points out that

> expansion of settlement, sales and mortgages, leases and rewards,
> inheritance and family arrangements, forfeiture, piety, illegality must
> have given to estate and village history a vitality and movement which
> could not fail to complicate the relative simplicity of the early estate, and
> to obscure and ultimately destroy that unity of lordship and settlement
> on which it was based.

It is no criticism of Aston's thesis to point out that he largely ignores
the fact that in their turn Anglo-Saxon colonists were not in fact
settling an empty landscape: they had beneath their ploughs a
heritage from earlier patterns, and the work of Glanville Jones
points to the survival of ancient multiple estates beneath the manors
and vills of Domesday Book.[19]

This complex relationship between settlement in 1086 and its
antecedents can best be demonstrated by means of a specific example (Fig 18). The distribution of population and woodland in Warwickshire reveals a striking dichotomy between the south and east
and the north and west; the former, known by later topographers as
the Feldon, emerges as a well-populated zone, rich in terms of
population, plough-teams and meadow resources, while in the
north-west the forest of Arden emerges as a zone of generally
smaller settlements, widely dispersed, with fewer plough-teams yet
paradoxically rich in terms of woodland. It was this portion of the

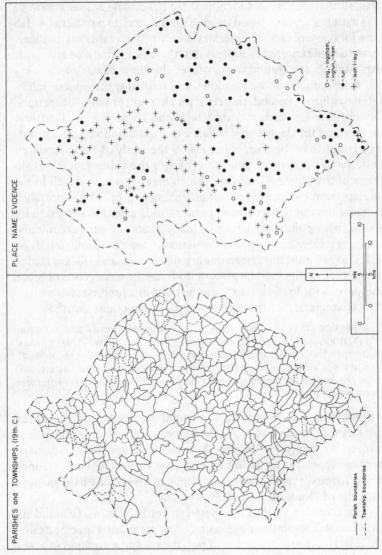

Fig 18 Early Settlement in Warwickshire. Parish and Township Boundaries, Place-Name Evidence, Domesday Plough-Teams and Woodland in Warwickshire, after Darby (1954); J. E. B. Gover, A. Mawer and F. M. Stenton, *The Place-Names of Warwickshire* (English Place-Name Society, XIII, Cambridge, 1936); the map of townships and parishes is derived from the work of Mr D. J. Pannett.

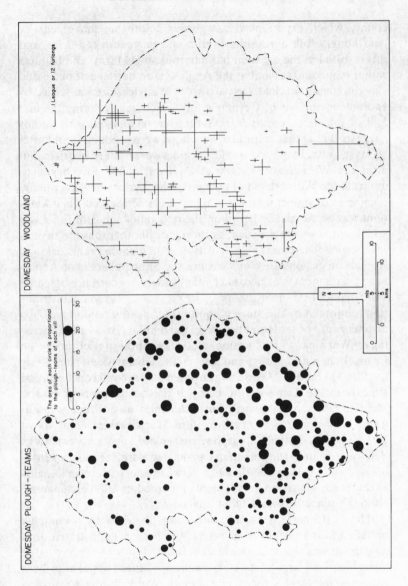

county which experienced a vigorous colonizing movement by land-hungry folk during the twelfth and thirteenth centuries, and this resulted in the creation of numerous single farms and hamlets rather than villages, so that the Anglo-Saxon heritage of nucleated *vills* still stands out clearly as parish foci. Warwickshire was settled by sporadic incursions of Germanic folk which began during the first half of the sixth century. Grave-furniture associated with burials suggests that at first cultural connections were predominantly from the east, and that the Avon valley settlers were eastern in origin, but after the West Saxon victory at Dyrham in 577 folk began to infiltrate the Worcestershire portion of the Avon valley, eventually coming into conflict with the Anglian kings of Mercia. Their kingdom was economically based on the rich valley lands of the Avon and Trent, a territory which, as recent air photographs are revealing, possessed a remarkable density of settlement in prehistoric and Roman times. Within Warwickshire the principal areas of Anglo-Saxon settlement are indicated by the scattered occurrence of 'early' place-names terminating in -*ing, -ingaham* and -*ingaton,* a distribution reinforced by the more ubiquitous terms -*ton,* and -*ham.* Two distinct zones of settlement emerge: the middle Avon valley, focusing on Warwick, with extensions along the southern tributaries (the Leam, Itchen and Stour) and also taking advantage of sites along the Lower Lias and Marlstone scarpments. A second concentration appears in the Tame-Blythe basin to the north, focusing on the Mercian capital of Tamworth, but such names are noticeably absent from those portions of north-western Warwickshire lying above 120 m (400 ft). In these areas they are replaced by such elements as -*ley, -worth* and -*feld*, elements associated with secondary settlements. The striking relationship between the pattern of Anglo-Saxon place-names and settlements recorded in 1086 is apparent, although space forbids a fuller analysis.[20]

The basic pattern of occupation was overlaid by a complex pattern of administrative divisions: the basic administrative unit was the township, and Domesday Book shows the grouping of townships into larger estates. Significantly, there appears to be a tendency for estates focusing on south Warwickshire to possess outlying dependencies in Arden, and as early as 704–9 Nuthurst was a dependency of Shottery. This arrangement is also reflected in the grouping of townships into 'hundreds', for Kineton Hundred, centring on the Stour valley, has a substantial outlier within Arden, composed of the portions of several estates which in the post-Conquest period emerged as separate townships in their own right.

Townships represented what can be termed the 'economic area' of individual cluster settlements; in some cases this was coincident with the parish (an ecclesiastical division superimposed on the basic pattern of townships). At times several townships were grouped together to form a parish, and indeed there is the suspicion that the gradual establishment of the parish system between the late-seventh and twelfth centuries sometimes led to a reduction in the number of small *vills*, and the concentration of folk in one true village around the church. Warwickshire contains few true strip parishes, such as are found in Lincolnshire and Wiltshire (Fig 22), placed across the grain of the countryside so as to obtain a share in the varying types of land available, but there is a striking contrast between the smaller townships and parishes of Feldon and the generally larger areas of townships and parishes within the late-settled Arden. While there are grounds for arguing that the parcellation of the countryside into townships, parishes and estates continued into the post-Conquest period, the pattern seen in Fig 18 is almost certainly in its essentials inherited from the Anglo-Saxon period, and, for a number of Feldon parishes, surviving charters of tenth-century date confirm the survival of early boundaries, as at Wormleighton, Warwickshire, in Fig 21.

Much of the argument of this chapter depends on a tacit assumption concerning place-names, namely that the settlements referred to in the documents are in fact still occupying the same site — that Preston, Southam or Kirby of the modern map are the settlements of the same name appearing in Domesday Book. This assumption is probably essentially valid, but it begs many questions, and the problems associated with it will be more fully considered in the two chapters which follow. The reader will be aware that the sources so far discussed reveal nothing of the *forms* of settlements, and indeed the term *vill* has been used to evoke a picture of a smaller, more primitive, version of the familiar village, a usage which is at best imprecise. A similar sort of problem is raised by the question of the relationship between the initial Anglo-Saxon settlements and their antecedents of Romano-British date, and the contribution of the centuries before AD 410 to the pattern. It is too easy to see the antecedents of the Domesday pattern as a scatter of village settlements established in the 650 years between the arrival of the first raiders and 1086, but it is becoming increasingly clear that documentary evidence is too often interpreted in the light of preconceptions. How can we know, for instance, in the case of Tysoe given at the beginning of this chapter, precisely to what settlement form the thumbnail sketch relates; there are today no less than three villages called Tysoe, but the settlement in 1086 could have been a single farm, perhaps the demesne farm, called Tysoe, to which rents and services were rendered by a peasantry living in farms as scattered as those depicted in Fig 48. Domesday Book tells us nothing of settlement forms, and in interpreting the available facts extreme caution is needed. This question must be considered more fully in Chapter 5, but to some extent preconceptions concerning settlement are always derived from our view of the nature of change and the pace at which it can and does occur. To what extent are we dealing with an independent succession of forms and patterns created by different and distinct folk-cultures superimposed upon each other, and to what extent are the hard outlines blurred by continuity between periods and phases?

The Continuity Problem

The student concerned with problems of 'continuity' is, when considering the patterns of Anglo-Saxon settlement, faced with two extreme alternatives: on the one hand, he can argue that 'the Conquest involved a complete break with the agricultural past' and that the 'villages of Saxon England have inherited no legacy whatever from Roman Britain'; on the other, he can see the institutions, settlement forms and agrarian systems of Saxon England as 'the compound product of barbarian and Roman institutions'. In the words of Hoskins, 'It yet remains to be proved that any English village has had a continuous existence since Romano-British times', but as in so many academic disputes the answer is to be found, not only between the two extremes, but varying spatially across the complex and intricate landscape varieties within these small islands.[21]

'Continuity', as Finberg clearly shows in his essay on 'Continuity or Cataclysm', could take many forms and have many meanings, but for the present purposes four aspects may be distinguished. The problem of territorial occupation is particularly significant, and the degree to which it is possible to generalize depends on the scale of the enquiry. An examination of the map of Roman Britain quickly demonstrates that the Romano-British and Anglo-Saxons were attracted to the same regions, avoiding the negative uplands above 244 m (800 ft), while the disposition of Roman towns, whose hinterlands we can only guess at, is a strong pointer to a degree of continuity of occupation. It is interesting to recall the point made by

A. L. F. Rivet concerning the resurgence of such Roman towns as Colchester, Gloucester, Worcester, London, York, Dorchester, Chichester, Leicester, and Canterbury and Cambridge, which are still county towns to this day:

> The implication of this must surely be that these places both as adminis-
> trative centres and as markets, were as well sited as they could be in
> relation to the agricultural exploitation of Britain not only in Roman
> times but in the conditions that prevailed in the Middle Ages and later;
> and as a corollary, that the exploitation of Britain's agricultural wealth in
> Roman times was neither so limited nor so primitive as we sometimes
> tend to assume. The pattern is strikingly modern.

The discordance seen between Romano-British and Anglo-Saxon settlement in the chalk country may be more apparent than real, and recent work, already discussed in Chapter 2, is suggesting that the so-called 'Celtic' field systems are in fact the survivals of a system which originally spread down off the chalk on to the heavier soils of the valleys; they have in fact survived only because they spread *above* the limits of medieval open-field cultivation. While no one would dispute that Anglo-Saxon folk pushed new villages into areas on heavy soil which had remained forested, there is frequently a striking coincidence between areas of primary Anglo-Saxon settle-ment and earlier occupation, as Fox demonstrated in the Cam-bridge region. In this context it is well to recall the contribution of Iron Age folk to forest clearance suggested by the palynological record (Fig 6); paradoxically long-tilled areas are now less produc-tive of archaeological finds than are marginal areas. No one who examines the OS 1″ map of the Ilchester area, Somerset, can doubt that Somerton and Low Ham, West Coker and North Coker, Drayton and Kingsdon, Yeovil and Ilchester are Anglo-Saxon vil-lages using land tilled and depastured in Roman times (Fig 12).[22]

The survival of Celtic population and language is too complex to be discussed at length here; that Anglo-Saxon affected native speech is indisputable and if a substantial Celtic element persisted it is difficult to see why more basic words associated with agriculture and settlement do not have Celtic roots. There is, however, an increasing body of evidence to suggest a bilingual phase, while Celtic influence in the artistic fields of ornament, brooch and pot-tery design strongly suggests a substantial degree of cultural over-lap, and references to Welshmen in seventh-century Wessex laws, coupled with the powerful influence of Celtic christianity seen in literary and chronicle sources, may all be taken as pointers to a highly complex period of cultural intermingling. More pertinent to our theme, however, are the questions of continuity of site and continuity of territorial organization. How many English settlements overlie Roman-British or even older sites? At Wharram Percy, Yorkshire (Fig 3) the excavation of a deserted medieval village has produced clear evidence for Roman and Iron Age occupation, but one might ask why more evidence for this does not come to light in the tilled gardens of many villages. There is no simple explanation, but the answer is partly to be found in a negative response; how many such villages, undoubtedly on the same site in the Middle Ages, or even the seventeenth century, produce much archaeological proof of this existence? The archaeology of existing villages is too little explored. Continuity of settlement, furthermore, does not necessarily imply continuity of site, as is illustrated by Maxey in Northamptonshire. The present village lies some half a mile from the twelfth-century church; there is documentary evidence to suggest a twelfth-century nucleus around the church, yet the present village, known as Maxey East in 1611, has produced eleventh- and twelfth-century Saxo-Norman pottery. Between these two nucleations archaeological evidence has demonstrated the presence of a village considered by the excavator to belong to the Middle Saxon period. The settlements occupy a gravel ridge which has produced a complex of crop marks which may range in date from ritual sites of the Neolithic period to medieval ridge and furrows. It may be that this concentration is wholly exceptional, caused by the attractiveness of the gravel ridge lying somewhat above the surrounding alluvium, but it is significant that other sites in the Welland, Trent, Severn, Avon and Thames valleys are producing evidence of comparable continuity of occupation, and there are as yet no good grounds for assuming that this complexity is a prerogative of river gravels. To point out that settlement history is complex may appear trite, but it is nevertheless valid, and this point must be kept constantly in mind when the past is being interpreted.[23]

As long ago as 1883 Seebohm was arguing Roman roots for the English manor, and Finberg has suggested that 'The tradition of Roman estates could not be entirely swept away . . . It would be preposterous to suppose that Roman landmarks and arrangements were wilfully destroyed and no advantage taken of the existing stock and labour arrangements!' There are grounds for arguing that from a very early date Anglo-Saxon kings levied tribute and taxes from their lands, and it is reasonable to assume that British resistance was based on armies supported with tribute levied by native rulers; to postulate a complete breach between the two systems is not wholly reasonable, especially as both sets of rulers must have been familiar with the *tributum*, the land-tax of the later Empire. Finberg argues that there is no reason to suppose that the British princes would have abandoned so familiar and convenient a levy, and it may have been taken over by the English who stepped into their shoes. Part at least of this *tributum* was, in the late phases of the Roman Empire, rendered in produce, and in this we may surely detect the origins of the Welsh *gwestfa* or the English *feorm*, food rents. There is here more than a hint of administrative conformity. The work of Glanville Jones has been touched upon on a number of occasions in this chapter; in a stimulating series of articles he has argued convincingly for the survival, in Anglo-Saxon, and thus in Norman and medieval England, of multiple estates of ancient origin. He points out the essential similarity between the grouped hamlets of Wales in the Early Middle Ages, the estates of Domesday Book with their widely scattered *berewicks* and *sokes*, and the northern shires with their *vill* groups, and he has marshalled an impressive range of evidence in the form of parallels between rents and services to support his case. He has in the author's opinion established 'a weight of probability', arguing that such estates were present not only in Roman times but also in the Iron Age or even earlier, and that they underlie the building of the Iron Age hill-forts, and even such monumental ritual sites as Stonehenge or Avebury. His ideas constitute a unifying theme which pulls together many disjointed facts concerning early settlement, and the multiple estate may be viewed as the logical territorial manifestation of social stratification found within European society from the Bronze Age onwards, with warrior kings, priests and other territorial lords receiving a flow of tribute from humbler folk.[24]

It is clear from the arguments presented in this chapter that England, indeed Britain, in 1086 was truly in Lennard's words an 'old country' in which patterns of settlement had already been securely established, patterns which form the recognizable antecedents of those we see today. The eleventh century was a period during which, in spite of local setbacks, settlements continued to multiply as a result of dispersion from the nuclei established during earlier phases of colonization. The pattern of settlements established by 1086 laid the foundations of a system of rural settlement which was to persist with some modifications until the Industrial Revolution and the Agricultural Revolution accelerated processes which fragmented the old order by creating rural depopulation, a powerful solvent and force for change.

4

Patterns of Village Settlement

THE MAP OF DOMESDAY *vills* (Fig 13) emphasizes the broad links between this settlement type and terrain conditions and, as has already been emphasized, cluster settlements are most usually associated with the lowland portions of Britain. In the two chapters which follow it is proposed to delve more deeply into certain questions concerning villages, in particular the forces generating and changing the overall patterns of village settlement and the factors concerned in the appearance of differing village plans. In as much as the village in former centuries was little more than a mere cluster of farms, the nature of the farm will be examined, although this theme will also be explored in Chapter 6. In the preceding chapter, using Domesday Book, it was shown that *vills* could vary very greatly, both in size and social structure, and it is appropriate at this point to ask the question, What is a village? There is at the outset the fundamental problem of whether a definition should be based on formal or functional criteria, but in practice the long time-perspective discussed in this volume raises further problems of definition which are almost insoluble. There is much to be said for the circumlocutory dictionary definition of a village as an 'assemblage of houses, etc., larger than a hamlet, but smaller than a town'. Without attempting to define exhaustively the causal factors underlying the nucleation or clustering of houses in a village, it is essential to see grouped settlement forms as product of man's struggle to wrest a living from the natural environment; in the words of Homans, 'men must live on and off the land as the first condition of their survival.' The importance of this fact in a 'difficult' environment such as the Scottish Highlands has already been stressed by a quotation from the work of Fraser Darling in the previous chapter; in the same context he continues:

> The system [of township organization] was one of essential co-operation by people living near the fringe of possible human existence. Man is essentially a social animal, and where life has to be lived and subsistence gained from the land around the dwelling sociality becomes a necessity. Digging by one's self is drudgery, but shared with three others with only elbow-room between them, it can be joy.

Although, as he points out, the introduction of the plough into Scottish crofting settlements was a disruptive element, his essential point is nevertheless valid for all agricultural communities, and even in the eleventh century the work was no doubt lighter when the assembled ox teams of the whole *vill* set the ploughs 'singing in the soil' and gave the earth that 'smooth raw lustre, Of fruit or flesh newly cut'. It is in this co-operation that we see the essence of the village.[1]

The distinction between a village and a hamlet can by no means be easily defined, even in terms of the modern world; population size is a continuous variable with no detectable break occurring between hamlet and village, and although there is a level of services which are characteristically associated with the latter, the distinction is in practice rarely clear-cut. One hundred years ago, however, such functional distinctions between village and hamlet would have been even less sharp, and although villages generally possessed churches, smithies and specialist tradesmen and craftsmen not found in hamlets, all had a basic dependence on the land which distinguishes them from the modern village which, in many cases, has a high proportion of non-agricultural population. In such circumstances settlement size becomes a more manageable criterion; two hundred or five hundred years ago functional distinctions would have been even less evident, and the information on them more scanty, while as one moves backwards through time there is a steady decrease in the amount of data reflecting even the size of settlements. A thousand years ago the use of the term *villa* (village) by a monkish scribe may reflect little more than a misconception: indeed there are grounds for thinking that north-country scribes used this term for settlements consisting of no more than a manor house surrounded by the cottages of a few dependants. To adopt another viewpoint, Thorpe, writing on rural settlement in Britain in 1962, took a hamlet to be a nucleated settlement, with or without a parish church, having from three to nineteen homesteads i.e. dwellings with dependent buildings and ground. He argued that this definition, discovered empirically, applies as well to the small clearing settlements of the Anglo-Welsh border and East Anglia as to the clustered clachans of Scotland or north-east Ireland. In contrast, he held a village to be a nucleated rural settlement of twenty or more households, a large village being distinguishable from a small market town by its paucity of services. The mixing of formal and functional criteria in these definitions may be noted. It is to be doubted if any definition derived from the modern map can usefully be projected backwards in time; nevertheless Thorpe's criteria did serve to produce a map (Fig 1) which sets forth certain fundamental contrasts in the settlement of Britain, contrasts which have their roots deep in the past. In practice it is virtually impossible, when dealing with a period of over a thousand years, to impose on the terms 'village' and 'hamlet' any absolute consistency of meaning, more particularly as there has been a tendency in historical writing to see hamlets as 'secondary' settlements, smaller clusters, arising after the principal villages were already established, a usage strongly supported by the dictionary definition of a hamlet as 'a small village, especially one without a church'. This usage, which will as far as possible be adopted within this volume, requires the further qualification that a settlement validly described as a hamlet in the fourteenth century may, by the eighteenth century, fully warrant the term 'village', and by the nineteenth century be a mere suburb in an expanding town. The qualification 'church-hamlet' can be reserved for situations in which a parish church is related to a very small cluster of dwellings, often no more than a hall and appendant cottages (Fig 2). Furthermore, the point of separation at which individual houses cease to be part of a cluster and become single farms has never been accurately defined: indeed it is doubtful if any one definition would possess universal validity.[2]

In the introduction to this volume it was argued that settlement patterns and forms can be explained in terms of differing combinations of three groups of variables: physical factors, economic factors and cultural factors, and it is the unique combination of these factors at one location which gives to settlement its diversity and character. Fig 2 demonstrates the increasing sharpness of focus as one moves from patterns to forms, but the wider view has, nevertheless, much to tell us, for it poses questions. The first series of diagrams in Fig 2, based on the work of Ian Evans, attempts to classify all the types of settlement pattern found within Britain; no doubt some are extremes which rarely occur in reality, while others found in reality would show a mixing of these ideal patterns, but they do provide the basis for a simple question: Why do all these variations occur? Quite clearly in a regular linear pattern the villages or farmsteads are strung out at regular intervals along a routeway, while in clustered linear patterns and linear random patterns — differing facets of the same type of pattern — the settlements are responding to a markedly uneven distribution of resources, clinging perhaps to habitable valley lands within an inhospitable upland region: such distributions can be closely paralleled in the highlands of Wales, northern England or Scotland. To obtain a view of the factors creating these differing patterns in differing environments, however, it is necessary to begin with a study of the basic requirements of a cluster settlement.[3]

Site and Situation

In a region dominated by villages the relationship between man and land can be seen in terms of the simple model reproduced in Fig 19.

The model relates specifically to the medieval period, a time when, in theory at least, outside links were minimal, although the author holds strongly to the view that the isolation of medieval villages has been much overstressed. In so far as this model omits any consideration of dispersed settlement which may have lain around many villages, it cannot be viewed as entirely accurate, but it does serve to distinguish between three broad categories of man-land relationship; none is simple, and, although it is possible to define each with some precision, all are in reality inseparable. Firstly, each village settlement possessed a finite area, clearly definable in terms of the break between the house-plots, gardens, and the fields proper — the site. It is only in comparatively recent times that this relationship has been irrevocably blurred by the expansion of dwellings over the farmland surrounding the village, although close studies of village plans show that the area covered by the houses and gardens has at times fluctuated quite considerably. Secondly, attached to each village was a territory from which the inhabitants obtained subsistence by farming — what can be termed the economic area. This would consist of arable fields and the necessary grazing lands, often waste lands. Thirdly and finally, each village had, outside this territory, a variety of links with other settlements and wider communities, and links with urban and administrative foci occupying a higher status in the hierarchy. Artificial as these divisions may appear, it is significant to note that Duby cites an author who wrote at the end of the twelfth century of his childhood memories, recognizing three concentric zones — the village enclosures; the *coûtures*, that is the arable fields; and finally, surrounding all, a broad, uncultivated belt. These were three zones in which the effects of man's labour became less and less visible as the distance from the inhabited centre grew greater, but which were of equal importance to him as a means of subsistence.[4]

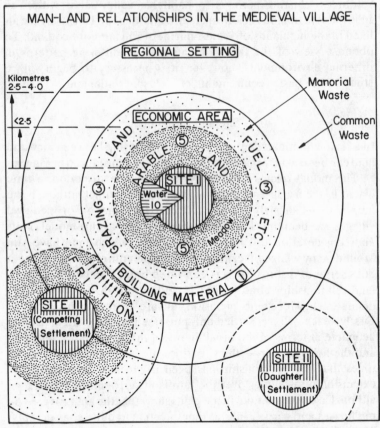

Fig 19   Man-Land Relationships in the Medieval Village

The site of the village is relatively easy to define; it is simply the area occupied by the houses, outbuildings, adjacent yards and small enclosures. But when evaluating a site, when asking, Why did men settle here? one is immediately faced with two intertwined sets of value judgments — what may be termed an intrinsic set, concerned with the particular qualities of the site, and an extrinsic set, taking note of the position or situation of the site relative to the resources of the surrounding area. The traditional importance of water in the location of settlement serves to illustrate this point: if the houses are clustered closely around a well or a spring, as for instance in the scarplands of Oxfordshire, where water-bearing sands are inter-bedded with limestones and clays, and villages cluster thickly along the spring lines, quite clearly it is reasonable to argue that the folk who founded the villages selected sites at or very near springs, and water represents an intrinsic factor. In contrast, on the Oxford or Lower Lias Clays or more starkly in the Fenland, villages are perched on drier 'island' sites, and, although shallow wells may tap the underground water, in this case water is more properly regarded as an extrinsic factor. There are thus good grounds for viewing the situation of a village as a multi-variate product in which environ-mental factors were evaluated in a particular socio-economic con-text, and it is important to appreciate that man, the rational being, would at times tolerate a poor site because of the advantages offered by a good situation. At this stage, however, it is well to pause and ask what particular qualities might be sought in a site. In Britain there are rarely strong grounds for claiming that village sites were selected for defensive qualities, although many have churches sited on sharp rises of ground, so that in times of need the church could perhaps have been used as a strong point, like pele towers along the Scottish-English border. Some of the massive church towers in Wales and Herefordshire were undoubtedly built for defensive purposes, and at Bedale in Yorkshire the stairway in the tower was protected by a portcullis. Such phenomena are, however, the excep-tion rather than the rule.

It is remarkable how few published studies exist which permit any degree of generalization about site. The reasons for this are not difficult to find. It is a daunting task to appraise a site through the eyes of earlier generations of farming folk, and indeed too little is known of village growth to permit a systematic study of early sites, using the evidence of the landscape. Nevertheless, in considering village sites three environmental factors do seem particularly important: flat land, shelter, and free drainage. For building pur-poses, particularly if a village was to be constructed, a flat site was desirable, but it is important to realize that flat land need not mean an area large enough to accommodate the entire village; a plot no more than a dozen or so feet square will accommodate a house, though this be part of a gradient which in general inhibits house construction. It is surely no accident that planned settlements of later centuries, needing larger areas of flat ground, tend to occupy sites which in practical terms are often both exposed and poorly drained, and would have been ignored by any self-respecting early farmer. Shelter and drainage are particularly important, the second of these being the dominant factor in areas where the environment was generally favourable to human settlement. In hill country, the Pennines, Wales, Dartmoor and Scotland, especially where heavy winter snows, high winds and heavy rainfall tend to be normal, sheltered, relatively flat land became a matter of premium, and site drainage was rarely a problem. Although it is difficult to prove, there may have been a tendency to select locations exposed to sunlight, but rarely, if ever, at the expense of increased exposure to wind. In the kinder lowlands, the scarplands and clay vales of the east, particularly in areas of heavier soils, well-drained sites were sought, such as valley slopes, terraces and hill tops. Ridges of glacial sands and gravels were characteristically occupied in the Midlands; more specifically, in the Vale of York pioneer settlers seem to have favoured three categories of sites: firstly, along the moraines and on the boulder-clay bench around the edge of the Vale; secondly on high terraces along the major rivers, or the higher banks on the outer edges of meander curves; and thirdly, on isolated hillocks and banks of better-drained material within the Vale itself. Minor fluctuations in climate may, in time, have affected some sites, but these were also probably marginal in economic terms. If the importance of a drained site seems overstressed, it must be remembered that the rain falling on the modern village is channelled away in the form of absolute run-off from roofs, paths and road surfaces, into underground drainage lines where it causes no inconvenience: drains have, in more ways than one, improved the habitability of villages, a contention which is supported by the frequent discovery of open drainage ditches in medieval deserted villages, and, indeed, by the numbers of these which lie on heavy clays.[5]

The study of site is an aspect of settlement geography which has not received the attention it deserves, and there is much need for basic observation and measurement. Accurately levelled contour maps and profiles of large numbers of villages have much to teach us about site selection, especially if combined with work on drift geology, slope mapping, studies of drainage lines and local soil conditions. These observations must of course take place within a framework designed to provide a rational descriptive understanding of the cultural landscape, and it must be appreciated that the ultimate goal is probably unobtainable; the land-cunning or land-folly of our forebears cannot be easily rediscovered. The ability to see the land with the eyes of its former inhabitants, from the standpoint of their needs and capacities, is about the most difficult task in all human geography; indeed, the matter is even more difficult than has been indicated, for quite the hardest task in assessing any site is what may be termed 'hazard perception'; few campers have not experienced this problem — the most inviting slope, even if not actually exposed to flood, can suffer a startling degree of run-off, even in moderate rain.

> In all settlement foundation it is important to grasp that a long pro-tracted form of trial and error must have been involved, and hazards, real or imagined, must account for many failures. Only the slow cycle of the seasons experienced over several years could confirm or deny the initial appraisal of site qualities, and by this stage inertia could be seriously restricting a willingness to move and begin anew.

Hazard perception can thus be defined as the ability to assess the long-term potential of a given site, and it is probably only achieved in the more mature stages of colonization, when the incomers have become thoroughly familiar with the environment and its difficulties.[6]

Village Territories

In the territory or economic area attached to the houses of the village we see the origins of the township; it must be distinguished from the parish, for although on our modern maps many townships are undoubtedly fossilized by the parish boundaries, it is important to appreciate that parish and estate or manor were, in some senses at least, superimposed upon a basic unit of production, and represent later administrative creations, one of ecclesiastical origin, the other representing a body of land and rights severed from its natural context by being under the control of one lord, who might or might not control the surrounding estates. Chisholm has argued, convincingly, that the process of selecting a situation in which to establish one or more farms is an exercise in least-cost location analysis, and hence the rationale of site selection may be very much determined by extrinsic factors. Furthermore, as Lennard points out, mistakes were made, and the land-cunning of our village founders was never infallible, as is manifest in a toll of site changes and desertions caused by a gradual mutation of the initial patterns to the logic of a securely established and fully-developed mature system, well adjusted to the character of the terrain. In his study of village location Chisholm begins his analysis of the relationship of the settlement to its lands as follows:

Let us imagine a people of modest cultural achievements, such as the Anglo-Saxon colonists who settled widely over England. Such people, in seeking places in which to build their abodes, would have to bear in mind the availability of arable and grazing lands, the supply of water for man and beast, fuel resources and the ease of obtaining building materials.

Incorporated in Fig 19 are these five basic elements of a settler community's economy; as the disadvantages posed by distance in conducting various enterprises are very variable, Chisholm has assigned to each a hypothetical value showing the relative disadvantage of distance. For example, the removal of water one kilometre is equivalent to ten units of cost, whereas if the source of building materials is that far away it represents only one unit of the cost. Water was given a high value on account of its traditional importance and the fact that it is needed by man and beast at frequent intervals; arable land is more greedy of labour than grassland, requiring more cultivation, more transport of inputs and products, while in the traditional rural economy over much of medieval Europe, grazing and fuel were closely associated, both being found on the commons. Finally, building materials have been given the least weight because, although bulky and awkward to handle, they are only required at infrequent intervals. To put these weighting factors more concisely, the site of a settlement will bear a relationship to the availability of water, arable land, grazing land and fuel supplies, and although there has always been a tendency to select a piece of sheltered, flat but well-drained land for the site, there will be circumstances — the presence of a large land-hungry population, for instance — when the demand for arable land is so great as to override all other factors. Similarly, although arable land has been given a weighting of five, it is now virtually impossible to appraise soils through Anglo-Saxon eyes, and it is probable that certain soils could rate as high as eight in terms of cost-distance factors, whereas at the other end of the scale potentially poor arable land would merge with grazing land at a rating of four or three. Early medieval colonists appear to have sought lighter and intermediate soils, and, as Clark points out, 'from the earliest times pervious soils have been sought for settlement, but the mere disposition of settlements on gravels and sands by no means precludes the cultivation of neighbouring claylands, particularly in regions where such are traversed by river valleys.' Thus, a detailed examination of the distribution of villages anywhere within Lowland Britain will often show that the great majority are sited either on the margin of claylands, or on the gravels and sands of river valleys, taking advantage of small areas of drift which may appear on no geological map. There are indeed increasing signs that some of the heavier, richer soils were already being taken into cultivation before the end of prehistoric times in parts of temperate Europe. However, while these hypothetical ratings do help to frame an argument, it must be stressed that decisions were not always necessarily rational; we can only guess what other factors must be taken into account; what taboos, dreams, fears, priestly deliberations or feminine intuitions overrode the practical considerations. The Saxons, for instance, were clearly well aware that where they saw 'snapped rooftrees, towers fallen' and 'the work of the Giants, the stonesmiths' there once stood 'halls . . . high, horngabled, much throngnoise; these many meadhalls men filled with loud cheerfulness' and we may guess that to them such features were indicative of the presence of fertile ploughland in the vicinity, although the ghost-haunted ruins themselves were no doubt to be avoided. The irrational element present in the siting of settlements must never be underrated, although it would be a foolish man who attempted to produce an estimate of the importance of this irrational component in the present state of our knowledge.[7]

The question of the actual extent of a village's territory or township can be examined in more precise terms. Turning first of all to a theoretical consideration: if settlement were occurring upon a completely uniform plain, then the territories attached to the villages, or nodes, would tend to assume a pattern of regular hexagons, and indeed the settlements would themselves be regularly placed (Fig 20A). Such resources as water supply, arable land and grazing land are, however, rarely uniformly distributed and the regular lattice is correspondingly distorted when particular resources are localized. In the second case (Fig 20B) a limited resource is shared between the surrounding villages, as were Dunsmore Heath in Warwickshire and portions of the Fenlands, or, on a vastly larger scale, the common rights upon Dartmoor were shared amongst the surrounding townships. Fig 20C represents townships clustering on such arable lands as are available, a common feature throughout the uplands of Britain, while in 20D the resources are distributed in a linear fashion, characterizing the remarkable series of strip parishes on Lincoln Edge (Fig 21), one set with villages occupying a scarp-foot location, the other set with villages at the junction between dip-slope and fen, both sharing the limestone heath of the Edge itself. The linear resource in 20E could represent a routeway or river, and good examples of this type of pattern are found in the chalk country of Wiltshire and Dorset, where settlements tend to occupy the valley-bottom benches in close proximity to the permanent streams. In the final case a point resource is assumed, a single well, a defensive site, a well-drained site in a fen area, or, in cultural terms, the attraction of a church or the hall of a lord, encouraging strong concentration at one location; examples are found in the 'island' settlements of Chedzoy, Weston Zoyland, or Muchelney on the Somerset levels. We have here gone full circle and returned to the question of intrinsic and extrinsic factors, and it will be appreciated that the models in Fig 20A–F could apply as well to

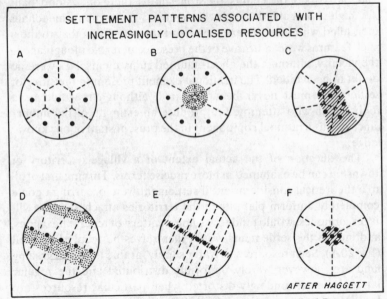

Fig 20   Settlement Patterns Associated with Increasingly Localized Resources, after Haggett (1965)

single farms and their territories as to villages and hamlets, case 20F representing the clustering of farms in a large village. One further point needs stressing. When explaining settlement, a 'resource' can also be a cultural factor, such as the attraction of proximity to a church or the presence of seigniorial pressure to occupy nucleated *vills*; this is an important point which helps to explain the presence of differing settlement forms and patterns within fundamentally similar physical environments.[8]

In practical terms parish boundaries often show an adjustment to the zonal distribution of the basic resources — arable land,

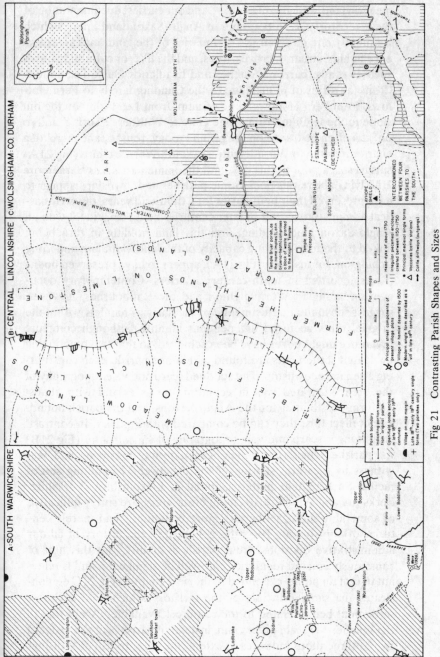

Fig 21 Contrasting Parish Shapes and Sizes

meadowland, and grazing land — and our earliest documentation of these territories is to be found in Anglo-Saxon land grants, which frequently cite in detail the boundaries of the land, making reference to hills, streams, groves, trees, and the like, or cultural features such as roads, barrows, ditches and headlands. Such descriptions 'from the strips of ploughland of the Cunding family to Fern Hollows, from Fern Hollows to Lea Camp, from Lea Camp on the hill slope to Stone Gate, from Stone Gate to Wulfhere's spring' and so on, can often be traced on the ground today: thus 'Crane mere' of a charter relating to Wormleighton in south Warwickshire (Fig 21A) survives as a pool to this day, and the name persists as 'Granmore Hill' lying above this pool. Some parishes and townships appear to have preserved their boundaries for a thousand years, the ecclesiastical administrative unit of later centuries being coincident with an Anglo-Saxon land holding, and this land holding in turn being linked to the folk-carrying capacity of the land. Southam and Long Itchington, for instance (Fig 21A), appear to have preserved boundaries recorded in tenth-century charters. Contemporary documents relating to Wormleighton and the Radbournes, however, suggest substantial adjustments, particularly as hamlets within the original units acquired independent identity, although complete severance might never have been achieved, so that two functioning nucleated settlements are found within one parish, each constituting a separate township. The subdued scarp and vale topography of the area illustrated was in economic terms a land with almost uniform possibilities for the Anglo-Saxons, and the parish boundaries reflect this; they can be compared with Fig 20A. In contrast, the stronger scarp and vale topography of Lincolnshire (Fig 21B) has parishes which reflect the linear pattern of resources, and bear witness to a careful sharing of these between competing settlements. Such regular patterns, found in Lincolnshire, Yorkshire, Berkshire and Wiltshire, to cite but four areas, are surely indicative of something more deliberate, more conscious, than merely centuries of adjustment. Too little is known of the history of all our administrative divisions, from parish to county, but this hint of consciously created regularity may well be significant, and is relevant to certain points examined in the next chapter. Fig 21C demonstrates the same principle of the territory attached to a cluster settlement being related to the resources available, except that in the uplands the scale differs and, instead of parishes of the order of two to three thousand acres in extent, the great parish of Wolsingham encompassed 8,903 ha (22,000 acres). Within all three regions residual areas occur, not appropriated to any township or parish, and in Wolsingham such lands are to this day still inter-commoned between the surrounding communities. In Lincolnshire a lord of the manor who had control over the heaths of Lincoln Edge was able to put them to use by granting them as a block to the Knights Templar, so creating a separate and distinct parochial area. In densely settled and long-occupied south Warwickshire the extra-parochial Wills Pastures is a reminder of a situation once more fluid. Fig 12B incorporates an illustration of the complexity of this crystallization process, including certain details derived from a late Anglo-Saxon perambulation of an estate at Hawling in the Cotswolds. The *woodland* and *feldland* (or open-pasture) portions of the estate are described in detail, and Finberg has suggested that these in turn define the arable land of the village. The complete territory incorporated portions of at least seven later parishes, and the present boundary of Hawling includes within it the former parish and deserted village of Roel, itself carved out of the woodland of the original Hawling. The territories which supported individual villages in former times were thus by no means necessarily the result of a single deliberate act of creation; those which finally emerged were frequently the product of centuries of adjustments, some small and some large. In a sense these adjustments continue, as parish boundaries are altered to meet changing population conditions, but such changes no longer have economic significance. The territory of a village, its economic area, was formerly vital to its existence, and we must now turn to the differing modes of exploitation which evolved.[9]

Village Field Systems

The peasant farmer, seeking to carve a living directly from a given environment, is at once producer and consumer, dependent on the practice of agriculture, the knowledge of his craft, the technical aids at his disposal, and his ability to apply these. There is thus, in a given environment, a definite relationship between farming technique, population and the area exploited. Furthermore, the effect of the environment is not negligible, and while it is improbable that any great changes have occurred in climate during historical times, there have undoubtedly been fluctuations, runs of wet summers, long cold winters, or periods of severe drought, when farming, at least in some regions, has been seriously affected; for example the extra frequency of wet autumns around 1300–50 and 1650–1700 probably had some effects on farming throughout Western Europe, in the first case contributing to the general population decline which began in the second decade of the fourteenth century. The types of crops grown by a farmer are determined by both climate and the type of soil, but in Britain it is the amount of rainfall and variations in temperature, in combination with the patterns of relief, which determined whether stock-farming or tillage was the chief source of livelihood, and which defined the altitudinal limits and transition zones between the two enterprises, although the balance on an individual farm was frequently the result of prevailing social and economic conditions and the decisions of the individual farmer. During and immediately after the Middle Ages one can distinguish three principal methods of cultivating the farmland, depicted diagramatically in Fig 22.[10]

In the first case (Fig 22) we have an arrangement in which only a small proportion of the available land was continuously cultivated, without any fallow period, but it was maintained in good heart and fertility by heavy manuring. Such an area has generally been termed an infield. The waste around this nucleus was used in two principal ways: firstly, it provided grazing land for the maintenance of stock, and secondly, portions of it were temporarily brought into cultivation by the farmers holding shares in the infield area. Such intakes were cropped for a few years and then allowed to revert to waste, the land so used being termed the outfield. These arrangements have a two-fold importance. They represent a stage between true shifting agriculture and the development of more complex cropping and field arrangements, using fallowing to maintain fertility of an extensive arable acreage, and such arrangements, with many local variations and adaptations, were characteristic of much of upland Britain, Scotland, Wales, the Pennines, together with the late-settled areas of the lowlands (i.e. those areas containing much woodland and waste in 1086). Because of climatic restrictions and the limited availability of land suitable for arable use, these arrangements represented a system of land usage best adapted to upland areas, although they possessed a degree of flexibility, in terms of the area of outfield cultivated and the intensity and organization of grazing activity, which enabled them to adapt to changing population conditions. Pressure of population on the available resources would tend to ensure permanent cultivation of the outfield areas, or the better portions of them, and in any particularly favourable circumstances more complex systems evolved, as in south Wales, the Pennines or lowland Scotland. It is a common

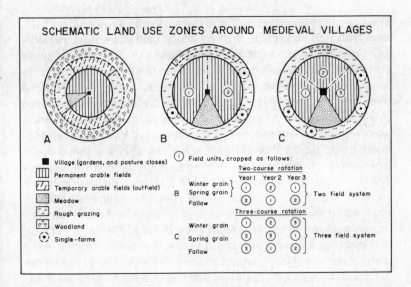

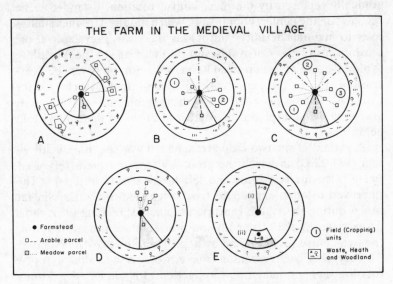

Fig 22   Land Use and Farm Structure in the Medieval Village. (i) Schematic Land-Use Zones around Medieval Villages (ii) The Farm in the Medieval Village

practice when discussing Scotland to equate infield/outfield with the term 'run rig', an arrangement by which field strips were periodically re-allotted amongst the co-partners; the equation is quite erroneous, and has arisen from misunderstandings. There is, from *some* areas of Scotland, evidence for periodic re-allotment, but the term 'run rig' may mean no more than the division of land into strips, and there are no grounds for assuming that the redistribution was ever universal or indeed of great antiquity. An arrangement for maintaining the fertility of larger areas of arable was found in the two-course rotation, which may have an origin in the Iron Age (Fig 22iB). Under this system the arable land was divided into two sections, which were alternately cropped and fallowed. Winter-sown wheat was grown on a portion of the crop field, the remainder being put down to spring-sown barley or oats. This arrangement, with frequent fallowing or resting of the soil, was documented in the tenth century by Gray, but not before, and was widespread by the twelfth and thirteenth centuries. Although on the better soils it was gradually replaced by the three-course rotation, it tended to be retained on the lighter, poorer soils, which required frequent fallow rests to maintain fertility, and it was therefore prevalent on the brashy soils of the Cotswolds and on the chalk of the Yorkshire Wolds. This relationship to soil type must not, however, be over-stressed, for on the heavy clay soils of south Warwickshire the two-field system persisted until the seventeenth century, only gradually being displaced by rotational practices demanding four fields.[11]

A variant of the two-field arrangement was the three-field system (Fig 22iC) in which the ground was more intensively used, being tilled for two years and left fallow every third year. This improved rotation appears to have originated in the Carolingian realm during the eighth century, gradually spreading throughout Europe during the thirteenth and fourteenth centuries, replacing the two-course rotation (and by implication the two-field system). The advantage of a transition from a two-course to a three-course rotation lies in increased production, for under the former arrangement one half of the land lies fallow in any one year, in the second barely a third; hence a greater number of folk can be supported from the same area of arable land although, of course, on certain soils, the more intensive system can result in a reduction of yields, so that the two-course rotation is more advantageous. It cannot be overstressed that there are no grounds for attributing the three-field system or indeed the two-field arrangement to the

Anglo-Saxons. Pre-tenth-century evidence, notably a law of Ine, does perhaps indicate the presence of a form of communal cultivation in Wessex in *c*. 690, but there is no evidence to demonstrate the universality of such arrangements in Wessex, let alone in Anglo-Saxon England. Safe ground is to talk of the antecedents of the developed field systems of medieval England. Two further cases are shown. In Fig 22iiD the arable strips of an individual farm are grouped in one part of the fields, an arrangement associated with sophisticated manuring arrangements, in particular the folding of sheep, and not linked with rigid cropping units. Such a system was found in East Anglia, and it will be noted in Fig 4 that East Anglia is a zone of what in the next chapter will be called fragmented villages, settlements made up of several nucleal clusters. A link can be assumed between these distinctive field arrangements, the less rigid manorial control throughout this part of England, and the particular type of settlement pattern. The final case (Fig 22iiD) shows two block-farms, in which the lands are consolidated and surrounded by a ring-fence, and while in the one instance the farm remains in the village, in the other it has migrated out to the consolidated fields.

The village, as has already been stressed, is the sum of a cluster of individual farms, and we must now pause to examine the relationship between the farm as the basic unit of production and the generalized patterns of land use already outlined. Fig 22ii indicates a range of possibilities which can occur, the central point being a farm located in the village, and the rectangles being units of landholding, or parcels. Each farm may be seen as a *share* in the village territory and its resources; one man might have more of these shares than another, but the shares themselves were equal. Cases B and C show the normal peasant-holding of the Middle Ages in an area of subdivided fields, prevalent throughout most of the lowland areas densely settled by 1086; such farms, consisting of a number of separate parcels of land scattered throughout the fields, often equally divided between the two or three cropping units, were traditionally assessed in *virgates* (yardlands) or *bovates* (oxgangs). These fiscal units could then be combined in groups of four or eight to form a hide or *carucate* of about 60 ha (120 acres). The origins of these assessments cannot be considered here, but it may be noted that the term *virgate* (or yardland, one term being Latin, the other Anglo-Saxon), reflects the use of the land-rod to lay out such farms, while the term *bovate* or oxgang reflects land assessed in terms of the ploughing capacity of oxen, an eight-ox team being considered able to plough about 60 ha (120 acres) in one year, a *bovate* being one eighth of this and a *virgate* one quarter. The importance of these arrangements lies less in their local diversity and complexity than in their universality and implications in terms of the standardization of farms for the purposes of taxation. Vinogradoff in his volume *Villainage in England* summarized the principles underlying the fiscal and physical characteristics of open field villages in the following terms:[12]

i The principle upon which the original distribution depended was that of equalizing the shares of the members of the community. This led to the scattering and intermingling of the strips. The principle did not preclude inequality according to certain degrees, but it aimed at putting all of the people of one degree into approximately similar conditions.

ii The growth of population, of capital, of cultivation, of social inequalities led to a considerable difference between the aritificial uniformity in which the arrangement of the holdings was kept and the actual practice of farming and ownership.

iii The system was designed and kept working by the influence of communal right, but it got its artificial shape and its legal rigidity from the manorial administration which used it for the purpose of distributing and collecting labour and rent.

A late-surviving example of a farm scattered thoughout a subdivided field is shown in Fig 23 at Crimscote, Warwickshire, and although this township nominally possessed four 'quarters' or fields by 1844, the structure of the furlongs strongly hints at the former presence of two fields. Such a complex scattered holding, was, for the individual farmer, greedy of labour, but the arrangements ensured that, given the desirability of a nucleated settlement, each tenant possessed an equal share in both soil quality and cost-distance load. It was of course, possible to have a holding which took a block form, radiating out from the village (Fig 22iiE) but in practice such farms only developed after enclosure at a later stage in the history of the system, although the lord's home farm, the demesne, probably tended from earliest times to form a block, and even in the thirteenth century such holdings were not entirely unknown. Throughout the twelfth and thirteenth centuries, however, as a result of rising population and land subdivision, there was a clear trend towards fragmentation, and while late twelfth-century charters talk in terms of half-acre or even acre strips, late-thirteenth-century documents deal with minute parcels sometimes smaller than half a rod in width. In Kent and East Anglia, because of a different history and distinctive agricultural practices, the holdings, assessed as *sulungs* or tenements, tended to be concentrated in

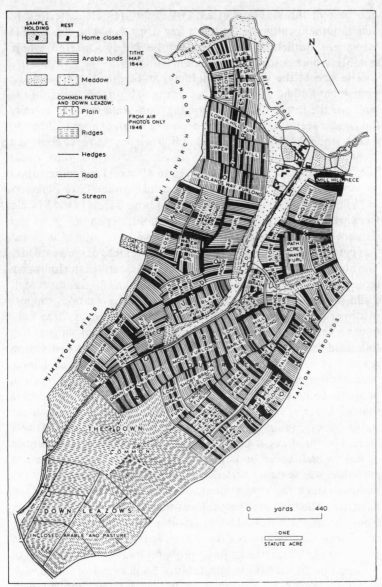

Fig 23   The Township of Crimscote, Warwickshire, after D. J. Pannett, in Roberts in Baker and Butlin, (1973), 196

one part of the arable (Fig 22iiD); in an area characterized by infield/outfield cultivation, while a few strips would be clustered in the infield, outfield shares might well be widely scattered, where suitable arable lands were available.

The size of the individual holding, and hence the area of the permanent arable, would vary according to both the quality of the land and the return obtained upon the seed-grain sown. In practice the *virgate* seems to have varied around a mean of about 12 ha (30 acres), while the normal peasant holding in a bovated area consisted of two *bovates* each of about 15 acres; the 'normal' farm could fluctuate from about 4·8 to 16 ha (12 to 40 acres) depending upon the size of the acre involved, but a *virgate* of between 10 to 14 ha (25 to 35 statute acres) seems a reasonable norm. Yields in the Middle Ages were of the order of two- to fourfold, depending upon the clemency of the season. This is only a small margin, and it meant that periodic food shortages were a marked feature of medieval life. The importance of this fact can be expressed clearly in the following terms: the traditional peasant holding of 12 ha (30 statute acres), could, under threefold yields and a two-course rotation, support just over two folk, and with a fourfold yield, just over three folk; under a three-course rotation threefold yields would support five folk, and fourfold yields approximately six folk. If a bad season resulted in depressed yields, only a small proportion lower, famine would result, and a year with only twofold yields would result in peasants being compelled to eat their seed-grain for the coming season. Clearly, such a precarious balance could be made more stable by extending the area cultivated, but in practice this was limited by the draught-power available for ploughing; the number of oxen which could be kept, and hence the amount of manure available, was severely curtailed by the necessity of carrying these beasts through the winter months on the precarious yields of the hayfields. The medieval peasant was thus caught in a vicious circle from which escape was all but impossible. Furthermore, it is well to remember that in practice by no means all peasants possessed thirty-acre holdings; the majority probably had less. In the manor of Taunton in the late-thirteenth century 56 per cent of the tenants had under 6 ha (15 acres) each, while only 7·6 per cent had more than 12 ha (30 acres), and Titow has calculated that while there were 1·32 ha (3·3 acres) per person in 1248, by 1311 this had dwindled to some 2·5 persons per 0·4 ha (i.e. per acre) a truly desperate state of affairs if the inequalities of distribution are remembered. Many peasants, particularly those in densely populated regions, must have been living at or below subsistence level, and this comes out very clearly in the close correlation that existed between mortalities and years of bad harvest at Taunton. In addition to the vital shares in the arable lands of a village, the peasant cultivator also possessed shares in the meadowlands, and had also rights in the wastes, marshes and woodlands to supply his needs in building materials, fuel and grazing for stock. These rights were, ideally at least, securely attached to the arable holding and were divisible with it. Finally, the peasant possessed a share in the village, having a house plot and access to the communal facilities such as the village well or spring, the common oven, the forge, the lord's mill, and the obligation to partake in such communal organizations as the local manorial court or *halmote*. It will be noted that all the various models postulated above assume a uniform distribution of resources, and medieval and post-medieval surveys amply attest that was the intention. But economic resources are never uniformly distributed, either in space or within the community, and in this respect the ideal situation expressed by such simple models becomes a useful tool of analysis, for in explaining the variations between model and reality one is brought to a closer understanding of interrelationships within the real world.[13]

The Spacing of Villages — Colonization and Diffusion

A further aspect of the application of these simple models to reality was indirectly discussed by Chisholm when he examined the spacing of villages in Lincolnshire, and this work must be considered in more detail, for the results have a direct bearing on the precise definition of the actual extent of the economic area around each settlement. He measured the maximum distance from the village to the parish boundary in all the parishes of Lincolnshire, using parish boundaries in default of township boundaries, and found for all rural districts the median distance from the named villages to the furthest point on the parish boundary. For the county as a whole this figure was 3·2 kilometres, but the range was from 2·3 to 8·2 kilometres, the latter being accounted for by some very attenuated parishes along the Fen edge in Boston, Elloe and Spalding. He concluded generally that some 70 per cent of the parishes have their furthest point only some 4·0 kilometres from the village, about 2 miles. These figures are open to question.

As Chisholm points out, they ignore the fact that parish boundaries are not township boundaries, and that deserted villages occur, but nevertheless it must be remembered that this estimate can only mark the extent of the commons and grazings attached to the village, and in the majority of cases, at least initially, all the arable land would have been substantially nearer. Chisholm accepts the figures $0 \cdot 8$ to $1 \cdot 6$ kilometres as the limiting distance at which the cost of cultivation rose high enough to warrant a shift of abode, giving rise to the hiving off of part of the group and the establishment of a satellite or daughter settlement, either within or outside the economic area of the mother village — what in Fig 19 has been termed the regional setting. However, measurements derived from an accurate map of open-field land in Warwickshire in about 1700 show quite clearly that the median distance from village centre to the furthest point on the perimeter of the open-field land was in fact $2 \cdot 4$ kilometres, and the median distance to the most distant point on the township boundary was $2 \cdot 5$ kilometres. This fission was no doubt usually amicable, and two forms can usefully be recognized: on the one hand a satellite settlement was separate physically, but retained close social and economic ties with the mother, while a daughter settlement became a separate and independent community.[14]

The regional setting would, during the initial stages of settlement, consist of true 'common waste' which, unlike 'manorial waste', was not appropriated to any estate; but inevitably, as villages multiplied and this basic resource was depleted, competition arose between adjacent settlements, sometimes between mother and daughter villages. Most of the documentary material relating to commons post-dates 1200 and concerns periods when control over them had unquestionably passed to the lord of the manor, but occasionally there are records of the division of a great common between townships and lordships in the twelfth or thirteenth centuries. Such partition was sometimes amicably arranged, but there are frequent cases where the men of intercommoning *vills* resisted the proposals by force and insisted upon their ancient custom, which antedated lordships, manors and ecclesiastical parishes. The history of common rights in England may be viewed as that of an increasing limitation of rights to a more sharply defined class of user; as population pressure on land increased, so men became more jealous of their rights. The degree of pressure, and hence the chronology of the limitation of rights, varied according to local circumstances, but even within the Forest of Arden, Warwickshire, a region where much unsettled land still survived in 1086, we find Ingulf, Warden of Rowington (on behalf of Reading Abbey) coming to an agreement (*c.* 1140) with Hugh Fitz-Richard of Hatton concerning 'what common of pasture there ought to be between us' in Shrewley and Rowington. In friction between villages and between landowners, we see one aspect of the complex process of the adjustment of population to available land resources, and it is possible that some settlements, in favoured locations, were able to expand at the expense of their weaker neighbours, producing a concentration of population in a smaller number of larger nuclei.[15]

An important mechanism underlying this process of colonization, diffusion, and competition between settlements may be seen in terms of fluctuations in population, which largely involved periods of relative stagnation, when deaths roughly balanced births, and periods of growth, when births outnumbered deaths, so that there was an increasing demand for more living and working space. If we imagine a level plain, settled by villages, with agriculture satisfying food demands, and births just balancing deaths, then clearly we have a delicately balanced 'steady state' situation. An increase in births, however, will upset the balance and lead to the demand for an increase in the arable area, and ultimately to the need for new houses, either within the existing settlements, or outside them, stimulating the creation of new units, while a decrease in population might lead to land falling out of cultivation because of a slackening of demand. In practice, decade by decade there are always slight population changes which result in minor adjustments within the agrarian and settlement arrangements to meet the demands of the new situation. This response may be vigorous and immediately visible — the intaking of new land, the foundation of daughter settlements, the decay of existing farmsteads — or it may be purely organizational — a re-adjustment of the tenurial system, tighter rules over usage rights in the common lands restricting the number of beasts which could be grazed or the amount of fuel that could be taken — or it may simply make sure that existing rules and regulations are thoroughly obeyed, so that the changes may be reflected in the documentation in the form of an increased number of prosecutions for particular offences appearing in the court rolls of an estate.

The troubled question of establishing a precise chronology of village foundation and hence the possibility of identifying village 'generations' was touched upon in Chapter 4. If the assumption that the cluster settlements of later centuries were indeed present in 1086 is accepted, and it is broadly true, then during the twelfth century forces were at work which resulted in a gradual decline in the number of new villages established. Indeed after about 1200 the flow almost ceased. The pre-1086 contribution to our stock of villages is a substantial one in most counties and the problem of accurately differentiating between 'generations' of settlements before 1086 is one of outstanding difficulty. Place-names, as was indicated in the last chapter, afford some guide, and at this point it is necessary to return to the meaning of the more common place-names and assess what they can tell us concerning the multiplication of villages. A useful point of origin for this inquiry is, however, afforded by Fig 24 which attempts to map generations of villages within County Durham, avoiding the use of place-name evidence. This map depends on the basic assumption that a village which pays an old rent form is more ancient than one which does not, and hence all those villages paying the ancient cattle-rent of cornage, discussed already in Chapter 3, are counted as first generation; all those villages which appear in the documentary record before about 1200, but which do *not* pay cornage, are treated as second generation, while all those villages and hamlets appearing after 1200 but before 1400 form the third generation. All known shielings, temporary sites, occupied initially only during the summer months, complete the picture. The deficiencies in this map caused by inadequate or incomplete documentation are obvious enough, but the picture is both fuller and more reliable than one provided by place-name evidence alone. There are slight grounds for believing that the first generation of villages was present by the mid-eighth century, and there is a striking contrast between an early-settled zone in the east and south and a late-settled zone in the north and west. By the time of the enclosure of the village open fields — in Durham this took place between 1550 and 1750 — the east and south clearly formed a 'champion' region, dominated by open fields and village settlements, while the north-west retained much open pasture. It is tempting to see the settlement of the county in terms of three broad regions; as colonists thrust westwards seasonal occupance was gradually extended into permanent occupance, with subsidiary settlements, perhaps of a specialist nature, being transformed into separate communities: there may be a measure of truth in this. The shielings of the uplands represent the last 'generation' seeking the most remote, the most inhospitable localities. This hypothesis conveniently ignores the fact of pre-Saxon occupation, but with this Durham pattern in mind it may be profitable to consider the original meanings of the more frequent village place-name elements.[16]

The endings *-tun, -ham* and *-by* occur in some of the commonest English place-names, usually attached to villages. The word *tun*

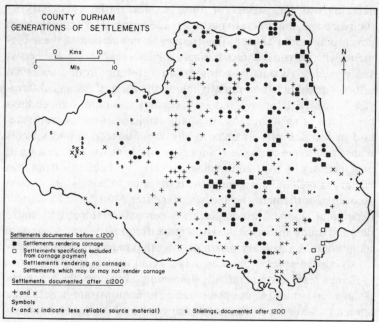

Fig 24   Village 'Generations' in County Durham

seems originally to have meant 'fence or hedge', being extended to imply 'that which is fenced in, an enclosed piece of ground'; from this, other meanings evolved: 'an enclosure with a dwelling', then 'a farmstead' and finally 'a hamlet or village' as well as 'manor or estate'. A *tun* appears to have been a smaller unit of settlement than a *ham*, whose root means 'a safe dwelling', which was extended to cover 'a dwelling-place or a house' and finally 'a village, a collection of dwellings'. Smith suggests that the word *ham* belongs to the 'earlier period of English settlement' while *tun* relates to a wider time-span, extending to form an element in place-names of post-Conquest origin. It was probably less common in the earliest days of English settlement, and is linked with the extension of areas of occupation, becoming more used as *ham* fell into disuse. The word *worth* and its derivatives -*worthig* (-*worthy* in south-western place-names) and -*wordign* (-*wardine* in West-Midland place-names) show the same variety of applications, meaning 'an enclosure', particularly one in individual and personal possession, 'a home plot', although they survive today incorporated in village and hamlet names. In these changes we see not only words altering their meaning with the passage of time, but also settlements changing their size and character, in particular the homestead or single farm developing into a cluster. The frequent combination of these elements with personal names strongly suggests that we are not necessarily seeing secondary colonization resulting from communal effort, but colonization initially taking the form of dispersed farmsteads, which later evolved into clusters. Scandinavian endings reveal the same trend: -by originally implied 'dwell' or 'cultivate' and in Sweden place-names in -by are clustered round villages whose names are of an even older type, implying the exploitation of new territory by the parent village or certain inhabitants from that village; in colloquial language the term came to be thought of as 'a secondary settlement, an outlying farmstead', or 'a small hamlet dependent upon a larger place': a context reinforced by more detailed study in that it survives more frequently as a secondary name than as a primary parish or township name; indeed in many surviving examples it denotes only a small hamlet.[17]

It may seem a comparatively simple matter to carry the argument a stage further and to use place-names to demonstrate in detail the spread of settlement; this is not the case, and the problem is that each element can in practice occur over such a wide time-span that detailed conclusions must necessarily be subject to many qualifications. Nevertheless, the names indicate a process by which individual footholds were gained in the waste some distance from the parent settlement. Note, however, that we are not normally dealing with such specialist elements as the Middle English *scele* 'a temporary hut', especially a shepherd's hut on the summer pastures, a summer pasturage; *denn* 'a woodland pasture, especially for swine'; and the Norse *erg*, 'a shieling, or hill pasture'. Rather we are seeing a continuous gradation from dispersed farmstead to joint village, composed of loosely organized groupings of farms. Significantly, this sequence of development has been traced in seventeenth-century survey maps in Sweden, and in this context it is interesting to note Erixon's conclusion that the infield type of open-field arrangements was derived from the amalgamation of fields formerly farmed independently. Do we see here an echo of the origin of settlements such as the Arden village of Tanworth, on place-name evidence 'Tanna's homestead or enclosure', but later a village with open fields (Fig 42)? One thing is clear: it would be dangerous in an English context to view these initial pre-village footholds in terms of specialized shielings or outpastures. To understand the movement from single farm to cluster, it must be appreciated that, before the Norman Conquest, we are dealing with a society in which pressures towards communal effort were steadily increasing as population rose, but the colonizable reserve was sufficiently great, lordship less absolute, and the times, intermittently it must be admitted, sufficiently stable to permit the occurrence of single-farm dwellings, even within the presence of a viable framework of communal obligation and group settlements. We are, however, some distance from the classic village of the Middle Ages, for not only is there an infinite number of gradations on the scale between single farm and village, but also the all-important iron hand of seignorial power, although undoubtedly present, is perhaps less universal, less total.[18]

What of these 'single-farms-to-become-villages?' The discovery that nearly one hundred Anglo-Saxon deserted settlement sites are known, in what is at present open country, is part of a growing body of evidence for fundamental changes in settlement patterns in the later Saxon period. Many of these sites are little more than large single farms or small hamlets. The late Saxon and Norman period may well have seen a process of 'balling', with villages evolving from more scattered units under the heavier hand of new lords; indeed Hurst, Sheppard and Roberts suggest that many villages may well have been substantially replanned in the centuries after the Conquest, and the process probably continues right through the Middle Ages, its final echoes being seen in the estate villages of the eighteenth and nineteenth centuries. This conclusion, to be discussed more fully in the next chapter, could well encourage a critical re-evaluation of what Domesday Book really tells us about rural settlement. However, this is no answer to the question of how a single-farm became a village, and two processes were no doubt involved in the development of village clusters with open fields (albeit simple ones): on the one hand land could be granted to dependent tenants, while retaining in hand some proportion of the reclaimed land. In this we see not only echoes of the *demesne-villein* land relationship of later centuries, but also the possible significance of the law of Ine that he who had twenty hides of land must show twelve hides settled with tenants; that he who had ten hides must show six; that he who had three must show one and a half. Men, settled on land, were of interest to both Crown and landowner. Aston has linked the strong personal element in so many place-names with incipient 'seigniorial' activity as an important force in the moulding of rural society and the spread of settlement. A further law indicates that the acceptance of a house from a lord commits the tenant, if the lord so wishes, to the performance of labour services; it may well be that we see here the beginnings of the highly organized village settlements to be described in the next chapter. On the other hand, the sharing of land between kin could result in the appearance of a joint-farm village; at Upthorpe, Worcestershire, a late-seventh-century charter shows acres getting intermixed, with two brothers so dividing two hides of land (about 90 ha, or 240 acres) that in all places the elder had three acres while the younger had a fourth. The motives for establishing the 'original' single farms are of course virtually impossible to ascertain. Of Eardisley, in western Herefordshire, Domesday Book tells us that it pays no geld, renders no customary payment or service, does not belong to any hundred. In spite of the proximity to Wales, 'It lies in the middle of a forest, and there is one house'; it was 'Aegheard's clearing', but within a hundred years, according to Hoskins, it had developed into a parish. If Aegheard was, either just before or soon after the Norman Conquest, willing to settle alone in a woodland clearing near the Welsh border — or, if not alone, with only his family — then we may presume that such single farms were being founded elsewhere. The motives for their foundation were no doubt many, but the same pioneer spirit which sent colonists in the Americas into lands often bordering on hostile Indian tribes was no doubt present; such regions offered freedom, either real or illusory.[19]

Competition between Villages — Settlement Desertion

If the processes of colonization and diffusion underlie the spread of settlements in England before 1200, then these foundations have in subsequent centuries undergone competition, and economic, social and political forces have combined to eliminate the weaker growths. Fig 25 shows the remarkable pattern of deserted settlements mapped by the Deserted Medieval Village Research Group. It is likely, indeed probable, that others have escaped the net, either by reason of their small size or by virtue of deficient documentary or field evidence; this is particularly true of such settlements as disappeared before 1250. If Fig 25 is compared with Thorpe's map of rural settlement (Fig 1) it can be seen that, with few exceptions, the large majority of sites lie within the rich lowlands, on the river terrace, clayland, chalk and limestone terrains of midland England; we are not in fact dealing with rash ventures into the difficult environments of the west and north, although close study reveals that these

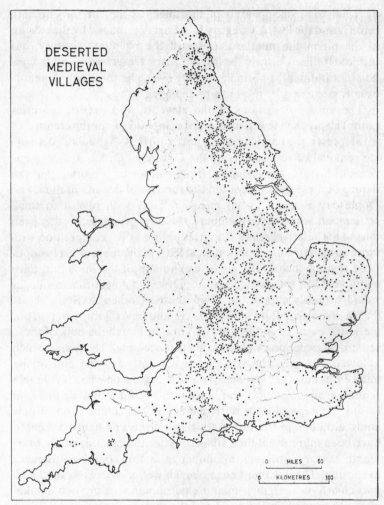

DESERTED
MEDIEVAL
VILLAGES

0   MILES   50

0   KILOMETRES   100

Fig 25   Deserted Medieval Villages in England, after Beresford and Hurst (1971), 66

regions have added their tithe. The numbers of deserted villages are such that we are quite clearly dealing with something more fundamental than the mere accidents of history: these large numbers, over 2,000 in fact, represent physical evidence of the constant adjustment of patterns of village settlement to changing circumstances, and Hound Tor on Dartmoor, Wormleighton in Warwickshire and East Howle in Durham have more in common than might at first appear; all are deserted villages, although one was deserted by 1300, one disappeared in the final decades of the fifteenth century and the last, a 'category D' village, marooned by the closure of the pit in the middle decades of the twentieth century, has suffered its final decay in the last ten years. Desertion is a phenomenon of settlement, a normal, possibly even a healthy, phenomenon, usually occurring in response to changing needs.[20]

The village desertions of the eleventh and twelfth centuries cannot always be viewed in terms of competition, for the creation of royal forests, the harrying of the north in 1068–70, and the deliberate removal of settlements by the Cistercian Order, are the accidents of history. Nevertheless, it must never be forgotten that the nature of these events ensured the survival of documentation, and Domesday Book is by no means reliable with regard to small settlements which were members of larger groupings, so that even during the relatively dark centuries before 1086, competition with more successful neighbours may, at least in the more densely populated regions such as the great river valleys of the Midlands, have eliminated less successful ventures. Deserted Anglo-Saxon villages would certainly support this hypothesis. Domesday Book shows that William I's military activities created havoc locally in parts of the south-east and in the Vale of York, although the bulk of these settlements were probably eventually reoccupied. The period which followed, between the end of the eleventh and the end of the thirteenth centuries, was one of notable expansion when favourable economic circumstances combined with a kindly climatic phase to favour the expansion of settlements and the colonization of new lands, although in frontier zones single farms and hamlets seem to have been more usual than villages. After the opening of the fourteenth century, however, a number of factors combined to check expansion. The weather became much wetter, harvests failed and, particularly in marginal upland environments, many new intakes were abandoned. In the middle of the century the disastrous Black Death of 1348–50 was associated with, but not necessarily the cause of, a major economic recession which shook the foundations of the medieval order. Without doubt some villages disappeared during the fourteenth century; climatic change (the onset of a wetter, more stormy phase); the Black Death; and, in the north of England, destructive Scottish raids all played a part. It is the economic changes, however, initiated during the latter half of the fourteenth century, which had the greatest impact upon village settlements. Landowners faced with low cereal prices and high labour costs, and tempted by high wool prices (for the domestic woollen industry was

Fig 26   Garmondsway, County Durham. The date of this desertion is unknown, but Garmondsway was once a one-row village (for there is no trace of a second row). The former toft boundaries are still clearly visible, as are traces of the long-houses which once lay in eaves-orientation along the edge of the green, while the village boundary bank along the toft tail line is almost submerged beneath a great double plough-ridge. The farm is characteristic of North Eastern England, with its great complex of byres, loose boxes and stores arranged around several open yards. The structures range in date from the late-eighteenth century to the present day. Photo: N. McCord and University of Newcastle.

expanding) began to lay down to grass great areas of arable land. To do this they were, by the middle decades of the fifteenth century, willing to evict tenants and to depopulate settlements. It is worth citing a portion of the preamble to an act of 1489, for by the late fifteenth century the newly established Tudor government was very much concerned with the overall effects of individual policies of depopulation:

> Great inconveniences daily doth increase by desolation and pulling down and wilful waste of houses and Towns [i.e. villages] within this realm, and laying to pasture lands which customarily have been used in tillage, whereby idleness, — ground and beginning of all mischiefs — daily doth increase, for where in some Towns two hundred persons were occupied and lived by their lawful labours, now be there occupied two or three herdmen, and the residue fallen in idleness; the husbandry, which is one of the greatest commodities of the realm is greatly decayed; churches destroyed; the service of God withdrawn; the bodies there buried not prayed for, the patron and curate wronged; the defence of this land against our enemies outwards feebled and impaired; to the great displeasure of God, to the subversion of policy and the good rule of this land.

It would be difficult to pack more into one sentence, but, as Beresford aptly puts it, the big fish had escaped the net and the act was too late. In Warwickshire, for example, some seventy-two sites were abandoned between 1450 and 1485, and only twenty-one between 1485 and 1680. In fact, the period of village depopulation was probably more extended than these figures indicate: thus in Lincolnshire some twelve villages went before 1350; soon after 1350 a further fifteen disappeared; the early fifteenth century saw eighteen go, while the latter half of the same century saw twenty-seven. A close study of Fig 25 and Figs 1 and 3 shows that the village-strewn claylands of the midland counties were the most prone — claylands which are equally valuable down to grass and under a corn crop; indeed in many instances a run of wet winters could well have been a critical factor in tipping the scales. Three other factors are important, however. Firstly, Beresford has argued that it was the smaller villages which tended to go, and Fig 18 shows that small parishes were certainly involved; secondly, the social structure of the settlement had to be favourable — copyholders were easier to evict than freeholders; and finally family links were possibly important in spreading news of the advantages, economic and social, of depopulating. The short-term economic advantages were obvious enough: a village of cultivators was replaced by a few herdsmen, and the profits from the sale of wool or stock accrued to the lord, who was often able to enhance his own status by constructing a fine new manor house on or near the depopulated village. The results can, at times, be quite astonishing, and villageless zones occur in Yorkshire, Warwickshire, Leicestershire, Oxfordshire and Buckinghamshire, areas where depopulations were particularly successful and the pattern of villages has been replaced by a scatter of single farms. The frequent survival of lowland parochial areas which contain no village but still retain boundaries and name are almost infallible indications, while on the ground it is often possible to trace the old house-places, plots, gardens, and roadways as low embankments and hollows; sometimes the old church survives, either as a ruin or incorporated into a secular building, while the local system of tracks and footpaths often preserves the lines of old roads converging upon the village site. There are, of course, many gradations of change between total desertion and some measure of decline. A modern village may be flourishing, but still show some signs of deserted house-plots round its edges. Again, a site may consist of a large farm or manor house with many former house-sites scattered round close by. These minor variations, however, have a more proper place in the next chapter, which is concerned with village plans, for deserted sites and the excavations of these constitute valuable sources of evidence for plan variations.[21]

The processes of village depopulation have of course not ceased; some late removals of villages were carried out by great landowners in the late-seventeenth, eighteenth and nineteenth centuries when they wished to remove them further away from their residences when they were creating parks. Examples can be found at Burton Constable in Yorkshire, Milton Abbas in Dorset, Westonbirt in Gloucestershire and Chatsworth in Derbyshire. Similarly the clearances in Scotland during the nineteenth century, and the subsequent depopulation of coastland clusters as the result of emigration, have resulted in many deserted settlements, while the mining villages of the north, declining as pits close, represent a modern generation of deserted villages, like the railway settlements such as Waskerley in the Durham foothills, which has suffered its final decay within the last decade. The pattern of village settlements which has survived to appear on the present Ordnance Survey maps is the end-product of a protracted process of competition in a hard world of economic and environmental facts in which the weakest necessarily went to the wall, and, just as the temporary camps of Mesolithic hunters can have no meaning for the modern world, so the somewhat more permanent camps of certain nineteenth-century industrial communities have, in some cases at least, outlived their usefulness. The patterns of village settlement we have inherited are the product of at least nine hundred years of constant adjustment to new demands and new pressures, and there are surely no grounds for assuming that this process of adjustment will not continue in future centuries, although increasing mobility is proving a powerful preservative, particularly when associated with an increasing awareness of the 'sanctity of place', and the need for roots and continuity which is probably as strong today as it ever has been.

5

Village Forms

THE REMARKABLE VARIETY of village forms seen on the modern map is a reflection of the long period of time involved in their development, and it is this characteristic above all others which gives to British rural nucleations a diversity and fortuitousness in which lies much of their visual charm. The appearance of the village, often beautiful, always varied, is the product of many centuries of historical change. The evidence of Domesday Book points to nearly one thousand years of continuous existence for many settlements, while archaeological and documentary evidence can easily add another half millennium to this.

Three types of evidence are relevant to the historical appraisal of village settlements: documentary, archaeological, and morphological or landscape. The evidence derived from documents has for many years been the mainstay of historical studies of rural settlement, and falls into two main categories. The first is the evidence of maps, at many scales, both manuscript and printed, enabling both patterns and forms to be studied with some accuracy as far back as the early decades of the seventeenth century and, more rarely, the sixteenth century; this can be supported and illuminated by the great wealth of the second category — documents, rentals, surveys, deeds and administrative material from both national and private archives. Before 1600 the researcher must rely on what he can cull from non-cartographic sources, and in the study of rural settlement the evidence of archaeological excavation becomes increasingly important. The period between the Norman Conquest and 1600 provides unique opportunities for a combination of the two approaches to be applied.[1]

One further source remains available, the evidence of the landscape itself, and although a recent authority has written that 'the joys of tramping fields and roads or of flying over the countryside, are more likely to benefit the searcher's health than his knowledge', the evidence of settlement morphology is a valuable and virtually untapped source. As M. R. G. Conzen pointed out 'settlement is the geographical record of its own evolution', and although the heritage of the last century in terms of visual landscape is undeniably large, much of the substance of former centuries is still with us. The fieldworker is frequently able to evaluate hypotheses more realistically than the student in the library or on the map: slopes have a habit of being steeper than the eye of the mind appreciates; the lie of winter snows can reveal the land-cunning shown in the placing of the village, while the desirable settlement site can emerge as bleak, shelterless and inhospitable; the continuation of an existing building line or fence line as a soil mark or break of slope, or the presence of slight banks indicative of former house-foundations can be of vital importance in interpreting the history of a particular settlement. To repeat a well-known metaphor, the landscape, that 'marvellous palimpsest' is a document, overwritten not once but repeatedly. It can reveal facts not discoverable from parchment or paper. To learn to read it involves observation and discipline. Nevertheless, morphogenetic analysis, the technique of basing a retrogressive study on the settlements and field structures found both in the present landscape and on large-scale maps, is not a tool for the uncritical, and the evidence has to be read, sifted and evaluated as carefully as the 'tedious rubbish' of monkish moralizers or the intricacies of bailiffs' account rolls in order to reveal the grain of truth. The evidence from the landscape — the boundary, just visible, but shown on no map; the earthworks of a small unknown farm or hamlet; the distinctive patterns of field and hedgerow can lead to a fresh evaluation of conventional documentary sources, and all evidence, landscape, documentary and archaeological must be woven into the completed picture, for each complements the other.[2]

Rural House Types

The most obvious signs of settlement in the rural scene are the dwellings and associated buildings which make up villages, hamlets and farms, but important as these are, and large as is the literature dealing with them, it is not the purpose of this volume to dwell in detail on domestic architecture, and a brief review of some of the issues and questions must suffice before we turn to the contexts within which these structures occur. Houston has argued that in the rural landscape the traditional house is an important element, 'providing evidence of the complex relations between man and his environment'. Building materials and house-types adopted do undoubtedly illustrate some of the interactions between physical and human factors, while the plan of the house and the layout of the farm buildings (Figs 2 and 41) are valuable visual clues to the functional aspects of settlements. The evidence available for British house-forms in a pre-1600 context is derived primarily from archaeological sources, although there is a surprising number of late medieval structures still standing, and a careful study of documentary material can greatly illuminate social and economic contexts for these. There is an increasing volume of evidence to show that throughout medieval Britain the long-house formed an important if not a dominant house-form at the peasant level, although it underwent substantial modifications. The characteristic features of this type of house are illustrated by Figs 2 and 29; such structures usually possessed a width-length ratio falling between 1:2 and 1:4, and were designed so as to house both men and beasts under the same roof, one end of the building being for human habitation, the other end, usually equipped with some form of drain and frequently lying on the downslope side, for stock. One or two entrances in the middle of the dwelling were shared. There are indications from many sites that, between the twelfth and the fifteenth century, two parallel sequences of change can be observed. First, broadly between late-Saxon times and the fifteenth century, there was in general a progression from a small, single-roomed cottage, to the long-house, and thence to the true farmhouse, a building specifically designed for human habitation, and provided with separate barns, stalls, byres and other outbuildings. Second, the same time-span also saw the change from timber construction using post-holes and sleeper beams, to stone footings to carry timbers, and finally to substantial dry-stone walls or clay walling, depending upon the locality. The repeated rebuilding of peasant houses has been demonstrated at a number of sites, not least at Wharram Percy, although the complexity of the pattern overlying the demolished twelfth-century manor house in toft 10 (Fig 30) may be the result of the unusual status of that particular site.[3]

The Anglo-Saxon antecedents of these peasant house-forms are gradually being revealed, and recent finds are emphasizing the sophistication of pre-Norman timber structures; at Maxey, Northants, a Dark Age settlement was discovered during gravel quarrying and partially excavated, to reveal at least seven rectangular buildings ranging from 9 m to 15 m (30 ft to 50 ft) in length and 5 m to 6 m (16 ft to 20 ft) in width. They were all of a post-hole construction, but examples of wall trenches and beam slots were found. Nearby were small ancillary structures, including pits surrounded by postholes, perhaps representing storage huts. The excavator did not consider these main structures to be long-houses; indeed he placed them in a class in which separate buildings have separate functions. Dating evidence of small finds places them in the middle Saxon period, and there were hints of Danish affinities. At West Stow (Suffolk) and Mucking (Sussex) the excavation of two pagan Anglo-Saxon villages has shown that the sunken-hut or *Grubenhaus* is the most common type of building, and it may be that we have to reckon with social variations between villages, as well as economic contrasts. Any consideration of the origins of English villages and their associated structures must mention the important site at Feddersen Wierde, near Bremerhaven, where early in the first century AD a settlement was established consisting of houses laid out in parallel rows running east to west. In the course of the first century the village was several times rebuilt, and an artificial mound was deliberately created to lift the houses above the gradually rising water-table as the sea encroached, and during the second century the village assumed the characteristic radial plan of a *Wurt*, as such mounds are termed. The houses of this settlement were aisled long-houses, with the living quarters at one end, centred around the hearth, and the stalls for the beasts at the other. These structures were impressive, between 15 m to 24 m (50 to 80 ft) long, and 8 m to 10·5 m (25 to 35 ft) wide, and there were successive rebuildings between the second and the early fifth century, when the rising sea level stimulated the final abandonment of the *Wurt*, and the inhabitants, it has been suggested, probably joined in the general migration towards the shores of England. It was the blending of these continental traits with 'native' British traditions which gives the development of building types and village plans a particular complexity and interest.[4]

At the opposite end of the time-scale, Hoskins has demonstrated how, during the period between 1570 and 1640, there was a revolution in housing, which led firstly to the physical rebuilding or substantial modernization of the medieval houses which had come down from the past, a movement accompanied by a remarkable increase in the household furnishings and equipment. Hoskins has

gone so far as to postulate a sequence of events which he sum-
marizes as follows: 'savings — rebuilding and enlargement of
houses — decreased mortality and perhaps higher fertility (linked,
one might comment, with greater opportunity?) — rise of population — new building and development of congestion — rise in
mortality rates', a cycle which carries us from the late-sixteenth
century to the mid-eighteenth century. Space forbids an examination of these linkages, but this cycle serves to emphasize the importance of domestic buildings in any consideration of the past. The
post-medieval vicissitudes of traditional building styles have been
admirably outlined by Professor Maurice Barley in his volume on
the *English Farmhouse and Cottage;* it is sufficient to say here that
most visible structures found within villages post-date 1570, the
beginning of the 'great rebuilding'; indeed in terms of absolute
numbers there is a progressive weighting towards the later centuries, particularly the late-eighteenth and nineteenth century.[5]

As Houston points out, the rural dwelling, like the agricultural
systems themselves, belongs to a domain where a kind of collective
conscience is more effective than individual initiative, and although,
within any one cultural group, a variety of house types may reflect
social status, economic prosperity, or regional variations in the
availability of building materials, the form of the house not only is
closely related to the nature of the particular farm and the needs of
the individual but was also, as Hoskins shows, intimately linked with
socio-economic and demographic trends within the society as a
whole. The appearance of the courtyard farm at peasant level must
be seen as a form already prevalent amongst farms of higher social
status; thus the moated farmsteads of the lesser knights and wealthy
freeholders probably had separate dwelling-houses even in the
late-twelfth or early-thirteenth century. The ordinary villager
tended to retain the long-house until well into the thirteenth century; indeed the form persisted until the fifteenth century in some
settlements and some regions where opportunities for economic
upgrading were limited, and it survived into this century amongst
the highlands and islands of western Scotland.[6]

The archaeological, architectural and cartographic evidence currently available concerning village buildings makes one point abundantly clear: buildings represent the most ephemeral component of
any plan, for not only are they modified and adapted by each
generation, with new doors, new windows, new internal arrangements and new wings being added as fortune and occasion demands,
but also complete rebuildings can occur within the span of no more

than a few years. Our present stock of vernacular buildings is the
end-product of centuries of change for, as T. S. Eliot noted in his
poem 'East Coker' quoted at the beginning of this volume

> In succession
> Houses rise and fall, crumble, are extended
> Are removed, destroyed, restored, or in their place
> Is an open field, or a factory, or a by-pass.

A building's capacity to survive is a reflection of two principal
factors: its position on the social scale, and the changing fortunes of
the owners, the settlement and the whole region. Thus the higher up
the social scale a building is, the more chance there is of it surviving,
so that great houses from as early as 1200 are still with us, but there
are relatively few cottages from before 1800. In a prosperous context, however, even the great house will experience rebuilding. The
work of Brunskill covers these questions in a most systematic way,
but in practical terms, in a village, the property boundaries and road
lines are often very much older than the buildings they contain.

Village Plan Types

In all villages the dwellings and subsidiary buildings, each usually
surrounded by one or more small enclosures, are always grouped in
some way, and geographers have traditionally been preoccupied
with classifying the various types of village plan. C. T. Smith discusses at some length the classification of settlement forms within
Europe, concluding that the usefulness of classifications devised by
such workers as Demangeon or Christaller depends on the scale of
application, and even within an area as small as Britain many
possible classifications exist. G. Schwarze classified grouped settlements on the basis of size, compactness, shape and regularity, and
while recognizing that a variety of classifications is possible —
their usefulness depending upon the nature of the study undertaken
— forms do vary and the variation can be significant to the geographer. Conzen, with reference to urban forms, has emphasized the
need to recognize the 'compositeness of town plans which can give a
clue to distinct stages in town growth of which a defective historical
record may give no hint'. Such analyses can be extended to rural
forms, although not without pitfalls: the material must be handled
with care. When faced with the task of studying the forces which
have created a profusion of forms, one must needs generalize in
order to see order and tendencies, but it is essential to appreciate

that this process of classification distorts the reality which is being studied: the disorder *is* reality.[7]

Fig 28 illustrates one way of treating village plans: all villages are made up of an individual, but not necessarily unique, assemblage of public space (the roads, tracks and open spaces), and private space (the houses, gardens and other structures and enclosures). Two basic village shapes can occur (Fig 28a): either the assemblage of structures and enclosures can be linear, forming a row, or non-linear, forming an agglomeration. The quality of this overall arrangement can vary enormously, but can broadly be described as regular or irregular (Fig 28b), a subjective measure ultimately involving comparison with a geometric shape, so that a village with straight roads, eaves-oriented rows of buildings and rectangular house-plots would be regular, as indeed would be an agglomeration based upon a series of wedge-shaped plots, or upon a rectilinear grid of roads. In contrast, and Braithwaite, Cumberland is an example of this (Fig 28a), little geometric order can be detected in some settlements. Furthermore (Fig 28c), many settlements contain large open spaces within their plans, spaces that are too large to be merely streets, and thus warrant the term 'green', i.e. an area of open land used by the community for special and closely defined purposes, notably for grazing beasts (cattle, horses, sheep, geese, chickens and ducks) and playing lawful games (for football may have originated upon such open spaces). Figure 28 does two things: first, it demonstrates this classification of plans diagrammatically in the sequence 28a–c, using symbols which in their developed form (28c) can be used for mapping purposes (Fig 32). Secondly, it incorporates a series of examples of village plans derived from the three northern counties of Durham, Northumberland and Cumberland.

If work on the morphology of rural settlements is to progress, it is essential to pass beyond mere classification to explore structural-functional relationships in both the present and the past, to define the processes at work influencing village plans, and to examine their origins. Classification, however, laying emphasis upon the forms as objects to be observed and studied, is only an essential preliminary step, leading towards a relatively uniform terminology which can then form the basis of comparative studies. The classification outlined here, used by the author in the north of England, appears to have a more general applicability, and is based upon descriptive terminology found in documentation used as far back as the twelfth century in Durham sources. Nevertheless, it is only a classification, a working tool, to be used flexibly and to be abandoned when no longer useful. It represents no more than a personal attempt to bring some order into the morphological diversity of village plans, and it has proved to be of value to the author.[8]

A number of qualifying points must be kept in mind when studying Fig 28:

 i The classification is entirely based upon form: function is excluded as it represents an entirely different dimension of reality. Furthermore, the fact that two settlements have virtually identical forms need not mean that they have a common origin: similar or identical forms need not have similar or identical origins.

 ii The ten plan types defined by the three principal variables (for the moment ignoring the problem of additional factors) are sharply drawn in theory: in practice no village ever accords completely with the most regular ideal (although in the USA and Israel, for example, perfectly regular settlements can be found), and the axes of the grid may be thought of as a scale; thus regular two-row villages, like Culgaith, grade gradually into regular two-row green-villages (or regular two-row street green-villages) like South Charlton. Similarly villages like South Charlton grade gradually into irregular two-row green-villages like Whickham. The distinction between a wide street and a narrow green must always have been one of mere convention, and it must be remembered that the addition of tarmacadam to roads has sharpened this distinction during the last hundred years. In practice the location of a village on the grid may be altered during study, as the eye and the documentation reveal the details of the plan, the former presence of a green or the creation of apparent irregularity as the result of cottage infill.

 iii The ten plan types indicated are merely representatives of plan families: take the two rows at South Charlton, remove one, and a single-row village appears; move them apart, however, and add two extra rows, one on each side, and a multiple-row village with a broad green emerges; push the rows apart at one end of the village to produce a wedge-shaped green, then add a head-row, and a triangular village results. All, the author would contend, are variants of the same plan, the basic building blocks of which are rows; all belong to the same plan-type family.

 iv A final point is perhaps the most important. Village plans are frequently *composite*, that is to say they are made up of two or more of the basic plan types of the grid. A good, well-documented example, is to be found at Kirk Merrington (Fig 27), but the plans of Grassington, Mawbray, Embleton, Whick-

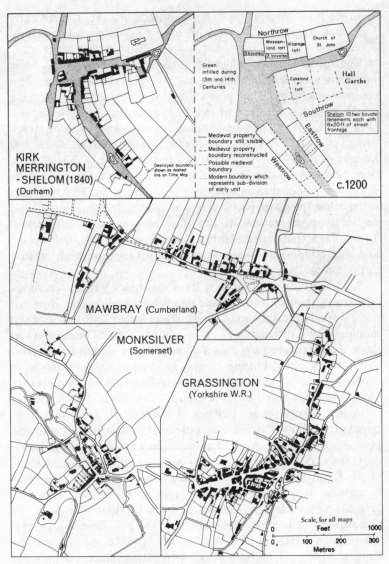

Fig 27   Village Plan Contrasts

ham and even Culgaith are worthy of closer study, for all of them may be to some extent composite. To complicate matters further, two or more plan types, or two or more composite clusters, separated by distances of up to several hundred yards, can sometimes be regarded as one village (they may for instance possess a single-field system) and such settlements are conveniently termed fragmented clusters or, to use Taylor's term, polyfocal villages.

The three variables which form the basis of the grid — basic shape, the degree of regularity, and the presence or absence of a green — are the principal plan variables; to these must be added a fourth important one, size for, as Fig 28a suggests, at the lower end of the scale, a rural cluster may consist of no more than three farms, while at the other end there are clusters the size of small towns, and Longtown, Cumberland, clearly lies in this category. The distinctions between hamlets and villages, villages and towns tend to be functional rather than morphological, although the final variables listed below the maps, particularly complexity, building density and degree of fragmentation, are all status-linked i.e. relate to function. Thus villages that once had urban status tend to have complex plans and high-building densities. Nevertheless, they are clearly related to their rural cousins.

A study of forms along these lines very quickly raises questions concerning their socio-economic significance and origins. How can these varied forms be explained? What forces and factors have moulded their development? How old are they? The answers to these questions are rarely easily attained and cannot be covered within this volume, but Fig 28 may be used to illustrate the basic problems. For the purposes of discussion let us assume initially that villages are influenced by three groups of variables: those deriving from the physical characteristics of the site; those arising from population change within the settlement; those linked with the presence or absence of lordly power. Each group is in itself complex, and of course all three groups may well influence the development of a single settlement. It may with some validity be argued that in a linear village, Culgaith, Greysouthern (Fig 28e) or Mawbray (Fig 23) physical factors, the presence of a dry ridge such as a levée or a strongly defined spur may condition the plan morphology; in a very regular village, South Charlton for instance, we may see the expression of lordly power — the classic estate village, but may this not account for the regularity in Culgaith? In irregular settlements lordly power may not have concerned itself with ordering the dwellings and outbuildings, while in the case of tangled agglomerations such as Braithwaite and Tantobie even physical constraints seem to have conspired to create disorder. All of the settlements in Figs 27 and 28 appeared because there were sufficient people to create them, but at Whickham in particular, set on the Durham coalfield,

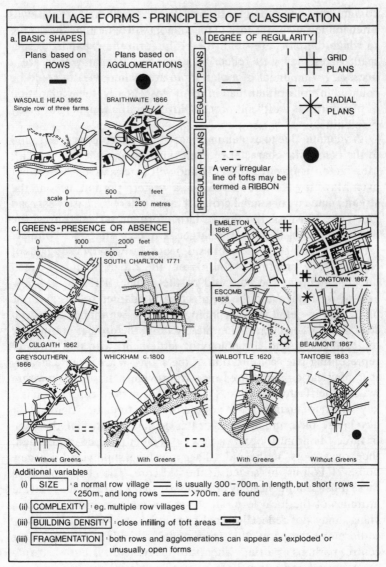

Fig 28   Village Forms, Principles of Classification

may we not suggest expansion caused by population growth, haphazard because of weak control? Quite clearly these three groups of variables cannot provide a complete explanation: for instance, population expansion will (in a purely agricultural context) be closely related to the economic resources available to the community, while the inheritance practices followed (themselves often influenced by the lord of the manor) will determine the degree to which the plots are subdivided. The form the expanded settlement takes may well reflect its economy, so that greens are a necessary component of a plan in an area where wealth could be counted in stock rather than in cornfields. Clearly, the explanation of plan forms is a difficult process, involving the weighing of many possibilities.

A valuable clue to explaining what can be observed is to be found in the composite character of even simple plans: the case of Kirk Merrington is obvious (Fig 27) and will be examined below, but even Mawbray has three elements; a western portion, beyond the stream, made up of a small group of farms where the east-west road meets the coast road; a line of farms forming the north row, the northern side of the street; a larger farm consisting of a compact group of buildings on the south side, together with two straggles of cottages, one creating a south row, the other fringing a small integral green at the east end of the village. The site is a low east-to-west ridge and the form is clearly adapted to this, but it is likely that in detail the morphology reflects two things: the social structure of the village — i.e. the big farm, the ordinary farms and the cottages — and chronology of settlement, with the 'sea end' representing later colonization of the shore. What is quite clear is that physical circumstances merely provide a framework within which other factors operate. Population growth or contraction is a key factor, for an increase in population will stimulate a demand for new house-plots and holdings; if this demand is satisfied, then one of three things must occur: a new settlement must be established; the house-plots of the old village must be subdivided; or new house-plots must be added to the old core. The choice between these must be influenced by both the size of the existing unit and the attitudes of the local lord. However, an increase in the size of a village may not reflect internal population growth; lordly power could move the population from outlying hamlets into the larger centre, perhaps at a time when the village field system was being re-organized and rationalized so as to maximize production.[9]

Population Trends

The question of population, an essential and integral part of the preceding discussion, must now be considered more fully. Domesday Book provides a unique opportunity for estimating the population in 1086; by adding together all the recorded tenants it is possible to multiply this sum by a factor and obtain a total for England. This estimate falls between 1·5 and 2·0 million folk, while the population in 1377 has been estimated from Poll Tax records to have been 2·2 million. Population trends between these two fixed points were very succinctly summarized by Sir John Clapham when he wrote, 'An opinion often expressed, which is perhaps near the truth, is that the population of England and Wales doubled between 1100 and 1300; fell sharply with the Pestilence (the Black Death in 1348–9); and rose again to its former maximum by 1500, when it was perhaps 2,500,000 or 3,000,000 people. But it is all a perhaps, and statisticians are wary about it'. There is even less data for Scotland, but he cites the figure of about 500,000 in the fifteenth century. The following table is a summary of numerous estimates, and extends from Domesday Book to the period of census records:

England and Wales: Estimates of Population (in millions)

Year	Population
1100	1·5
1200	2·2
1340	4·5
1470	3·0
1620	5·0
1740	6·0
1800	9·0
1900	33·0

From the seventeenth century onwards these figures become increasingly reliable; figures from the Hearth Tax returns, various episcopal censuses, figures of actual births and deaths taken from parish registers, and argument backwards from the census of 1801 can all be utilized. It is, in Clapham's words

a fair estimate that in 1700 the figure was between 5,000,000 and 5,500,000 and in 1750 about 6,500,000; it had then taken about 250 years for it to double. It doubled again in a little more than 70 years, being 12,000,000 in 1821. The most rapid growth came between 1801 and 1821; but between 1750 and 1801 there was a growth of 40 per cent. After 1821 the next doubling took less than sixty years. The Scottish figure for 1801 was 1,608,000. If it had moved parallel to that of England and Wales, it would have been about 1,200,000 in 1750 and approaching 1,000,000 in 1700. Its course has not been so carefully studied as the English, but these figures cannot be far wrong.

The tremendous upsurge in the second half of the eighteenth century was of course associated with the Industrial Revolution, and

the vast proportion of this growth has occurred in urban populations. Indeed, migration to the towns has steadily depleted population numbers in purely rural areas. The recent trends are complex.
The drift to the south is well known, and commuters, seeking
pleasant rural homes, are helping the towns to tighten their tentacu-
lar grip on the surviving countryside, while to the north and west the
hill farms are becoming bird-haunted shells as the flight from the
countryside continues.[10]

We are, however, here concerned with the trends before 1500.
The period up to 1310 or thereabouts saw a relatively rapid and
sustained growth, as is clearly seen from the eagerness with which
men sought new land to reclaim; the period between 1310 and the
mid-fifteenth century was a period of declining or stagnating population. It will be noted that this decline begins before the Black
Death, or indeed before the great famines of 1316 and 1317; by the
early years of the fourteenth century medieval society had, given
the technology at its disposal, outgrown its resources, so that the
relatively sharp population decline of the second half of the fourteenth century may be seen as a Malthusian check. From the viewpoint of rural settlement, the period between 1100 and 1310 saw
the establishment of many hamlets and single farms and, as has
already been shown, by 1200 the foundation of new villages had
virtually ceased. Nevertheless, these population trends form an
important backcloth or mechanism against which changes within
the village must be viewed. The problem of population trends
before Domesday cannot concern us here; it is not unreasonable to
postulate a period of intermittent expansion occurring between AD
700 and AD 1000, but to speculate further is fruitless.

These general trends form a useful framework, but it must be
stressed that each village possesses its own population curve. Hoskins has published his conclusions concerning the Leicestershire
village of Wigston Magna; in 1086 the village was a substantial one,
containing no less than 83 families and he has argued that in the
second half of the fourteenth century the number of households lay
between 110 and 120. A knowledge of general trends suggests that
in the late-thirteenth and early-fourteenth century this total would
have been exceeded, possibly by as much as one quarter or even one
third, but we have no measure of the severity of plague mortality in
Wigston. Tax quotas of the early fifteenth century show a decline in
the ability of the village to pay tax, and a continuing population
decline is confirmed by an estimate of a population of 60–70
families based on the Lay Subsidy Rolls of 1524 and 1525, while an

episcopal census of 1563 suggests the presence of some 70–80 families. Hearth Tax returns of a century later, however, demonstrate that Wigston then had some 161 households of varying size, and this is supplemented by a contemporary religious census of 1676, which shows that on average each household consisted of just over 4 folk, in all some 683. In the first census return of 1801 Wigston had 354 families, totalling 1,658 persons, an average of nearly 4·7 persons per family, and the 354 families occupied nearly 336 houses.[11]

This data produces a crude population curve, expressed in terms of households, and while it is not proposed to follow any further Hoskins's necessary elaborations and qualifications, two particular points may be noted. First, the way in which the local trend reflects the national trend, although once again one must remember that each village was unique, each had a tithe of good fortune and bad which would be reflected in population figures. Wigston, it must be noted, has always been a large prosperous settlement. Both Hoskins and Titow have written about the close links between population trends and harvests, Titow demonstrating how, on the estates of the Bishop of Winchester in southern England, bad harvests in the thirteenth and fourteenth centuries were invariably followed by a rise in the number of *heriots* or death-duty payments rendered to the lord, while Hoskins has traced in more general terms the links between harvests, mortality, disease, food prices, agrarian legislation, social unrest, and perhaps even the fundamental process of economic growth during the period between 1480 and 1619. Second, these population changes found a physical expression in the expansion and contraction of farm, village and town. Within the village a rising population would lead to the subdivision of existing tofts or the addition of new ones, while a falling population would mean the reconstitution of larger units as groups of small tofts were amalgamated, without necessarily resulting in the reappearance of the same larger units as had existed earlier. There would also be a tendency for the desertion and destruction of tofts located on the periphery of the settlement, much as the modern farmer in possession of more than one farm will allow some of the buildings he cannot use to fall into decay. There are few villages that do not reveal traces of this contraction, and Fig 36 illustrates a fine example of a shrunken village. There has yet to be a study which relates population trends to changes in village morphology, largely because of the problems of accumulating sufficiently accurate data, but the general relationships are clear, and the 'mechanism' of population, the balance between births and deaths, between expansion and contraction, is clearly fundamental to any study of the morphology of rural settlements.[12]

The interaction of some of the variables affecting individual villages can be demonstrated in the studies which follow. In the literature of settlement in Britain there is a remarkable absence of detailed morphological studies, and Professor Harry Thorpe's paper on Durham villages still remains an outstanding milestone; furthermore, even where detailed work does exist it relates to areas where regular plans predominate. At the present time it is almost impossible to redress this imbalance. The studies which follow lay particular stress upon the analysis of plans, but it must again be emphasized that morphogenetic studies form but one tool for illuminating beginnings and functions, and it will be noted that there is in the argument a gradual transition from the pure description of changing form to a consideration of its significance.[13]

Case Studies

The site of Jarlshof in Shetland is remarkable in that, superimposed on each other, lie the remains of three prehistoric and protohistoric village settlements. We are not here directly concerned with the Bronze Age and Iron Age settlements, but Fig 29 shows the evolution of the third cluster, a Norse Viking settlement, between the ninth and the thirteenth century. In detail, the houses were sited on sloping land or upon a small rise, where the drainage was freer; if possible a sheltered location was selected. Jarlshof was truly agglomerated, with each farmstead being placed downslope from the parent farm (which presumably occupied the 'best' site) to take advantage of the local lie of the land rather than in any obvious consideration of the adjacent structures. We may guess that there were strong family ties between the parent and two daughter farms, for each would necessarily partake of a limited range of resources; as the maps show, these secondary farms were eventually abandoned, leaving only the parent, but another generation of secondary farms was established nearby. The site of Jarlshof was occupied for well over three thousand years, and one might well ask what qualities attracted Neolithic and Bronze Age peasants, Scandinavian pirates and seventeenth-century lairds to this particular location. Without doubt the key factor *was* the location, at the southernmost tip of Shetland, yet within easy sighting distance of Fair Isle. A shallow inlet offered good harbourage for seafarers, while the

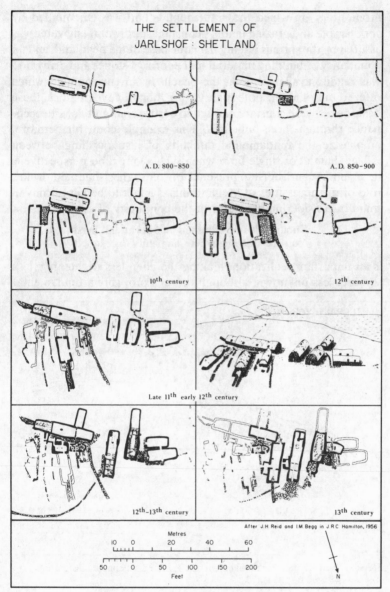

After J.H. Reid and I.M.Begg in J.R.C. Hamilton, 1956

Fig 29   The Settlement of Jarlshof, Shetland after J. R. C. Hamilton, *Excavations at Jarlshof, Shetland*, H.M.S.O. (1962)

promontory on which the settlements stood was surrounded by good arable and grazing land. A constant supply of fresh water was assured by the springs issuing from the base of the headland, and an abundancy of building material in the form of stones and driftwood was readily available along the beach. In an environment which offered only limited potentialities for human development, these basic needs were constant enough to ensure continuity of site occupance through three millennia. This example does, furthermore, emphasize the fundamental difficulty of distinguishing between village, hamlet or single farm when such a long time-perspective is involved. At Jarlshof the presence of ruins, ghost-haunted or not, told of the necessities of life, and this is a fact to be kept firmly in mind in considering problems of the continuity of settlement.

> Though all's now hushed and gaunt and harsh
> You are standing where humanity once stood

is an important realization, making the alien less frightening, less sombre, less unknown, although there is probably a fundamental

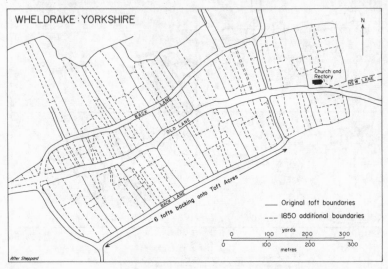

Fig 30   The village of Wheldrake, Yorkshire, after J. Sheppard, *Geografiska Annaler,* 48 Ser. B (1966), 73

distinction to be made between the recognizable, obvious, settlement site, and the dark horrors of graves or ritual monuments.[14]

Jarlshof, although complex in detail, is a relatively neat and clear-cut case, but Figs 30 and 31 provide a point from which to begin an analysis of more complex village forms, and each is charac-

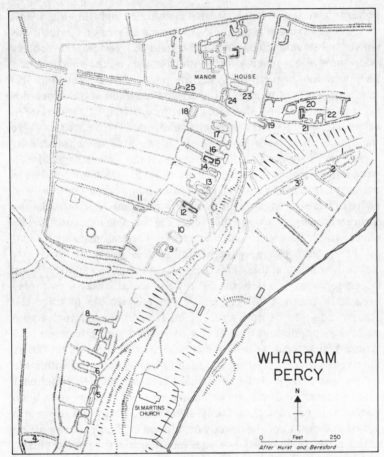

Fig 31   The Village of Wharram Percy, East Riding, Yorkshire, after Beresford and Hurst (1971)

teristic of the two classes of evidence upon which morphological studies are based. The evidence or early maps enables village plans to be projected back into earlier centuries, with confidence to the nineteenth and eighteenth centuries and, rarely, into the sixteenth century, while evidence from deserted settlements enables plan studies to be carried back to the sixteenth and fifteenth centuries and, with excavation, back to the thirteenth or even the twelfth century. June Sheppard's study of the Yorkshire village of Wheldrake is a model of its kind. The present settlement can best be classified as a regular linear village — that is to say the houses are strung out along a principal street some half-mile long, with the toft patterns forming a regular series running at right angles to this axis, and also lying at right angles to two back lanes or service roads which have developed parallel to the main axis. Nineteenth-century plans show about seventy tofts with frontages on the village street. Sheppard has argued from known population figures that this number could well be closely linked with the number of households present in 1348, and she reconstructs a pattern of some sixteen original tofts which were gradually subdivided. While we recognize that the devastation of 1069–70 provided ample scope for starting afresh, there are grounds for thinking that the sixteen original tofts were laid out in pre-Conquest times — firstly, the figure of sixteen perhaps implies a link with a fiscal assessment based upon units of eight, *bovates* or oxgangs, with eight units combining to make the *carucate*; secondly, around the village she was able to reconstruct an area of arable land surrounded by a turf dyke, demonstrably present by 1140, and probably representing the limits of the early eleventh-century arable. This area was sufficient to support some fifteen to twenty households. So regular an initial layout strongly suggests a planned village, and it proved possible to trace the gradual addition of newly reclaimed land to the original arable nucleus as population rose during the twelfth and thirteenth centuries. At first these were closes or fields held by individuals, but by the fourteenth century they are seen to be incorporated within the furlongs and strips of the subdivided field parcels. How the inner core of arable land was worked in the eleventh century is an open question. It was almost certainly divided into strips, but it is worth noting one point not specifically developed by Sheppard: a portion of this early arable, which was later incorporated within West Field, was known as Toft Acres on eighteenth-century field plans, and hence perhaps bore some distinct relationship to the village tofts. In fact, this arable unit abuts on to six tofts on the southern side of the village, six tofts clearly demarcated by the southernmost back lane. Is it pure coincidence that in 1086 the manor of Wheldrake possessed only six tenant households? If this correlation is correct it need not detract from the allocation of the entire sixteen tofts before 1086. Domesday Book makes it clear that while the *vill* once had four ploughlands, in 1086 it only had one plough, and what more logical than that the peasants in the depleted *vill* should concentrate their dwellings and ploughed lands in one part of the settlement?[15]

This study leads us towards a remarkable picture of a Domesday *vill*, albeit a reduced one, for instead of a disordered cluster we find the peasant tofts arranged in a row, each backed by a portion of arable land, and this is a form which occurs repeatedly in tracing the origins of village settlements; the arrangement is essentially similar to that found in an infield, with the houses clinging to the perimeter of the good arable land. Before attempting to assess the general significance of Wheldrake, let us turn to a site which has been studied by means of a very different technique, the deserted or 'lost' village of Wharram Percy, also in Yorkshire. As Fig 27 shows, the village plan is more complex than that of Wheldrake, and is exceedingly difficult to classify precisely. There are in fact a series of well-defined toft groupings forming what can be termed toft complexes — for example, tofts 1–3, 4–8, 9–18, 19–22 and 23–25. The settlement was deserted in the sixteenth century, and we see on the ground the pattern of this period, but several seasons of excavation have revealed three major growth phases: first, the Saxon village, whose form is at present unknown, seems to have lain around the church on the slight terrace above the stream. Secondly, tofts 5–8 appear to represent twelfth-century expansion on to the ridge top. Excavation has shown that at this stage toft 10 contained a fine, stone-built manor house. Tofts 9–18 are associated with what must be seen as a third phase of planned expansion in the thirteenth century, when the manor house was moved to the north — tofts 23–25 — and there are good grounds for arguing from morphology that tofts 1–3 and 19–22 are linked with this particular phase of development. However, this is not the whole story, for recent excavation has shown that between tofts 6 and 7 the still visible boundary overlaid earlier foundations, indicating that during the late-thirteenth and early-fourteenth centuries there was a greater density of houses than just before desertion in the fifteenth century.[16]

These two Yorkshire examples raise an obvious question: how typical are they of English villages as a whole? There is no short answer to this. We are still a long way from understanding the regional variations in medieval village settlements, let alone their relationship to the patterns of manor and estate. Major village excavations from sites as widely separated as West Whelpington in Northumberland, West Hartburn in Durham, Faxton in Northamptonshire, Thaxton in Norfolk, Upton in Gloucestershire, Gomeldon in Wiltshire, Hound Tor in Devon, and Tresmorn and Lanyon in Cornwall suggest that, physical limitations of site aside, the complex history of change in Wharram Percy is in no way exceptional, and in a summary of this work Beresford and Hurst have laid particular emphasis upon the changes which occur in both house orientations and property boundaries. They are of the opinion that village plans were constantly changing throughout the Middle Ages, and indeed archaeological evidence does raise serious doubt concerning the extent to which Sheppard is correct in arguing a case for stability in plan structures over eight or nine hundred years; at first sight there would seem to be ground for a sharp conflict of views between archaeologists and geographers. In the author's view such conflict is both unnecessary and probably unproductive. Reason suggests that within the English landscape there is a very wide range of possibilities, from total plan-destruction to total plan-survival, and it is probable that the proof for the latter will always be more difficult to establish beyond all reasonable doubt than the proof for destruction. The evidence for phases of expansion at Wharram Percy reflects one response to a rising population: there must be many others — the creation of smaller holdings within the old framework, the hiving off of subsidiary units creating fragmented nucleations or separate hamlets. Each will occur within a particular socio-economic context which, even within one small region, may vary from estate to estate. Denman's remark that 'if we fail to recognize that land use is a function of property rights in land our cognisance of the truth is deficient by a whole dimension of reality' is equally true of settlement, and in the transition from generalizations on the scale of Fig 13 to Figs 27–30 we necessarily become involved in the detail of settlement. Peter Wade-Martins, in his study of East Anglian villages, has been able to demonstrate from pottery scatters that during the middle and late Saxon periods village cores migrated, often over only short distances, a process of mutation that continued into the Middle Ages, and indeed is still in some senses continuing. Movement may be as much a characteristic of 'permanent' settlements as change, but as Wade-Martins stresses, his conclusions are applicable only to the parts of East Anglia he has studied, and the story elsewhere may be quite different.[17]

One solution of the dilemma, but not of the problems, is to be found in the recognition of plan elements, the basic structures which, when combined, make up the series of distinctive plan types already discussed. These plan elements may possess different 'survival' qualities, and comprise distinctive morphological components which can be isolated, defined and then used as tools for further analysis. So far as is possible they are not 'culture-bound' nor 'time-bound' and they provide a means of looking at form, largely free of functional and genetic criteria. These plan elements may be briefly listed as follows: the buildings are usually situated in

house-plots or tofts, to which separate small enclosures or crofts
were attached, the tofts frequently being grouped into toft complexes, ribbons, or rows; the arrangement of the tofts may or may
not be linked with a building line, and the structure of the whole
cluster is given definition and form by the presence of streets, lanes
and footways, although open spaces such as greens are often an
integral part of village plans. Finally, in most true villages there are
to be found buildings with a specialist function, the most obvious
example being the church, but the demesne farm or hallgarth, the
common forge or smithy and the common oven would fall into this
category. Each village combines these basic formal ingredients in a
unique way, and in analysing villages it is possibly more useful to
recognize these elements as distinct and separate features than to
attempt to treat the total assemblage. This is why the basic classification of forms outlined earlier in this chapter was kept so
simple. Within the village these plan elements do not and cannot
exist in isolation, of course, but they are interconnected in the sense
that each conditions the other's form, origins, physical relations and
functional significance, not just in historical perspective but at present, and indeed in the future. Thus the earliest elements and those
of more general functional significance, like street spaces, tend to
act as morphological frames conditioning the genesis and growth of
subsequent forms, and are often modified by them in turn. One
further question remains, and this is the most important. Given the
variety of forms which exist, is it possible to make them tell a story;
is it possible to associate particular forms with particular generations of settlements; are there regional variations which are of
significance? No clear-cut answers are yet possible, and before
discussing these wider points we must equip ourselves with more
facts, facts which can be derived from a close study of plan elements.[18]

Plan Elements

i) Tofts, crofts and building lines

After the houses, the tofts and crofts are the basic stuff of the
village. As Duby remarks 'these plots were undoubtedly most productive and the atmosphere of garden care which they cast over
their surroundings did much to anchor the village to its site', and as
long ago as 1789 Gilbert White was noting the 'black malm' of the
tofts of Selbourne, speculating that the soil there seemed highly
saturated with vegetable and animal manure, and that 'these may

perhaps have been the original site of the town.' In practice it is never easy to differentiate between toft and croft, but the former is taken to mean the plot of land specifically allotted to the house, and crofts are perhaps best viewed as accretions to this. The problems arising when assessing the continuity of property boundaries in a village have already been touched upon, and it will be sufficient to state here that toft boundaries were important, for they delimited a share of village lands in the hands of an individual or a family, and ensured the right to partake in the life of the community. Just as town holdings were divided and consolidated, so were tofts. While the materials used in their construction, a bank and ditch topped by a fence or live hedge, gave ample room for neighbourly dissension, their legal importance has been evident throughout the course of history.[19]

Broadly, toft complexes are of two types: a basic pattern, be this a rectangle or even a triangle, can be repeated, giving regular tofts, or a variety of shapes and orientations can result in irregular tofts. The distinction between these two qualities is frankly subjective, but it is none the less important, for regularity, the presence of an obvious order, as indicated by the appearance of a geometric toft shape, may suggest the pressure of deliberate planning. In practice it seems that regular tofts may be divided into short tofts, of the width-to-length proportion ranging from 1:1 to 1:4, and long tofts of the order of 1:10 or more. In the case of short tofts it will be noted that the field boundaries rarely accord with the toft boundaries, and the sharp line of discontinuity around the toft tail boundary delimits the outer edge of the enclosures before the parcelling up of the open field strips at a late stage in the village's history. Long tofts, in contrast, seem to represent a portion of field land securely attached to the house plot, and although they are too small to be strictly comparable with the great forest clearing strips or *Waldhufen* of Germany, we are again seeing a form of house-infield relationship discerned within the structure of a more complex village at Wheldrake and Wharram Percy (tofts 9-18). Examples of what can be termed false long tofts can be found; in these, particularly in enclosures of townfield land in the north during the seventeenth century, it was the practice to extend the original toft by the addition of land newly enclosed from the field strips. In the north such additions were often termed 'the Garrends' or 'Garthends'. The house-toft relationship would repay closer examination; for example how general is the trend visible in the Durham village of West Hartburn, where, by the thirteenth century, the long-houses were sited at the toft head, parallel to the street in eaves orientation? This causes a true building line to emerge as distinct from a toft frontage line. Except in the most irregular villages tofts are normally arranged in blocks, forming a row, and Roberts has suggested that a convenient way of classifying village forms found in Co. Durham is on the basis of the number of rows present, one-row, two-row or multiple-row settlements being usual. Order or regularity in the placing of tofts is usually linked with a regular building line, which may be straight or curving, open (i.e. not continuously built up for much of its length), or closed, notched or stepped, perhaps reflecting growth phases.[20]

Kirk Merrington (Fig 23) provides an illustration of the value of this type of reasoning. The village originated as two small but separate clusters, and in 1200 it consisted of two rows running east to west along a ridge, with the church garth forming part of the north row; nearby was the *vill* of Shelom, predominantly servile, and comprising two north-south rows. This settlement has been reconstructed on the basis of documentation relating to the estates of the Cathedral Priory at Durham and provides an example of what in Scandinavia would be termed a 'regulated' village. There were hints of this at Wheldrake in the sixteen original tofts. In a regulated village the toft sizes bore a metrical relationship to the fiscal assessment of the farm unit; and in the case of Kirk Merrington this was four eight-rod units, each of twenty feet (in all eighty feet), per *bovate*, but could vary from village to village depending upon the length of the land rod in use. Fig 32, derived from a diagram by Homans, illustrates an idealized regulated village, and is based on Scandinavian sources, for village regulation survived in Denmark and Sweden into the seventeenth and eighteenth centuries. The origins of such arrangements, with the field strips being measured with the same rod as the village tofts, are lost in the mists of time, but Göransson is of the opinion that England provided the source for the Scandinavian arrangements. He has demonstrated the distribution throughout Britain of such regulated or 'sun-divided' villages, so called because of the use of the terms 'towards the sun' and 'towards the shadow' to express cardinal direction. In Durham such arrangements were present by 1200, and both Roberts and Sheppard argue that the most regular village plans of Durham and Yorkshire, many probably associated with true regulation, are the result of settlement refoundation following the punitive campaigns of 1068–70. There may indeed be older generations of planned, regulated settlements, but these remain elusive.[21]

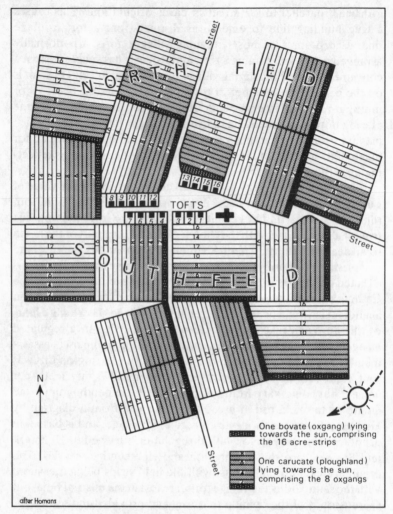

Fig 32   The Hypothetical Plan of an English 'Sun-divided' Village

To the modern mind these arrangements may appear to be unnecessarily elaborate, but bearing in mind the 'life-support' needs of villages, the share possessed by each villager was of vital importance, for with the ownership of the toft went rights to a share in the arable and meadow lands, a share in the common grazings, the right to take fuel, wood and peat, building-stone, reeds for thatch and fish from the stream. In modern terms, complex systems of division like *solskifte* (sun-division) represent a form of rationing, a sharing out of the community's piece of land and its potential fruits amongst those who had a just claim. It is the processes of the subdivision, amalgamation, and recombination of these shares which underlie much of village history, and, in Northumberland villages familiar to the author, these share units, termed 'husband-lands', are often traceable from the thirteenth century through to the nineteenth, being endlessly reassembled into differing patterns as the population of each settlement varies and the needs of individual families change. This introduces two complexities: first, the hand of the lord is invariably present, preserving the 'ordered reality' of the past and ensuring its continuation into ages when it was largely fictional, and second, our view of this 'reality' can vary greatly, depending upon the precise nature of the documentation; thus the careful land survey may well give a wholly different picture from the minister's account roll. True 'reality' may in practice never be attainable and we are left with a bewildering and often contradictory series of 'perceptional' levels of a village's landscape and organizational structure.[22]

The regular toft rows have so far proved most susceptible to analysis, but what of the less regular rows, with tofts of variable width and depth, perhaps more properly called ribbons? These are probably analogous to modern ribbon development, appearing in the absence of strong controls, perhaps in settlements on marginal land. If the Durham evidence is meaningful, there are slight indications that street-village forms, particularly the more irregular, represent a late generation of settlements. Agglomerations present even more problems, but it is probable that the final morphology is the product of the processes of amalgamation and subdivision of a set of original house-plots, in this case often highly irregular, and the addition of new units to an original core. The example in Fig 27 of Monksilver in west Somerset hints at possible lines for further analysis. In the West Country generally the deep hollow ways and massive hedgebanks represent an investment not lightly discarded by later generations; they form a skeleton around which the villages have developed, and preliminary field studies suggest that it may well be possible, in favourable circumstances, to identify a series of original units (farms), surrounded by irregular house-plots and separated by green areas and access ways, and often focusing on a stream which could provide water for man and beast as well as power for the mill. These are delimited in the present landscape by the edges of hollow-ways and massive hedge-banks. Continental scholars recognize that agglomerated villages develop in this way, and can be derived from loose clusters of single farms, often linked on a kinship basis.[23]

The importance of the tofts cannot be overstressed: together with the buildings, they were the basic stuff of the village. This view is expressed by Duby when he says 'these enclosures provided a haven for possessions, cattle, stocks of food, and sleeping men, protected them against natural and supernatural dangers, and taken together, constituted the kernel of the village, and expressed in terms of land and territory the essence of a society of which the family was the nucleus.'

ii) Streets, Lanes and Open Spaces

It is the relationship between tofts and access ways which provides the framework for describing a village as linear, green or agglomerated; tofts represent private land, but the streets, lanes and open spaces are common land, used by the whole community of the village. Linear and agglomerated nucleations represent the antithesis of street patterns found within villages: on the one hand the street dominated the plan, being a powerful determinant of form, while on the other hand there can be almost a superfluity of lanes, serving to disunite the settlement rather than help cohesion. One simple point aids the understanding of the patterns seen on map and ground: tarmacadam is a 'modern' phenomenon, and only recently have the most-used rights of way been surfaced for use by wheeled transport. To appraise fully the earlier pattern of communications, footpaths and field tracks must be taken into account; the 'back lane' or service road is characteristically a feature of many settlements, in some cases developing into a secondary axis parallel to the principal street, while, in sharp contrast, it may have degenerated into a mere footpath skirting the toft tails between chicken houses, dung heaps and the rubbish of twentieth-century mechanical farming.

Turning once again to the principal street, this can either be a true street, consisting almost entirely of road, or it can be broadened to form a large open space or green. The question of precisely what width of mud, stones and struggling grass originally separated a green-village from a street-village is academic, for in a pre-tarmac era the green must have lacked the sharp definition recently bestowed upon it. Green-villages are broadly of three types: where the green is a broadened street, where the green is a rectangle of land around which dwellings are placed, and where the green has no clear-cut form — and indeed dwellings may extend on to the green in the form of island enclosures. Functionally, the green is best seen as a specialized portion of the common pasture, and this is seen most clearly in certain north-country villages where green and fell grazings are continuous; where this relationship is absent, green and pasture are usually linked by means of a linear strip of common land, a cattle-track, outgang or driftway, passing between the former arable fields. There seem to have been controls over the erection of buildings and encroachment of gardens, although communal structures such as alehouse, smithy, church and pinfold could be conveniently sited on the green. Thorpe argued that the homesteads fronting on to the green possessed special and distinct rights, and that their status differed markedly from the peripheral dwellings, in that grazing rights for cattle, sheep, horses and the homely goose (pigs were usually excluded) were restricted to those facing the green. This is an important point: there was a fundamental distinction between those who were wholly integrated within the village group and peripheral newcomers, whose presence was tolerated, but who only participated in all the rights when they acquired a foothold amid the ancient homesteads, often no doubt by means of marriage or purchase.[24]

iii) Church and Manor House

A final category of plan elements that may be recognized is that of specialist buildings, the church and the manor house being the most obvious examples. The position of the church in relation to the village can pose many questions, more especially because this is the one structure whose history can be determined with some degree of certainty. Churches occupy a range of distinctive locations, the most striking undoubtedly being the central position on a green, raising by implication the fundamental problem of relative chronology. At Trimdon and Heighington, Co. Durham, Norman churches occupy such central points. In contrast, other churchgarths may be merely one of a row of tofts, suggesting in this instance contemporaneity between churchyard and row, while in the case of a peripheral location the church and churchyard occupy a site in proximity to the homesteads. This is probably the commonest church-village relationship. The final situation is particulary evocative where the church occupies a site some several hundred yards removed from the village, implying perhaps substantial site changes. At Hamsterley in Durham an Early English church lies half a mile from an irregular two-row green-village, and it is difficult to see any reason for this unless the settlement has changed its site. Too little is still known of our church sites, much-studied as churches are. The churchyard itself is worthy of close attention. What shape was it originally? What phases of expansion can be recognized? Detailed contouring will often show the cunning way in which the church is sited on a rise of ground — even when we allow for centuries of addition to the graveyard — with the homesteads clustering around placed with due regard for subtle variations in the physical characteristics of the site. It is worth recalling the letter from Pope Gregory to Abbot Mellitus, travelling to Britain in AD 601, in which he suggested 'upon mature deliberation on the affair of the English that the temples of the idols in that nation ought not to be destroyed, but let the idols that are in them be destroyed, let holy water be made and sprinkled in the said temples, let altars be erected and relics placed'. This was done on the pragmatic grounds that the temples were often well built and so that folk 'may the more familiarly resort to the places to which they have been accustomed'. Thus the continuity of the sacred place was preserved, although Beresford reminds us that churches could and did change their sites, as at Eaton Socon (Hunts.) and Pottene (Wilts.).[25]

Manor houses, or hallgarths, to use a northern term, occupy a comparable series of locations relative to the village. There seems, within Durham, to be a tendency, especially in very regular villages, for the site to occupy the eastern toft of the south row — an east-to-west orientation being common — and this may well be linked with village regulation. In former centuries many northern villages possessed a common forge and a common bakehouse, as well as a pinfold or pound, and the green, be it integral or peripheral, provided an obvious and suitable site for such facilities. The excavations at Wharram Percy have revealed dramatically the way in which the manor house was moved during the thirteenth century so that it remained peripheral to the village, and Toft 10 (Fig 31) became the focus of a bewilderingly complex series of changes in house orientation, overlying the remains of the twelfth-century manor house. At Northolt eleventh- to thirteenth-century superimposed layouts on different alignments were sealed by a fourteenth-century moat, representing a new manor house.

The General Picture

The changes in village form are clearly going to be a major research theme within the next few years, and there are apparently two stances; on the one hand is the archaeological evidence for changing village plans, and Beresford and Hurst have stressed this aspect in their recent volume on *Deserted Medieval Villages*; on the other hand, geographers, notably Thorpe, Roberts and Sheppard are arguing for a measure of stability. There is room for conflict here, and it is perhaps a little unfair to John Hurst to point out that in his recent analysis of the changes in Toft 10 at Wharram Percy he has in fact assumed that the property boundaries were largely static. Nevertheless, the case for change is supported by much archaeological evidence. Continuity of boundaries is very difficult to prove, but Roberts does appear to have concrete evidence to indicate the survival of late-twelfth-century row structures into the present landscape. As has already been stressed, 'reality' is sufficiently complex to cover an immense range of possibilities, and it is important to remember that the sum total of all village excavations and all village studies covers only a minute proportion of that reality. It seems preferable at the moment to attempt to define conditions which engender change and conditions which engender stability, and then to recognize that whole regions may be characterized by one or the other, while at the level of the individual village and farm the range of possible variations is, for all practical purposes, infinite. Conzen sees town plans in terms of three distinct complexes: the streets and their mutual association in a street system; the individual land parcels or plots and their aggregation in street-blocks; and the buildings, or more precisely their block-plans and the arrangement of these, in the town plan as a whole. This model can be applied to villages which are made up of streets and open spaces, the private enclosures and the building plans. Preliminary work suggests that these are listed in the reverse order of their susceptibility to change, and that while the fabrics and building plans mutate rapidly, the arrangement of public and private lands remains more stable, with the property boundaries of the garden plots being liable to a variety of pressures, some of which create stability or 'unchange', others which result in instability or change. What are these pressures? They are essentially the factors listed in the introduction to this volume: the physical, economic and cultural forces which mould settlement forms and patterns alike, operating at various scales, at the scale of Fig 1 and the scale of Figs 30 and 26.

This view of villages does provide data which can be analysed regionally and compared with other available evidence derived from both documentary and archaeological sources. There is, however, at present an almost total absence of detailed regional studies

of settlement forms, and Fig 29 illustrates the diversity of forms
found within Durham. This map, apart from illustrating the way in
which the classification outlined above can be adapted to the
specific circumstances of a single county, poses two questions. First,
is it possible to explain why the varied forms occur, and second, is it
possible to detect 'generations' of forms and to place these within a
relative and absolute chronological framework? In Durham an
elementary explanation of the forms is feasible: the villages in group
I are administrative centres; the villages of groups II-V are the basic
rural settlements, accounting for over two-thirds of the total; while
those of groups VI-VII present more problems, being a
heterogeneous group, some relatively old and some relatively new.
Groups II-V are all types of row settlements, and the fact that so
many villages take this regular form, indeed nearly one-third of all
the settlements in the county are *regular* two-row villages, does
indicate that a measure of planning is involved. The author has
traced this form back to the twelfth century and has suggested that
the villages may, in the Durham situation, be a product of replanning after the extensive devastations of the late-eleventh century;
perhaps it would be more correct to say that this particular phase
has contributed a 'generation' to the total pattern. It is as yet
impossible to associate particular forms and particular generations
with any clarity, and a comparison of Fig 33 with Fig 24 suggests
that there is no correlation between settlement generations
(revealed by rent forms and documentary reference) and the forms
visible in the present landscape; this is a powerful argument for
settlement re-organization subsequent to the growth of the pattern
of village settlements we now see. It is possible that in the enigmatic
'old town' sites and the garths and tofts — always in the plural, and
always occurring *within* the territory of an existing settlement, often
a regular two-row village — are to be seen the faint shadows of the
settlement system which preceded the one we now see, which has
been subjected to expansion, contraction, reorganization and
devastation.[27]

If the regular green-villages of Durham are indeed planned,
regulated settlements, re-established after the devastations of the
late-eleventh century, then two processes in particular are likely to
be of importance and to have a wider significance in the evolution of
settlement patterns; first, devastation, that 'sporadic, local and relatively ephermeral ingredient of no mean importance', destroyed old
settlements and provided the opportunity, indeed the need, to
re-plan; second, replanning was possibly dependent upon the pres-

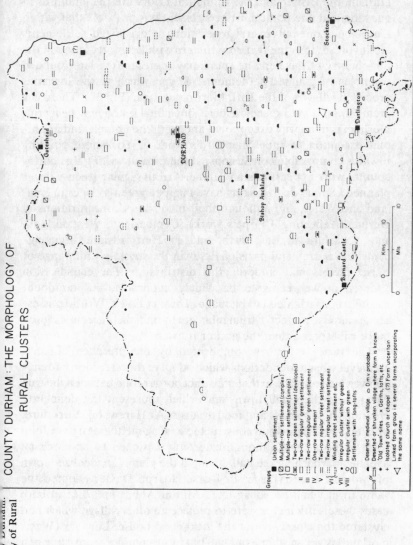

COUNTY DURHAM: THE MORPHOLOGY OF
RURAL CLUSTERS

Gateshead

DURHAM

Bishop Auckland

Barnard Castle

Stockton

Darlington

Kms
Mls

Groups

■ Urban settlement
□ Multiple-row settlement (complex)
▢ Multiple-row settlement (simple)
I Two-row green settlement
II Two-row regular green settlement
III Two-row irregular green settlement
IV One-row settlement
V Two-row regular street settlement
VI Two-row irregular street settlement
VII Winding street settlement etc
VIII Irregular cluster without green
○ Irregular cluster with green
⬭ Settlement with long-tofts

● Deserted medieval village □ D m v probable
◑ Deserted or shrunken village where form is known
× 'Old Town sites. × Garths, tofts, etc.
+ Isolated church or chapel (?) Form uncertain
▽ Linked form group i.e several farms incorporating
  the same name

Fig 55 County Durham:
the Morphology of Rural
Clusters

ence of a large estate under the control of a powerful landlord or
corporation who could *impose* a definite scheme during redevelop-
ment. These appear to be two important general causes, and in
Durham the Bishop and the Cathedral Priory are the landlords in
question, but one point must be stressed: it is probable that within
Durham not one but several generations of 'organized' settlements
are involved; thus the two-row villages with long tofts found in the
hill-country of the Pennine spurs may represent the late-founded
examples of planned settlements, a type which in the lowlands
preceded villages of the Kirk Merrington type (Fig 27). There is a
great temptation to speculate here, but a final lesson may be learnt:
Durham is in no way exceptional and, with the notable and important exception of June Sheppard's work in Yorkshire, pointing
towards comparable conclusions, at the time of writing this north-
country work appears to stand alone. Are all regular green-villages
planned? Stamp and Hoskins have mapped green-villages in England and Wales, and although their map shows concentrations in
Durham (reflecting Thorpe's work), Cumberland, Westmorland,
and Yorkshire in the north, and in Hertfordshire, Buckinghamshire, Surrey and parts of Essex in the south, a wide range of
causal factors may underlie this distribution. The classification
adopted above seems to be widely applicable, but no doubt
modifications will need to be made. Thus, in Essex, Writtle possesses an almost perfectly triangular green and such greens may be
more widespread than the author is aware.[28]

The issue is further complicated by the presence of post-
medieval village foundations which adopt earlier traditions, foundations which often lie in that indistinct border zone between the true
village and the small town, and which represent the deliberate
creations of landlords and industrialists. At Harewood, Yorkshire,
in 1760 Lord Harewood constructed a village to the design of John
Carr of York, and although ostensibly designed to lie along an
avenue approaching the hall, in detail the plan is an idealized form
of two-row street-village. In Dorset Joseph Damer adopted the
same form when he constructed Milton Abbas in 1786: in both
cases these settlements were to replace an older village which had
clustered too closely about the local great house. Lowther (Westmorland) is yet another example, but more complex, consisting of a
street with two cross-axes, terminating in a crescent at the east end
'with the implicit suggestion that the crescent was intended to be but
one half of a circus'. Tremadoc in Caernarvonshire, founded in
1798, and Blanchland in Northumberland, re-established on a

former monastery during the second half of the eighteenth century to accommodate workers in the lead mines on the neighbouring moors, are both rather more irregular, the former being T-shaped but incorporating at the junction a market square, while Blanchland is a 'thick L-shape', following the earlier foundation lines. These foundations, together with their nineteenth-century counterparts, Westonbirt in Gloucestershire for example, represent an 'idealization' of traditional regular villages, the 'ideal' combination of the plan elements described earlier in this chapter. They must represent but the tip of an iceberg, the documented cases, the clear-cut obvious examples, and it is probable that a map such as Fig 29 incorporates examples of late village restructurings as well as early ones. The author can point to no clear-cut cases in Durham, but he has a deep suspicion that the broad-green two-row village of Piercebridge, set squarely within the ramparts of the second-century Roman fort of *Magis*, is an estate village in this sense, even though it is present in 1729, according to an estate map in the possession of Lord Barnard.

The most perfect planned villages in Britain are to be found in Scotland. Largely of eighteenth-century date, they either represent villages or small towns founded for economic purposes or they represent settlements linked with the clearances, the reorganization of traditional farming patterns by landlords, too often resulting in the ruthless and brutal eviction of the tenantry. Tomintoul (Banff.) founded in 1775 is a long, low grey street-village, with parallel back-lanes, the pattern being broken in the centre by the square and by a regular series of cross lanes. The regularity extends beyond the settlement into the fields of the strip-crofts, and the plan is very similar to that of New Aberdour (Aberdeen), laid out during a period of agricultural improvement which fell between *c.* 1780 and *c.* 1840. The main economic basis of these planned settlements was often linen, but the domestic organization of the industry necessitated the provision of the croft-lands. Eaglesham (Renfrew), a 'cotton town' begun in the 1760s, consists of 'two rows of elegantly built houses, all of freestone, with a large space (15 acres) laid out in fine green fields, interspersed with trees and a fine gurgling streamlet in the middle'; the settlement is simply a very large two-row green-village.[29]

This final series of planned settlements is important. On the one hand they carry the rural theme into semi-urban foundations, industrial settlements, and there are threads here that manifest themselves in the 'garden city' concepts of the late-nineteenth century;

on the other hand they offer a warning that in dealing with planned villages we are surely faced with an immense time-span. Much of this ground is yet uncharted. Furthermore, in a sense the two-row planned rural settlement, with or without a green, is but a small section of a grid, a plan type characteristically associated with urban foundations, and one begins to formulate as yet unanswerable questions concerning the impact of urban forms on the rural scene. Beresford has demonstrated the scale of medieval town planning, and there are increasing signs that even Saxon towns were more carefully planned than has hitherto been appreciated. The roots lie deep, possibly even in the sighting staffs of the Roman land surveyors, the *agrimensores*, but much basic exploration remains to be undertaken. The research frontier has been reached.[30]

Within the last four hundred years, of course, village plans can be studied with the aid of cartographic evidence, and this permits the history of individual forms to be examined and their various vicissitudes to be charted but, perhaps more importantly, it also permits questions to be asked concerning the general processes of change affecting plans. Furthermore, and this point cannot be sufficiently emphasized, the study of village morphology is not an end in itself; what is necessary is a structural-functional approach, relating forms to the social and economic circumstances that have produced them. Cartographic evidence provides vital links between the landscape and the documents, allowing the tenurial status of individual tofts to be identified, for example. Plans reveal processes of change by showing their effects; in Fig 34, for example, seven villages with plans very similar to that of Earsdon (i.e. regular two-row villages) are shown, and while it is probable that in about 1600 all had essentially the same plans, the villages have experienced a variety of processes, of varying intensities, throughout the period from 1600 to the nineteenth and twentieth centuries. The latter phase, falling broadly between 1830 and 1920, is important because it is the period for which the earliest even tolerably accurate plans for most villages are universally available, and also a time when the plans are relatively free of comparatively recent changes, particularly the post-World War II move to the countryside. Such plans form the base line from which to begin retrogressive analysis, working backward to reconstruct earlier phases of plan development. As Fig 34 emphasizes, however, the centuries after 1600 (but before 1830–1920) saw many changes in village plans; East Hartburn, except for changes in the buildings, has survived virtually intact, there being merely some minor subdivisions of earlier, larger tofts,

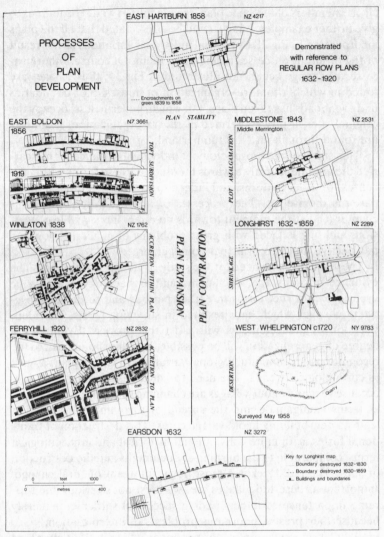

Fig 34   Processes of Plan Development

so that in 1600 toft X was one unit. In sharp contrast, on the right-hand side of the figure are to be seen the varied effects of plan contraction, while the left side reveals several degrees of plan expansion. The end-products are very varied, but all are recognizably allied to the simple seventeenth-century delineation of the plan of Earsdon, itself a deserted village by the early nineteenth century;

all are members of the same plan-type family. It would be tedious to give further examples, but it should be appreciated that all the plans incorporated in Fig 28 can reveal individual variations as the result of the different processes acting upon them. Of course, other processes of change occur, not illustrated in Fig 34; thus villages are found in which a total re-organization of houses, plot boundaries and even roads has taken place, but which, nevertheless, occupy the original sites, a process termed *in situ* re-organization. Examples are found throughout Northumberland.

This study of the morphology of individual settlements has carried the argument firmly towards the study of these forms within the context of wider patterns, and indeed towards a re-appraisal of the patterns themselves. The processes of analysis described in this chapter lead at the moment towards no direct manageable conclusion, and one is faced with great problems of generalization and perspective, but two principal points emerge.

i. There is a pressing need for the study of village morphology. The evidence of landscape, documents and archaeology needs to be used to reconstruct forms in earlier periods and to define subsequent changes which have resulted in surviving forms. The identification of plan elements will assist this process. Eventually a degree of generalization will be possible, and this should lead to the recognition of meaningful regional variations in village plans as well as chronological trends. The need for such basic work is pressing, because so many of our villages are changing their character rapidly as farms amalgamate and the spread of a commuter population leads to new building in old village cores. This destruction of traditional forms is, in more conventional historical and archaeological terms, comparable to the burning of documents and the destruction of sites. The bulldozer is a most powerful agent of rural change. Important as deserted villages are, we must not overlook the supreme importance of understanding successful settlements merely because they present enormous problems of interpretation.

ii. A fuller understanding of form is not an end in itself; it must lead to an understanding of the processes which have created the forms and of the functional arrangements within these structural and genetic frameworks. Two examples must suffice here. The driftway is an important morphological element in northern villages; is this merely a trait confined to the cattle-proud north, or has it a wider distribution, reflecting more uniform economic demands in ages before regional specialization? And then the recognition of stability or instability in toft patterns will resolve any unnecessary con-

Fig 35   Laxton, Nottinghamshire. This photograph, taken in 1946, shows the famous open-field village under snow. This stragling linear settlement is probably best viewed as a polyfocal village with shows the physical traces of a long and complex history in the relationship between its fieldlands (revealed by ridge and furrow ploughing) and its toftlands. Traces of both expansion and contraction can be found. Photo: Aerofilms Ltd

Figs 35 to 40 have been selected to demonstrate something of the rich diversity of village forms found within lowland Britain and are designed to complement and extend the geographical range of the material used elsewhere in this volume.

Fig 36 Newby, North Riding, Yorkshire. The principal plan element of this village is a row of regular tofts, clearly demarcated by a former back-lane. These tofts have been extended by the addition of 'garrends'. i.e. paddocks added at a later stage in the history of the village, and the boundary discontinuities along the back-lane may be noted. The head-row closing the green at one end may be ancient, while at the other end is to be seen a series of earthworks, possibly linked with a former hall-garth rather than peasant tofts. Worthy of close study, this plan raises more questions than can be outlined in a short note. Photo: Cleveland County Council and Meridian Airmaps Ltd

Fig 37   Deeping St James, Lincolnshire. Deeping St James is sited upon a levée along the river Welland and takes the form of a winding street settlement. Regularity is apparent in the succession of extended tofts and clear-cut back-lane extending on to the higher ground to the north of the river. The village appears to have been deliberately founded, some years before 1130, and represents part of a widespread colonizing movement affecting the western edges of the Fens during the twelfth and thirteenth centuries.

troversy over the persistence or obliteration of ancient boundaries. As yet we know too little to generalize.

Finally, as a more general proposition it can be argued that in the human organization of space, complexity is more usual than simplicity, and that in the analysis of forms and in retrogressive arguments great care must be exercised in the identification of the varied layers of organization and landscape present at any particular time. There is no substitute for terrain archaeology — the archaeological appraisal of a total landscape — but this approach imposes inevitable restrictions: it is expensive, exceedingly time-consuming, and it can treat only a relatively small area. There are grave dangers in the study of form without excavation, and these should not be minimized, but the historical-geographical approaches outlined in the preceding two chapters do offer one way, not the only way, nor even the most important way (for these things are relative), of blending the three types of evidence involved. Finally, if in this chapter too much emphasis has been placed upon the Durham material, it is because the author is using this as a testing ground for ideas, and experience proves the dangers of using examples from other regions where detailed studies, if they exist, are not readily available. Work outside Durham by the author and other workers does suggest that the general principles arrived at here are more widely applicable, and the field should prove a fruitful one: indeed Beresford and Hurst emphasize this when they point to the need for the study of shrunken villages.

6

Farms and Hamlets

DISPERSED-SETTLEMENT types, single farms, cottages, at times combined into small hamlets — dominate the rural landscapes throughout much of western and north-western Britain (Fig 1) and are indeed, a significant element within those areas where the general emphasis is upon nucleation. Just as there are practical problems of differentiating between large villages and small towns, and between villages and large hamlets, so the lower end of the scale, the boundary between single farm and hamlet, is often blurred. Take for instance the case of a small farm of twenty or so acres in the Pennine foothills in the sixteenth century; it is occupied by one man and his wife, and they have two sons. The elder marries and moves into a new house nearby; new land is added to the holding, and in time the father dies, the original farm being divided between the two sons. Nevertheless, the farm continues to function as a unit. The two families, however, may, in time, draw apart; perhaps they quarrel, and the inheritance is split so that separate and clearly distinguishable shares are created. At what point does the single farm become a joint farm, and at what point of size and degree of estrangement does the joint farm become a hamlet? This question is more than an academic one for the historical geographer, particularly when we remember that the documentation of the various processes may be absent, and reality is usually seen from the viewpoint of a rent collector (in whose eyes the 'original' unit may, decades later, still be undivided), or, at worst, may consist largely of a series of legal fictions whose relationship to reality is tenuous. Furthermore, a legal interest in a farm may have no relationship to the practical problems of management. These qualifications are relevant to any study of rural settlement in Britain. Furthermore, in

159

Fig 38   Fyfield, Essex. Fyfield is
characteristic of a type of village
which Christopher Taylor has
termed 'polyfocal', i.e. made up of
a series of, often discrete, plan
types. In the early nineteenth
century the regular row plan in the
foreground comprised only that
row between the stream and the
road; to the right can be seen the
outbuilding of Fyfield Hall, the
church being just out of vision,
while to the left a series of hamlets
straggles along a winding street.
The antiquity of this type of plan is
an open question, but the present
form is probably the end-product
of centuries of continuity,
adaptation and transformation.

most settlement patterns the severance of single farms and hamlets from village clusters is artificial, and in practice it is possible to recognize several distinct types of relationship between the components: a north-country shieling may have had, at least initially, a close relationship with the mother village, being integrated within an organized system of grazing activity; the moated single farm of a woodland colonist, in contrast, set amid the wastes of Arden or Essex, probably had few direct links with the long-established villages nearby, while the late-eighteenth-century stone or brick farmhouses associated with the late-enclosed landscapes of the Cotswolds, the Vale of the Red Horse or the Yorkshire Wolds represent the tearing apart of the village, a sundering of the old community, so that farmers and farm workers were physically separated. These essentially functional linkages or discontinuities may well offer the most rational way of classifying dispersed-settlement forms, but here it is proposed to rely upon traditional criteria, chronological and regional. Broadly speaking, in the centuries following Domesday Book, two principal periods may be identified during which particular groups of single farms and hamlets developed; the first phase, broadly medieval and Tudor, terminates in about 1600; the second, an early modern phase, falls between 1600 and the middle of the nineteenth century. Terms such as 'primary dispersion' and 'secondary dispersion' are to be avoided, on the grounds that they carry an air of spurious finality; we still know too little of Anglo-Saxon settlement. The date 1600 is in some senses quite arbitrary, and cannot be adhered to rigidly, but nevertheless the end of the sixteenth and the beginning of the seventeenth century mark a phase during which increasing regional specialization in farming, linked with improving husbandry techniques, provided a vital prelude in the move towards the 'take-off' stage of the industrial economy, a development which has had immense repercussions on rural settlement. Within this chronological framework the physical, biological and cultural contrasts discussed in the introduction lead logically towards a range of subdivisions, and provide the basis for the examples discussed below. Some discussion concerning the nature of the farm is, however, a necessary preliminary.

The Nature of the Farm

In the previous chapter the emergence of the 'modern' farm from the peasant long-house and the way in which this single unit was

Fig 39 Alverdiscott, Devon. This plan forms a marked contrast to the regular plans of northern England, for the hamlet of Alverdiscott (pronounced *Alscott*) is an irregular agglomeration, consisting of a church, mainly a fifteenth-century building but with a Norman font, a manor house (or *barton*) and a few cottages. The settlement was in existence in 1086, and probably originated as a single farm, 'AElfred's cot'. Like Monksilver (Fig 27) this church-hamlet is approached by a complex of lanes, whose hollow-way character attests the antiquity of the site. The surrounding fields, in the foreground and to the left, show slight traces of earthworks and crop-marks.

integrated within the economic system of the village were briefly discussed. The answer to the question 'What is a farm?' however, depends very much upon the facts we stress — legal criteria, economic criteria or social criteria, and, indeed, a single land parcel can have a place within a bewildering series of contexts. A farm can be many things: home, place of work, animal house, food store, manure collecting-point, a focus for produce collection, a taxable unit, a point in a marketing chain, a vital foothold on the soil, a source of wealth, a millstone of poverty, a plaything, or a way of life. In essence this chapter is concerned with the small, less important rural clusters, colloquially termed hamlets, and all classes of smaller groupings right down to an indisputable single farm, but in practice it is desirable to recognize a distinction between the farmstead — that is, the buildings, including the farmhouse, barns, byres, granaries, dovecotes, stabling and pigsties — and the farm — the total assemblage, buildings, land, stock and crops. This is not the place to examine the rich local diversity of building styles found throughout Britain, but one can at this point pause to ask what determines the essential character of a farm in any area. This is by no means an easy question to answer but, at the outset, shelter, water and flat land are as essential for a single farmstead as for a cluster, and the points made in Chapter 4 concerning village location are equally pertinent. Important determinants of farm character, however, are climate and tenure.

Climatic factors influence farmstead and farm in two ways; on one hand severe winters necessitate the provision of buildings to house the beasts throughout the more extreme periods of the north and north-east of Britain, while on the other hand rainfall and insolation affect the balance between stock and grain production, resulting in a broad contrast between the grain-producing south and east and the stock-producing north, west and south-west, each with specialized structural requirements (Fig 3C). As Marshall observed, the particular requisites of a farmstead 'are as various as the intention of farms. A sheep farm, a grazing farm, a hay farm, a dairy farm and one under mixed cultivation require different situations and different arrangements of yards and buildings'. He goes on to list the structures required for a mixed-husbandry farm, no doubt having in mind the great model farms of the late-eighteenth-century improving landlords rather than the smaller, less pretentious, units of the tenantry, which are nevertheless worthy of attention when we are considering the nature of the farm and its buildings. The basic requirements are, of course, a 'a suite of buildings, adapted to the intended plan of management, as a dwelling house, barns, stables, cattlesheds, cart-shed'. These are to be united by a 'spacious yard, common to the buildings, and containing a receptacle of stall-manure, whether arising from the stables, cattle-sheds, hogsties, or other buildings; together with separate folds, or straw yards, furnished with appropriate sheds, for particular stock, in places where such are required'. Liquid manure was to be collected in a 'reservoir or catchpool, situated on the lower side of the buildings and yards, to receive their washings, and collect them in a body for the purpose of irrigating the lands below them'. In addition, there should be 'a corn-yard, convenient to the barns, a hay-yard contiguous to the cow or fattening sheds and a garden and orchard near the house'. Finally (and this is a telling point), he recommends a spacious 'grass-yard or green, embracing the whole or principal part of the conveniences, as an occasional receptacle for stock of every kind, as a common pasture for swine, and a range for poultry, and as an ante-field or lobby, out of which the home grounds and driftways may conveniently be entered'. Such a complex, indeed idealized, farmery is a long way from a peasant long-house, but this ideal both underlines the diversity we may expect to find in farm buildings and suggests some of the functional inter-relationships which will have evolved empirically. Such practical problems in part explain the contrast between the house-over-byre farms of snowy Weardale, the small, neat courtyard farms of Cumberland, the great 'open' farms of the arable counties, and the spacious planned farmeries of gentlemen farmers from lowland Scotland to Kent. Fig 41 is based upon the work of R. W. Brunskill and shows a range of farmstead layouts, ranging from the traditional long-house form to the large courtyard farms of the agricultural improvers of the eighteenth and nineteenth centuries. Few systematic studies of farm plans are available, as opposed to those of building materials or styles, but as a previous chapter argued, the building plans are the most mutable element in any settlement. No doubt if sufficient data were available, local and regional contrasts would emerge in farm plans, but as Brunskill indicates 'a great deal of work remains to be done before we understand such meaning as there may be in the shape of the farmstead.' Clearly this work could be linked with a study of *site* and *situation* along the lines indicated in Chapter 4.[1]

The impact of tenure is no less direct than that of climate, and there is a clear-cut and obvious difference between the home farms of the landed gentry, be they in East Anglia, the valleys of Somerset

Fig 40 Ashmore, Dorset. It is possible that the village of Ashmore derives its name from its location adjacent to the Wiltshire-Dorset boundary, visible to the rear of the village as the densely-shrubbed hedgerow crossing the photograph from right to left, but more probably this settlement, already present by 1086, derives its name from the Old English *aescmere* 'the lake where the ash trees grew', for this chalk-country village is an irregular agglomeration around a large pond whose former importance as a water supply is surely attested by the close network of radially arranged roads and tracks.

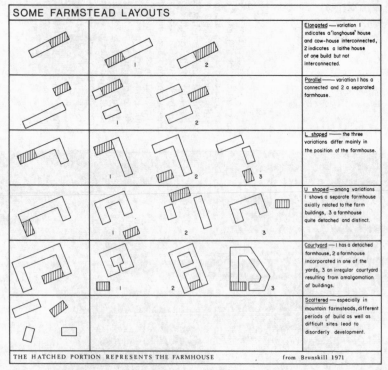

SOME FARMSTEAD LAYOUTS

Elongated — variation I indicates a 'longhouse' house and cow-house interconnected, 2 indicates a laithe house of one build but not interconnected.

Parallel — variation I has a connected and 2 a separated farmhouse.

L shaped — the three variations differ mainly in the position of the farmhouse.

U shaped — among variations I shows a separate farmhouse axially related to the farm buildings, 3 a farmhouse quite detached and distinct.

Courtyard — I has a detached farmhouse, 2 a farmhouse incorporated in one of the yards, 3 an irregular courtyard resulting from amalgamation of buildings.

Scattered — especially in mountain farmsteads, different periods of build as well as difficult sites lead to disorderly development.

THE HATCHED PORTION REPRESENTS THE FARMHOUSE   from Brunskill 1971

Fig 41   Some Farmstead Layouts, after Brunskill (1971), 139

or Devon, or the northern hill country, and the humbler establishments of tenants or owner-occupiers. One of the more striking visual manifestations of tenure is to be seen in Teesdale, where the whitewashed farms of the Raby estate contrast vividly with the emerald or acid greens of the rich meadows, themselves a product of estate-guided husbandry. Land-ownership and tenure, however, are four-dimensional, and just as the last thousand years have seen changes in the fabric and plans of settlements, so the same period has seen many tenurial changes. In general, three categories of tenure can be recognized: freehold, copyhold and leasehold. In the past two centuries copyhold, in origin a servile tenure, often 'at the will of the lord', has merged with leasehold or, through enfranchisement, with freehold. The variety of free tenures of former centuries has gradually given rise to simple freehold, the land nominally being held of the Crown, while leasehold has expanded from simple medieval beginnings to become an essential part of a complex web of land-holdings, and the contractual, economic agricultural lease was the basis of the traditional landlord-and-tenant system which emerged in post-Tudor England. Land tenure is a vital part of agrarian structure, and is interdependent with the pattern of cultivation and the terms of holding and scale of operations. For instance, a change in title may lead to a change in the terms of the holding, such as the status of the operator, the amount and type of rent he pays, and the scale of operation; it may also be linked with changes in farming practice and ultimately in farm structure. Some of the most graphic illustrations of the impact of tenure on farming are to be found in hill country. It is frequent to find striking contrasts between farms occupying the same terrain, one being well managed, well maintained and profitable, while its neighbour is a wilderness of coarse grasses, broken-down fences and ill-maintained buildings: superficially this is a management difference, but this in itself may be a reflection of deeper tenurial distinctions, and may indeed reflect the distinction between an owner-occupied farm and the tenanted farm of an absentee landlord.[2]

In England two tenurial developments may be selected as particularly important to a study of rural settlement: on the one hand the changing balance between collective and individual tenure and on the other the transition from servility to freehold or tenancy by contract, together with associated changes in the security of tenure. Both are sufficiently complex to lie far beyond the scope of this book, but both had powerful effects on landscape and society. The collective tenure of open-field villages was broadly an inherited phenomenon, although in the twelfth and thirteenth centuries, where villages were dominant enough to constitute the principal dynamic element in the pattern, individual clearings when they did occur were eventually incorporated within the open-field arrangements; this is well documented in parts of Yorkshire, and the author has found cases in the Midlands. Most of the new clearing taking place after about 1200, however, seems to have involved men who held their land as individuals, i.e. in severalty, a form of landholding which, as the result of the 'enclosure' movements of the Middle Ages, the Tudor period, the seventeenth, eighteenth and nineteenth centuries, eventually came to dominate. If villages tend to be linked with communal agriculture, then enclosures in severalty tend to be linked with single farms. As was indicated in Chapter 3, farms in severalty were probably present in the Anglo-Saxon period and the various swings of the pendulum have yet to be fully charted and explained. Similarly, the transition from medieval serfdom with its personal as well as tenurial connotations is an intrictate process, having roots far back in the Middle Ages; the driving force for this change could well have been the increasing importance of money instead of service as the medium of making tangible the obligations of society, and in this the rise of vigorous land markets and the development of leaseholds, creating tenant farmers much as we know them today, were important, in that they introduced an element of flexibility into the agricultural scene, and the contractual nature of the lease gave the tenant, in the right circumstances it must be admitted, an element of choice. These changes, taking place gradually between the fourteenth and the eighteenth centuries, when linked with enclosure, the development of ring-fenced, often compact, farms, held either as a freehold or by lease, created a context within which real and lasting improvements in the agricultural system could occur.

Medieval and Tudor Single Farms

As Chapter 3 pointed out, in spite of the fact that England in 1086 was an 'old country' and village settlements rarely more than five miles from their neighbours extended over the whole land, there were still areas which offered opportunities for agricultural colonization. Extensive woodlands still covered much of the Kent and Sussex Weald and the Arden area of the Midlands, while in Hampshire, Devon, Essex and Northamptonshire, substantial areas of woodland were in Crown hands as royal forest. Indeed, only Norfolk, Suffolk and Kent are known to have contained no land subject to forest law; drowned fen occupied most of the land between Cambridge and the Wash, and the high and windy uplands of the Highland Zone still for the most part deterred the pioneer. In the England of 1086 there was room to expand, and from the eleventh century onwards forces were at work which stimulated enterprise; landlords might be moved to make the most of their property, while the slow, steady growth of peasant population demanded that new land be won to fill the stomachs of more folk. The result was that from the eleventh to the thirteenth century there was a period of agricultural colonization, and certain important contrasts emerged between the old settled, village-strewn lowlands and the frontier regions, be these wood-pasture interfluves within the lowlands, or moorland pastures around the upland peripheries. Lords with extensive reserves of waste upon their domain were willing to make concessions in order to attract colonists, and the most significant, most universal concession offered was freedom, freedom from personal servitude, freedom from labour services and freedom from arbitrary demands. The typical colonist was a freeholder, rendering to his lord merely a cash rent together with nominal services. Significantly, there are only two areas where whole village communities can be seen benefiting from 'frontier' conditions, and these are found in those regions where, for quite different reasons, individual enterprise offered fewer opportunities. Firstly, in the Vale of York the reoccupation following the harrying of 1068–70 saw the establishment of arrangements more flexible than those found throughout the unwasted areas of the English lowlands, and secondly, the work of thrusting back the sea in the Fens demanded the sanctions and capital of whole communities. Elsewhere, however, the characteristic settlement forms of medieval colonization after about 1200 are largely single farms and hamlets, reflecting the free conditions, the individual enterprise and the piecemeal reclamation necessitated by the backbreaking toil of winning new fields from wooded clays or stony hillsides. In this way there emerged fundamental economic, social and tenurial contrasts between the predominantly servile cultivators of the old settled champion zones, and the predominantly free peasants of the woodlands and uplands.[3]

Woodland Colonization

The Arden area of north Warwickshire is characteristic of a late-colonized interfluve region and, although it is impossible to produce anything like a complete map of medieval conditions, Fig 42 is a reconstruction of the landscape of the parish of Tanworth in 1350. A network of winding lanes, scores of scattered farms, frequent hamlets, relict woodlands (the survivors of formerly more extensive blocks) all betray the arduous efforts of colonists in the decades between 1150 and 1300. There is little doubt that within Tanworth colonization was sponsored by the Earls of Warwick; charters indicate a standard rent of 2d per acre in the early thirteenth century (by 1270 this had risen to 4d) and the only service demanded was attendance twice yearly at the Earl's manorial court. Significantly, there are hints of such encouragement on the Gloucestershire estates of the Berkleys, and all over England lords of the manor with wastes to be colonized must have been making similar concessions, for more tenants meant an increased rent roll, increased judicial profits and ultimately expanded political power. Tanworth demonstrates three further points concerning the settlement forms and

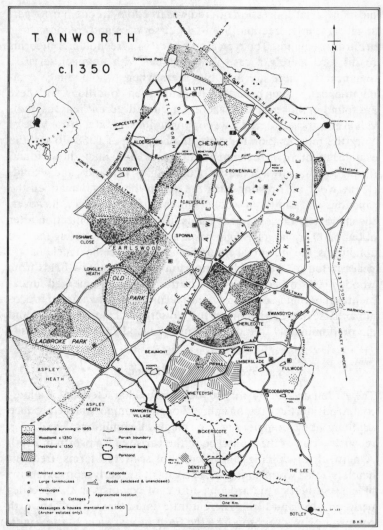

Fig 42   The Parish of Tanworth, Warwickshire, in about 1350, after Roberts, *Agricultural History Review,* XVI (1968)

patterns associated with medieval woodland colonization: first it resembled the ripples from a stone thrown into a pool of water, originating from long-established centres of Anglo-Saxon origin — *Tanna's worth*, the name of the village, probably originated late in the Anglo-Saxon period — and small, irregular areas of open sub-divided fields are usually found adjacent to such centres. Around this nucleus — the stone, so to speak — waves of clearing moved outwards, distorted by variations in terrain, by the presence of preserved parkland or woodland, and sometimes by a colonist leaping ahead of the main frontier to take advantage of a particularly advantageous location or simply because he received a grant of land in an isolated location. In this way a dense scatter of single farms was achieved within a few generations although subsequent centuries have seen the consolidation, concentration and desertion of medieval farms together with the multiplication of cottage holdings, resulting in a similar overall density.[4]

Secondly, even during the Middle Ages clusters of small farms and cottage holdings developed at crossroads, where a sliver of roadside waste offered opportunities for grazing a cow or two, and although later centuries, particularly the seventeenth and eighteenth, have reinforced this pattern, the 'Ends' and 'Greens' of woodland areas — Browns Green, Potters Green, Danzey Green — are a tribute to this medieval activity, and monuments to families (Warings Green), trades (Tile Green, Potters Green), and topographical features (Copt Green, 'a hilltop') are preserved in their place-names. Such settlements are to be found from Essex to Shropshire and from Somerset to Lancashire, where areas of late woodland colonization have occurred.

Thirdly, the frontier offered opportunity to men of enterprise, and this, coupled with the free tenure, the contractual bonds of society and an emphasis on cash in land transactions, encouraged social mobility and permitted the more ruthless, more able colonists to expand their farms and create small but prosperous estates. The moated homestead has a long and complex history of development, the earliest example of this type of single farm being the defended thegn's house found at Sulgrave Manor, Northamptonshire; but throughout the late-twelfth and thirteenth centuries this type of site appears in great numbers throughout the Midlands and East Anglia (Fig 43) and, if one may generalize from the midland evidence, it is to be linked with the emergence of prosperous freeholding families within areas of late-settled woodland. This is a characteristic example of an aristocratic fashion being slowly diffused to lower social levels, and the result is that the term 'moated homestead' embraces a range of sites, from small, splendidly appointed castles such as Maxstoke in Warwickshire, Weoley Castle in Worcestershire, or Allington in Kent, through manor houses, where the emphasis was upon (relative) comfort rather than defence, as at Birtsmorton Court, near Malvern, Worcestershire, or Markenfield Hall, West

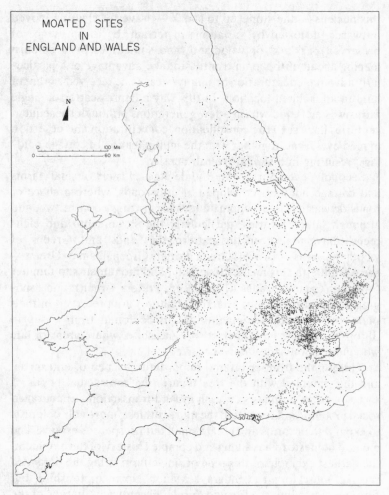

MOATED SITES
IN
ENGLAND AND WALES

N

0 ————————— 100 Mls
0 ————————— 60 Km

Fig 43   The Distribution of Moated Sites in England and Wales, based upon the work of the Moated Sites Research Group.

Riding, to the large number of sites which are no more than well-defended, or well-drained, farmsteads, densely scattered on the clayland of Arden and the East Anglian heights. Quite clearly, and Fig 43 reinforces this point, the moated site is a type of settlement particularly adapted for clayland terrains, where the wet moat, water-filled and probably sluice-controlled, offered some opportunity to drain the slightly raised farmyard on the island, while the waters of the moat, usually kept moderately fresh by maintaining a slight flow, were ideal for sewage disposal, the dumping of kitchen refuse, and the raising of fish. It is perhaps too easy to dismiss defence as an important cause in the building of moats, but their sheer numbers in some areas, together with their known socio-economic context, make it probable that we are seeing a form of ostentation dictated by fashion. In Devon, on the stone country of Dartmoor, wealthy freehold families such as the Cholwiches were constructing solid stone farmhouses rather than moated sites, and it is likely that the great bartons of Devon and Somerset represent essentially similar social phenomena finding expression in a different settlement form.[5]

A special case of woodland colonization is to be found within royal forests, for here there was conflict between the Crown officials, interested in preserving wasteland, both actual woodland and open rough pasture, as grazing for beasts of the chase, and the peasantry interested in extending their tillage and grazing. This conflict was particularly sharp within forest areas, and although such land, in theory at least, could not be effectively opened up until disforestation, the thirteenth century saw the diminution of royal forest as the Crown sold its rights to relieve financial difficulties. Between 1200 and 1280 large areas of Cornwall, Devon, Gloucestershire and Lincolnshire were thrown open for reclamation. The colonization of the woodland zones of lowland Britain was inevitable once they had emerged as islands, flanked, indeed surrounded, by open-field country and cluster settlements: ploughman and grazier followed charcoal burner and timber extractor, and from Devon to Lincolnshire and from Kent to Cheshire lords of the manor encouraged colonization.[6]

Upland Colonization

However, deliberate wastings apart, and setting aside for the moment the question of Wales and the more thorny problem of Scotland, the Highland Zone of England was in 1086 but thinly settled, and the rising population of the thirteenth century caused a tide of reclamation and settlement to creep up the hillslopes of the north and west, at first thrusting seeking fingers into the hospitable valleys and then rising slowly up the sides and valley heads to levels in excess of 242 m (800 ft) — indeed in the northern Pennines it certainly rose to 335 m (1,100 ft) and even over 380 m (1,250 ft), the limits of human settlement. In time this rising frontier swamped such specialist settlements as had been long established in the waste,

Fig 44 The Moats, near Caxton, Cambridgeshire. This splendid example of a complex moated homestead is characteristic of many hundreds of sites found throughout eastern and central England (Fig 32). The most obvious components are the two rectangular islands, one preserving its water-filled ditch, while an immediately adjacent second island is surrounded by a virtually dry moat. These two enclosures may represent respectively the house and farmyard areas. Finds of surface pottery include wares ranging in date from the Roman period to the thirteenth century, but the present site probably originated in the twelfth century as the seat of the de Scalers family. However, an exploration of the ground around the islands reveals traces of many other structures; the wooded eastern end of the island surrounded by water conceals many features, while in the foreground a curious group of earthworks, of unknown purposes, are now called the 'Asparagus beds'. To the east the scrub-covered boundaries of the two rectangular fields might repay attention, as they could well be part of the complex of earthworks surrounding the basic site.

notably the shielings, cattle-stations and isolated crofts of
shepherds, graziers, and mineral workers, and often involved the
permanent occupation of sites formerly occupied only on a temporary basis. Such a pattern of development is found throughout Wales
and northern England, but in detail each valley, each interfluve,
each plateau has its own history of settlement, and no single example is wholly characteristic. Nevertheless, the northern Ryedale
region of Yorkshire, extending from the marshy lowlands of the
Vale of Pickering to the bleak, rolling, heather-clad summits of the
North York Moors, beloved of Lyke Wake walkers, provides a very
useful case-study, and Hodgson's three maps have been reproduced
in Figs 45 and 46. A key point is provided by the pattern of
administrative boundaries, not the townships which represent the
most advanced stage of development (perhaps that achieved by the
late-thirteenth century), but parishes, church-supporting terrain
blocks, reflecting no doubt older frameworks, which form long
strips with their foci on either the Ryedale lowlands or the Tabular
Hills. This pattern surely echoes an ancient interdependence between lowland and upland, between arable fields and meadowlands
and summer grazings, and the pattern of cluster-settlements present
by 1086 has persisted to a remarkable degree, with few additions
and indeed few desertions. Within these villages, by about 1300, a
complex pattern of land-ownership had emerged, some being
dominated by lay landowners and others by ecclesiastical owners,
and Hodgson has mapped two distinct components in these upland
settlements which evolved during the thirteenth century: lay hamlets and single farms, lying near or above the 244 m (800 ft) contour,
both servile and free in character. In contrast to this fragmented and
piecemeal activity, monastic houses, notably Rievaulx, Rosedale
and Keldholme, had by the late-twelfth century acquired large
block grants in Rosedale, Farndale and Bilsdale. These areas,
linked administratively and economically to holdings in the Ryedale
lowlands, were subject to a more rational exploitation, in particular
the establishment by the Cistercian houses (notably Rievaulx) of
granges 'a collection of farm buildings which served as a sub-centre
or depot for the exploitation of the land'. These foci for economic
activity, found throughout upland Britain, could vary greatly in
character and economy: some were surrounded by compact
enclosed farms, others consisted of scattered parcels; some were
biased towards arable production, others were dependent upon
sheep; in Bilsdale, granges were even linked directly with iron
production. Northern Ryedale today is an area of scattered farms

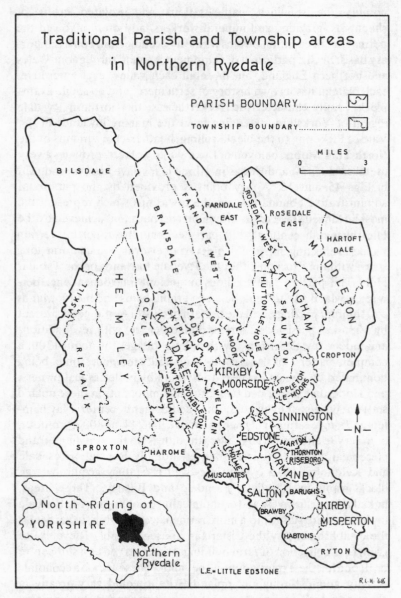

Fig 45   Parishes and Townships in Northern Ryedale, East Riding Yorkshire, after Hodgson, *Geog. Journal*, 135, pt 1 (March 1969)

and small hamlets, linked together by a distinctive pattern of roads which, because settlement on the whole avoids the dale floors, run parallel to each other through the two lines of farmsteads which tend to flank each dale. To what extent these girdles of farms are solely a product of medieval colonization and to what extent they reflect older patterns, Anglo-Saxon or perhaps even Romano-British, is impossible to ascertain (and this point must be returned to in a later context), for while within Yorkshire this question is muted, further west and north in Durham, Lancashire, Westmorland and Cumberland, areas containing the same dispersed medieval settlement types, it is sharpened by increasing numbers of place-names of Celtic origin.[7]

For two reasons, Weardale, Co. Durham, provides a useful point from which to begin an appraisal of these more complex problems of medieval upland settlement. Firstly, the land-ownership pattern since the twelfth century has remained remarkably static and until the mid-nineteenth century the dale was in the hands of the Bishops of Durham; secondly, the area is physically 'contained' by the surrounding moorland and is sharply distinct from Teesdale to the south and the headwaters of the Derwent to the north. Fig 48 shows the situation in 1438–9 as recorded by a Master Forester's account roll: settlement in the upper part of the dale consisted of a series of tenements to which grazing rights were attached, while lower down was to be found the ancient core of Stanhope, surrounded by subdivided fields and the assarted holdings of freeholders. At this stage it is probable that, although sublet by the Bishop, these upper-dale tenements consisted only of single farms: some have survived as such, but others, throughout the fifteenth, sixteenth and seventeenth centuries, were subdivided, giving rise to small cluster-settlements, hamlets such as East Blackdene, West Blackdene, and Daddry Shield, while the final element in the name of the last example suggests that the tenements of 1438 had in turn replaced an earlier generation of temporary sites, the place-names 'shield' (ME *shēle*) and 'erg' (ON *airgh*) being common in the dales, and implying temporary summer pastures (Fig 24). These earlier grazing arrangements, however, were by no means 'free-standing' for the High Forest of Weardale was part of Stanhope parish, focusing on the village of Stanhope. In turn this settlement, possibly as far back as the sub-Roman period, had been part of Auckland-shire, a territorial unit of great antiquity. This affiliation is shown by the fact that in Boldon Book the villeins of Aucklandshire constructed half a hunting lodge in the forest for the bishops, and, as the

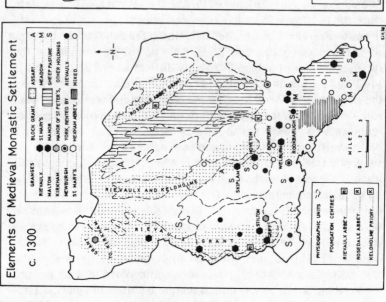

Fig 46 Some Elements of Settlement in Northern Ryedale, East Riding, Yorkshire, after Hodgson, *Geog. Journal*, 135, pt 1, March 1969

villeins of Stanhope constructed the other half, the ancient linkage appears certain. The *shēle* names probably relate to a period when the grazings of the high dale were utilized by an administrative unit based on the lowlands, some ten miles or so down-dale to the east. Rising population throughout the twelfth and thirteenth centuries, by stimulating the permanent settlement of this territory, already securely appropriated to Stanhope, led to an intensification of occupation. Had conditions been favourable, administratively, geographically and economically, separate townships would have emerged as independent entities, or even new parishes — indeed, by the early fourteenth century the Weardale records speak of the chapel of St John *cum villa sua* in the upper dale — the modern St John's Chapel — but in this case severance from Stanhope was never completed. A gradual intensification of occupation occurred; temporary shielings, permanent stock-farms, and finally the break-up of these from the fifteenth century, gave a scatter of hamlets and farms, followed later by the small-holdings of miner-farmers. This sequence appears typical of most northern uplands, and the significant point in this case is that the pattern of services indicated by Boldon Book in 1183 hints at great antiquity for the administrative framework within which occupation developed. The two peat bogs marked in Fig 46 at Steward Shield Meadows and Bollihope have indeed produced evidence for Iron Age and Romano-British landscapes in which tree-pollen amounts fall to as low as 10 per cent of the whole (Fig 4), (roughly the modern situation), while within the Great Park Iron Age fields are still visible. These pollen counts, of course, throw no light on the entire landscape; rather they give a picture of vegetation change within the area extending for about five hundred metres around each bog: the significant point is that these two sites, known to have been occupied in the Middle Ages, had in each case experienced an earlier occupation. In the uplands as in the lowlands it is unwise to assume that Anglo-Saxon and medieval colonization necessarily marks a complete break with what went before, and the girdles of small hamlets of three or four farms and the single homesteads found in this dale may well have origins as complex as anything found in the lowlands. The rising tide of medieval settlement described earlier is a pleasing and tidy picture, but is too ordered, too simple: the reality may be uncomfortably complex.[8]

Wales has long been regarded as an area of dispersed homesteads and farming in severalty, but Glanville Jones has, in numerous papers, demonstrated that the ancient pattern was made up of

Fig 47 Wasdale Head, Cumberland. In many senses this dramatic photograph is atypical of upland Britain, but it serves to emphasize that the question of hill-country hamlets is a fascinating topic in its own right. In this case three farms, Row Head, Middle Row and Row Foot form the most basic type of row-cluster (Fig 24). Two fields away lies an isolated chapel and a little higher up the valley the name of Burnthwaite applied to a farm hints at Scandinavian presence. Photo: Aerofilms Ltd.

small villages grouped into larger multiple estates — a situation already examined in Chapters 2 and 3; settlement dispersal is largely a product of developments since 1100, and is closely related to the emergence of free clans, joint proprietary units, having shares in what was termed a *gwely* — a number of homesteads, a small area of arable land, and rights, proportionate to the amount of arable, in the common grazing lands. Each *gwely* began with a grant of land to, or the appropriation of a piece of land by, an individual: after his death the partition of the original inheritance, arable land and pasture rights, amongst sons, grandsons and great-grandsons led to the subdivision of the original improved land, and frequently to the intaking of further parcels of land suitable for cultivation, which in turn were subdivided. In this way clans were created, all claiming descent from a common ancestor, and frequently bearing his name — the name Price (Ap Rhys, 'son of Rhys') being a good example, along with Prichard, Probert and Pugh. Characteristically, because of the relative scarcity of arable lands in Wales, the homesteads were built around the edges of the cultivated area, thus forming what Jones has termed a 'girdle' pattern, the shape of each girdle being flexibly adapted to local terrain. Subsequent consolidation has often destroyed the clarity of these patterns, but Jones has shown that, in portions of Wales at least, the dispersion of settlement, far from being explicable in geographical terms, is a function of the stage attained in the complex process of evolution from feudo-tribal to modern conditions of land tenure, and the modern farms are frequently the products of the consolidation of several earlier units. As Thirsk has pointed out, customs of inheritance and their effects on the distribution of land, and *sine qua non* settlement, have not been properly investigated for any part of England, but one cautious generalization seems to be justified, namely, that the custom of partible inheritance was more widely practised in highland England at the beginning of the sixteenth century than in the lowlands. She cites examples from Yorkshire and Lancashire, and it is probable that this particular mechanism may well be of more importance in the creation of dispersed settlements in upland England than has hitherto been recognized. This particular inheritance practice, so logical to the peasant but not to the feudal lord, was once clearly more widespread, and in the processes of subdivision associated with it we see a mechanism for producing farmstead girdles similar to those found in Wales: in this case it is not necessary to postulate any direct linkages. The Welsh system of *gwely* settlement evolved after the Norman Conquest, when a less extensive

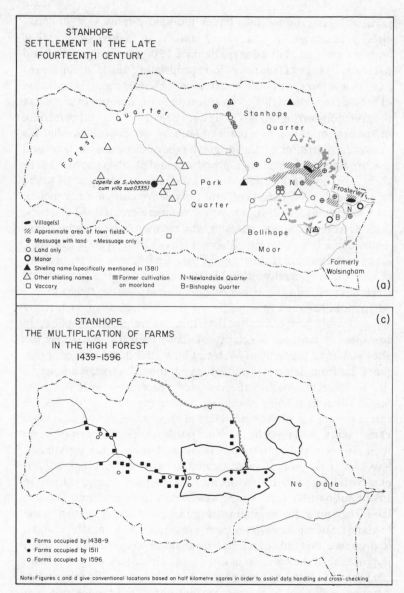

Fig 48   The Evolution of Settlement in Upper Weardale, County Durham, 1380–1799

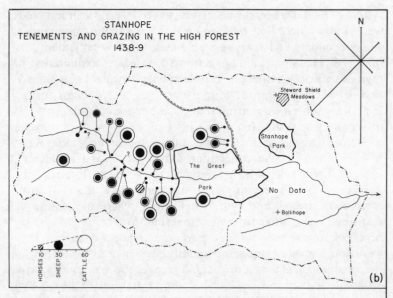

STANHOPE
TENEMENTS AND GRAZING IN THE HIGH FOREST
1438-9

N

Steward Shield
Meadows

Stanhope
Park

The Great

Park

No Data

+ Bollihope

HORSES SHEEP CATTLE
10   30   60

(b)

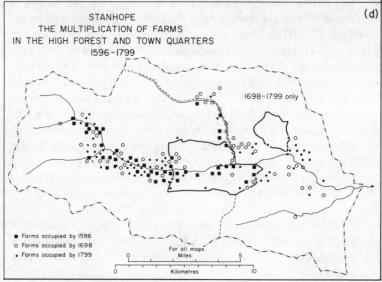

(d)

STANHOPE
THE MULTIPLICATION OF FARMS
IN THE HIGH FOREST AND TOWN QUARTERS
1596-1799

1698-1799 only

■ Farms occupied by 1596
○ Farms occupied by 1698
• Farms occupied by 1799

For all maps
Miles
0   5

0   Kilometres   10

system of land use became necessary; as the best agricultural lands were already occupied by long-established servile communities, whose economy had a strong arable bias, the new settlements, by reason of greater flexibility, permitted an easier exploitation of regions with only limited areas of fertile land available for cultivation. This exploitation of former pastures, and perhaps former temporary settlements, ensured that some echoes of older patterns of activity would survive[9].

Before leaving the single farms and hamlets of the Middle Ages, a word must be said concerning a type of upland settlement, touched upon briefly with reference to Northern Ryedale, the granges of the Cistercians. These structures were originally instituted as centres of husbandry of all kinds, where the land to be cultivated was too far from the monastery for the monks and lay brothers to make the journey out to work and back each day. They were not, it must be stressed, primarily given over to the keeping of sheep, although amongst the upland granges this was an important economic activity and, as Knowles points out, some of the isolated granges among the fells of the West Riding or on the moors of Radnor were merely centres of assembly for the flocks, just as the contemporary farms of these areas lack arable lands of any sort. The granges resembled large farmsteads, and the buildings contained quarters for the permanent staff, together with byres, cattle-sheds, dairies, sheepcotes, and shelters for poultry; and, particularly in the uplands, where unclaimed land was being colonised, they were surrounded by ring-fenced farmlands. Passing into lay hands at the time of the Reformation, these great farms survive less frequently than the proliferation of farms bearing the name 'grange' might suggest, for the term is now frequently used, as Briggs points out, to describe a large country house whose owners wish to proclaim their status as landed proprietors. Most true granges, in fact, perished by fire or decay and are now differently named[10].

Sufficient has been said to show that within England and Wales medieval dispersed settlement in both lowlands and hill-country had complex roots, although it is possible to detect certain general threads of continuity devolving from patterns of exploitation within which wood-pasture and open-pasture regions were integrated with the more productive lowland areas: these roots may well be exceedingly ancient, perhaps even prehistoric, and in one sense the rise of independent dispersed settlement within both types of area may be seen as a breakup of this ancient pattern. The difficult case of Scotland helps to carry this argument a step further and permits some notes of caution to be sounded. Before 1700 very little indeed is known. The Scottish countryside in its man-made aspects, either in the Lowlands or in the Highlands — and within the former the entire pattern of rural settlement, farmbuilding, fields, hedgerows or stone dykes, woodlands — all have been to a large extent laid out since the enclosures of the late-eighteenth and early-nineteenth centuries. However, the farming practice and settlement pattern of eighteenth-century Scotland was a comprehensible integrated whole; the characteristic rural settlement was the multiple-tenancy farm, at the heart of which was a patch of permanently maintained arable divided into intermixed strips and shared, on average, between three to eight tenants. There are here strong echoes of the medieval village, particularly in the eleventh century. The permanent arable, the infield (Fig 30) was maintained by manure accumulated in the byres during the winter months, byres attached physically to the farm dwelling — in effect a long-house — while in the surrounding pastures small patches of unmanured outfield were cultivated until exhausted and then allowed to revert to rank grasses. Throughout the summer months much reliance was placed on the surrounding common grazings in the uphill grounds, and it is still possible to locate the old shielings to which the cattle were sent. This transhumance was undertaken, according to Fairhurst, partly to utilize the more distant grazing and to conserve the grass near the parent settlement, but also to keep the cattle away from the growing crops. This farming practice may be regarded as a system in that it was closely integrated, for arable acres, rough pastures and shielings all played a particular part; but it was never a rigid pattern. While it represented a method of utilizing the particular environmental conditions — a cool, often damp, summer, with extensive areas of rough ground where stock-rearing tended always to take a more or less prominent place in the economy (and as Haldane has shown, the Scottish cattle trade had medieval roots), it was an adjustment to the environment not in any deterministic sense, but strongly influenced by age-old traditons. There is nothing specifically Celtic about the arrangements; rather we are seeing a system which at an earlier stage of development was more widespread throughout the relatively flat lands of southern Britain. As Fairhurst stresses

each element in the eighteenth-century Scottish complex may be regarded up to a point as a relatively simple agrarian expedient. The shielings utilizing the distant pastures may well go back to the Iron Age times and a semi-nomadic life (if such has ever existed). The infield was a simple device to utilize the same plot of land continuously by the regular application of dung, as in a garden. The outfield was a robber economy when dung was insufficient and the ground too rough for the infield method. Interspersed rigs are a common characteristic with communities using the common plough, and may be as old as the type of plough which requires a team of animals and is capable of dealing with heavier, deeper soil.

We are concerned here with deeply ingrained, age-old traditional practices, widely spread throughout Europe north of the Alps, although the difficult environment of parts of Scotland necessitated, as the quotations from the works of Fraser Darling in Chapters 3 and 4 showed, close co-operation, which has tended to preserve these fundamental patterns of human life for many centuries. Nevertheless, the significance of a different system of land tenure as a preserving agent must not be underestimated for, as Grant shows, in Scotland kinship bonds remained important right up to the late-eighteenth century, and although the clansmen seem to have occupied their lands as tenants-at-will, it was an understood thing that a chief must provide land for his clansmen, if necessary dividing existing holdings for the purpose. When, in the latter part of the eighteenth century, agrarian change came, taking the form of consolidation, enclosure or 'clearance', its impact was all the greater because it affected a traditional economy within which the seeds of change, possibly because of environmental limitations, had lain dormant. The severance of the chiefs from their folk was the hardest blow of all: traditional defenders became rapacious destroyers, and after the rising of 1745 the new generation of landowners found themselves short of money, particularly as tastes changed and aspirations rose; they forgot their old regard for their tenants as fighting men and kinsmen, and throughout the Highlands, notably in Sutherland, Argyll, Ross and Inverness, the multiple-tenancy farms were deliberately depopulated, some of the population emigrating, some being encouraged to resettle the storm-lashed coastal fringes, while others died in destitution. It was the destruction of an order that has its roots in Jarlshof and beyond, and although many questions undoubtedly remain unanswered in considering the eighteenth-century landscapes of Scotland, we must look, initially at least, backwards rather than forwards, for they have much to teach us concerning the nature of early economic systems throughout Britain.[11]

Agriculture and Industry

The case of Scotland carried the argument beyond the stated chronological limits of this section, and we must now return to the multiplication of dispersed settlements in the latter part of the medieval period. Even within the better-documented, closely-studied parts of Britain it is difficult, particularly in a general discussion, to draw a picture of the steadily increasing numbers of farmsteads. By the closing decades of the sixteenth century, population was on the upswing, pre-Black-Death levels had already been exceeded, and the pace of reclamation was again accelerating as economic activity quickened on both the agrarian and industrial fronts. The latter, never a negligible part of economic life, was expanding in response to increasing demands for basic iron, coal, pottery, salt and glass, while with rising incomes there was an increasing demand for manufactured goods. This is the place to stress again the artificiality of any temporal divisions, and one example, already discussed in part, forms a useful bridge between the two periods. Fig 48 shows the ancient tenements in the High Forest of Weardale in 1438–9 and the same figure continues the story until 1799, although only in the High Forest is the evidence completely reliable. A glance shows that the processes of reclamation were continuous, leading to both the growth of small clusters and the intercalation of new units amongst the old. Stoutly-built, chunky, slab-roofed, sycamore-shaded farmsteads multiplied, but at what rate? These maps are necessarily based upon available documentation, which, of course, merely records the latest possible date for the appearance of a farm — the time it first appears in the written record — but certain figures are instructive. Between 1438 and 1511 there was relative stability, with new units appearing only at a rate of one per decade; between 1511 and 1624 there was a rate of increase of about two per decade, and a survey of 1596 confirms both the addition of land to old farms and the creation of new ones; between 1698–1799 increases of the order of 2·5 farms per decade occurred. If these figures are at first sight low, indeed almost disappointing, such steady, slow rates of advance are a vital ingredient in colonization, each foothold being tested, consolidated and finally used for the next step. The High Forest farms have long been associated with a 'dual economy' — that is, many were smallholdings closely linked with a form of industrial activity which occupied the inhabitants for a significant proportion of their time. In Weardale this was lead-mining, and as early as 1438 the thirty horses grazed on the lands of Westerblackdene were 'galloways', pack-horses, used in the carriage of lead. The Weardale smallholding was traditionally worked by the womenfolk, and the small 'onsteads', to use the local term, supported a cow, a few sheep, and a pig or two by way of insurance against the risks of following the variable lead veins. It is this industrial aspect which imparts to post-1600 dispersed settlement a fascination and a dynamism, but its influence is very variable in character; it was quite direct in the establishment of specialist industrial settlements, mining clusters or cottage scatters specializing in particular types of textile production; it was more indirect in changing the character of the established system of settlement, and in stimulating the breakup of established villages and the dispersion of new farmsteads throughout the rural landscapes of Britain. In this latter case a key word is once again 'enclosure', and the remainder of this chapter will be devoted to a review of the modifications in settlement wrought by the large-scale changes in the structure of farms after 1600, changes intimately linked with distinctive enclosure movements, and hence indissolubly tied to the economic forces stimulating these.[12]

Single farms after 1600 — the Enclosure Movements

Village settlement in Britain has traditionally been supported by a form of open-field agriculture already described in Chapter 4. Within most upland regions the open fields tended to disappear silently before 1600; by 1700 almost all had gone, and because they represented such a small proportion of the land surface, these piecemeal enclosures, although often creating distinctive field patterns, had but little impact on settlement. Within the lowlands, however, especially the champion lands, dominated by open-field agriculture, the impact was at times cataclysmic. By the seventeenth and eighteenth centuries the disadvantages of such an agricultural system for commercial as opposed to peasant farming were becoming increasingly obvious; the dispersion and fragmentation of holdings, the necessity for communal action, the wasting of land in headlands and baulks, the promiscuous intergrazing of the beasts, the haphazard manuring, and above all the system of agriculture which involved extensive bare fallows — all these combined to make the arrangements inefficient in the eyes of the more proficient members of the farming community. The seventeenth century did indeed see some advances in husbandry techniques: the introduction of new fodder crops — clover, sainfoin, rye-grass and turnips and the improvement of rotations, either by replacing the bare fallow with turnips and clover or incorporating a period of grass ley, and there were also undoubted improvements in livestock. But these improvements were characteristically applied to the lighter soils on the chalk and limestones, light loams and sands. They could be, and indeed were, introduced on open-field farms, for the arrangements were sufficiently flexible and although, for example, turnips are not normally associated with open-field agriculture, they could be integrated into improved rotations. Increasing pressures towards more efficient farming and a more profitable use of the land, however, stimulated the spread of consolidation and enclosure. Significantly, one of the earliest English counties to suffer extensive enclosure of its open fields was Durham, and between 1625 and 1675 the majority of the open-field lands in the east and southeast of the county were converted into hedged fields. This early generation of 'enclosures by agreement' is distinctive, in that while the fields are large and square or rectangular, the roads remain narrow and winding, zig-zagging around the former headland tracks, in contrast to the regular roads associated with eighteenth-century enclosures. However, the vast majority of open-field enclosures were made by means of a special Act of Parliament and although no map is included in this volume their distribution is faithfully reflected by Thorpe's zone of 'predominantly villages with many scattered homesteads, occasional hamlets and market towns' (Fig 1). The following table, derived from the work of W. E. Tate, emphasizes the two distinct facets of this movement:[13]

Period	Open-fields and Waste		Waste only		Total	
	No. of Acts	Acreages (Thousands)	No. of Acts	Acreages (Thousands)	No. of Acts	Acreages (Thousands)
1700–1760	152	238	56	75	208	313
1761–1801	1,479	2,429	521	752	2,000	3,181
1802–1844	1,075	1,610	808	939	1,883	2,549
1845+	164	187	508	335	672	522
Recorded Total	2,870	4,464	1,893	2,101	4,763	6,565
Estimated Total	3,200	4,700	2,200	2,300	5,400	7,000

This table vividly documents a vast national movement, a movement having roots in the seventeenth century, culminating in a peak in the decades between 1761 and 1801, and dying away rapidly in the second half of the nineteenth century to leave behind a few fossil open-field villages, Braunton (Devon), Laxton (Northamptonshire) and Rhosili (Glamorgan), together with fossil strip-patterns in the Isle of Axholme and on Portland Bill. The scale of this enclosing activity can be grasped when it is realized that the probable final total, some seven million acres, represents 20 per cent of the total area of England. Of this 2·8 m hectares (7 m acres), some 1·9 m hectares (4·7 m acres) (two thirds), involve both open-fields and waste, a further 0·9 m hectares (2·3 m acres) involve waste only, and it will be observed that, while a large proportion of the open-field enclosures fell before 1801, those involving waste are in general more evenly spread: indeed the larger proportion fall after 1801. The enclosures of the eighteenth and nineteenth centuries were, throughout the whole country, undertaken by the larger proprietors, and their interest was often financial rather than agricultural; enclosed farms yielded much higher rents than did open-field farms, and while landowners undoubtedly recognized the relevance of more profitable farming to increased rent, and took steps to encourage their tenants to improve — often by incorporating their requirements in leases — they saw enclosure as a profitable investment which brought returns on capital as high as 15–20 per cent. Nevertheless, improved farming spread more rapidly as a result of enclosure, and by reorganizing existing resources output was increased to help feed the growing non-agricultural component of the country's population. This vital phase of agricultural development complex and protracted, varied immensely in impact, chronology and results, even within the bounds of one county. In some instances enclosure merely came as the final stage in a long-drawn-out story of rural change; in other instances it was rapid and cataclysmic in its impact. No single county, still less a single village, can be wholly characteristic of the movement but, in terms of settlement, enclosure and improvement led to the foundation of new, often idealized single farms amid the ruler-straight roads and field walls of the newly reclaimed wastes while, amid the village lands, enclosure represents a powerful solvent of the traditional cohesion of village life. It often encouraged the farmers to move out to new farmsteads set centrally within the newly created ring-fenced block-farms, and left behind in the villages a class of landless labouring folk — they are still remembered as *hinds* in many Durham villages — together with such shopkeepers and specialist craftsmen as had need of the advantages of a central location.[14]

Napton and Prior's Marston, Warwickshire (Fig 16), demonstrate the way in which this outward movement created a pattern of intercalated dispersion; in these two cases, although the movement has never been studied in detail, the contrast between the stone-built farmsteads and cottages of the village core (for not all farms moved, of course) and the brick-built outlying farmsteads is particularly clear in the field. The two parishes were enclosed in respectively 1779–81 and 1758, and Napton brickworks, opened in 1775 with the coming of the canal, provided a cheap alternative to local stone. Alan Harris has documented this process in the Yorkshire

Wolds. In 1771 most of the area was still unenclosed, but a mere fifty-seven years later a pattern of intercalated farmsteads had arisen, and in the sample area which Harris maps, dispersed dwellings seem to have appeared at a rate on average of about six per decade, although by no means all of these were necessarily farmsteads. On the Wolds a very common plan for the new farmsteads consisted of 'a dwelling house to the west; barns and stable on the north; stack-hovels, for cattle and implements on the east; [the whole] forming a square straw-yard, open to the south, having a high-brick-wall, with tall boarded gates'. As in Warwickshire, the new farms were of brick with red pantiles, gradually replacing the older, more traditional constructional techniques; in the Wolds mud, chalk and thatch were used and, more rarely, stone. Such observations could, with very few modifications, be applied to most of the regions experiencing late enclosure, and Marshall's observations on the requisites of a farmstead cited at the beginning of this chapter form a useful general framework, although there has yet to be a general or regional study of post-enclosure farmsteads as a group. Quite clearly this outward migration of farmsteads could have been avoided if a radiating or stellate pattern of ring-fenced farms had been established, focusing upon the village (Fig 22iE), but this was not usual English practice, although examples to do occur; even in Denmark, where it was common, the tedious journey to work has encouraged the migration of farms to centrally placed sites. Curiously enough, with the amalgamation of fields into vast arable tracts such as is occurring throughout eastern England, this form of division has positive advantages, for the concentration of folk in the village permits an adequate provision of services. Even in eighteenth- and nineteenth-century contexts it is possible to find cases where a deliberate twinning of new farms occurred, partly to use one source of water, often a new well (for the dispersed farms lay at some distance from traditional water-supplies), but no doubt sociality was a contributory factor. In practice, great contrasts are found in the density of intercalated farmsteads between one late-enclosed township and the next, and these usually reflect differing policies deriving from variations in landownership. There is a fundamental contrast between the open village with many small landowners, and the closed village, dominated by the local squire, and often containing the great house, a recurrent theme in English rural life and literature; in spite of two world wars and a revolution in social attitudes, the closed village is still with us, although the author would in this case hesitate to cite specific examples. Such villages are often characterized by an atmosphere made up of distinctive physical features; a uniformity and order; a lack of services, of community provisions, together with an attitude which is often surprising to an outsider; feudalism is far from dead in the English countryside. The effect of the presence of open or closed villages upon the appearance of intercalated farmsteads was well illustrated by J. A. Clarke in his prize essay on *The Farming of Lincolnshire*, published in 1851 and cited by R. C. Russell:

> The chief defect with regard to the houses of the poor is in their *number*, for in many localities on the Wolds, Cliff, and other districts the no-cottage system seems to prevail. . . . The population is very unevenly distributed and the cause invariably assigned is the unwillingness of parishes and proprietors to rebuild old houses or erect new ones. . . . They wish to keep down the population in their respective parishes, with a view of having less poor-rate to pay. At Winterton, for instance, are numerous freeholds and other small occupations of land, arising in a great measure from the reluctance of neighbouring landowners to rebuild or erect cottages. Labourers thus driven out of other parishes find a home here, and many are able to hire an acre or more of land (for perhaps £5 an acre), which their families, being out of the reach of paid employment, cultivate; while themselves are obliged to walk a great distance before and after their day's work.

No parish is an island and it is the dynamic interaction between open and closed villages which offers exciting possibilities for further work on the impact of the enclosure movement upon settlement.[15]

Complex Patterns of Change

In this volume a systematic study has been made of villages, hamlets and farms, following the broad classification outlined in Chapter 1 and represented diagrammatically in Fig 2; indeed it would be true to say that only villages and farms have received rigorous treatment, and hamlets have been treated as a sort of no-man's land between the two major groups. To have done otherwise would have demanded more specific regional studies, and careful consideration of the nature of fragmented clusters, settlements consisting of several small clusters (hamlets?) combined under one name, as for instance in the twin-loop 'villages' of Bedfordshire or the annular settlements of East Anglia; but Peter Wade-Martin's work on settlements such as Longham and Weasenham St Peter, Norfolk, and the Royal Commission on Historical Monuments work on the Upper Winterbourne valley, Dorset, show that fragmented clusters, or strings of small villages and hamlets, can be the end-product of a complex evolution. Furthermore in any region, lowland or upland, where there was a combination of late-surviving common waste together with — and this is an important point — the presence of relatively flexible manorial arrangements, the picture is further complicated by the presence of what may collectively be termed squatting settlements, cottages established upon a small plot of waste, legally or illegally.[16] Squatting settlements are found within all of the farming regions defined in Chapter 1 and mapped in Fig 3D. The importance of lordship, acting within the framework of a group of open-field villages has been illustrated by the example of Winterton, Lincolnshire, already cited, but it would most certainly not be true to envisage the 'reluctance of . . . landowners to rebuild or erect cottages' as the operation of a mere whim; it is likely, indeed probable, that in general landowners were willing to permit, if not to encourage, such piecemeal additions to the existing settlement pattern in those areas where there was an alternative form of employment. Thus while improved agriculture could only absorb a given amount of labour, where industrial employment was possible the landlord, often with a financial interest in the local industry, would be willing to allow cottages to multiply, even in areas of classic open-field farming. Hoskins has shown how, in Wigston Magna, the enclosure of the open fields in 1766 failed to stem the flow of people into the village. The reason for this is quite clear:

> It was an industrialised village that not only gave some sort of alternative employment to its own dispossessed peasantry but attracted those of the purely farming villages for miles around. Framework-knitting was a domestic industry and it required no capital to hire a frame from a hosier or an undertaker for a shilling a week and to knit yarn provided by him. And so, ever since the last quarter of the seventeenth century, the village had been attracting the dispossessed and unemployed from outside, and it continued to do so after its own fields and farms were taken out of the peasant economy.

Nevertheless, many of these cottagers were desperately poor, as Hoskins shows. By 1871 there were 600 inhabited houses in the settlement, as against only 336 some seventy years earlier, and up and down the four village streets, which enclosed a rectangle about forty acres in extent, timber-framed and brick-built farmhouses of the sixteenth, seventeenth and eighteenth centuries alternated with short terraces of red-brick cottages, erected by the score after 1800. In some senses Wigston Magna, one of the largest villages in the Midlands, was exceptional, but the process of cottage accretion visible at Wigston can be paralleled throughout the traditional open-field areas, particularly where a textile industry was present, as in the East Midlands and Wiltshire.[17]

In the wood-pasture areas, late-colonized zones, the creation of cottage settlements probably has medieval roots, but the seventeenth and eighteenth centuries saw the establishment of tens of thousands of small cottages, some placed within small intakes along the edges of the commons, others placed within plots intaken from the broad verges of the tangled network of roads so characteristic of landscapes reclaimed from woodland; these are still particularly evident in the lanes around Birmingham, and are betrayed by their long narrow gardens extending parallel to the present road. As one surveyor of a Midland estate wrote at the end of the seventeenth century, 'these cottages and inclosures doe yearly increase, yet these rents are very indifferently paid, they being a poore beggerly sort of people apt to run in Arrears, from time to time.' Many of these cottages were illegal, but it is probable that an element of connivance was often present, the agent turning a blind eye to the foundation of the building, and the tenant, when the encroachment was finally 'noticed', regarding any fine imposed as necessary for the legalization of his position. Although normally founded as individual ventures, these cottages tended to be strung out along roads, producing a characteristic fine stipple of isolated buildings on a map, but at favoured locations, notably at cross-roads or along the edges of the commons, small, highly irregular clusters appeared, and these in favoured circumstances acquired the status of hamlets, their names — Fen End or Stockley Bottoms — often being slightly derogatory, fit residences for 'a poore beggerly sort of people apt to run in Arrears'.

Alan Evirett stresses the links between such cottagers and their encroachments and the poorer labouring classes, pointing out their close associations with areas of woodland industries (the making of brooms, clogs, hurdles, wooden implements and containers), textile industries (spinning, carding, knitting, the weaving of flax, hemp and wool), together with more specialist trades like potting, tiling, nailing, coal-mining, iron-smelting and quarrying. Such cottages cluster thickly in woodland regions like Arden and Dean, the Weald of Sussex, Surrey and Kent, or the Welsh borders, Herefordshire and Shropshire. Additions to a pattern that was already largely composed of 'predominately hamlets with many scattered homesteads, occasional villages and market towns', they reinforced the older, more deeply rooted regional contrasts. It was a common belief that a cottage erected on the waste overnight entitled its builder to undisputed possession and rights to land as far as an axe could be thrown. As is commonly noted, axes could be thrown remarkable distances. J. Gareth Thomas comments

> This belief was present in many Celtic countries, and the fact that it was quite erroneous seems to have been no deterrent to the practice which was quite frequently encouraged by farmers and landowners as a method of keeping the landless poor 'off the parish'. The *ty unnos* or *caban unnos* (one-night house), or 'clod hall' or 'morning surprise', as these houses were called, with enclosed irregular encroachment, thus became a significant feature on the Welsh landscape.

This example carries the squatting cottage as a feature of settlement from the wood-pasture zones to the open-pasture fringes of upland Britain, and in such areas common-edge squatting during the eighteenth and nineteenth centuries is indissolubly linked with the opening of quarries or mines. At first these scattered moorland-edge communities frequently had a reputation for lawlessness that was not wholly undeserved. In Wales and the Pennines, however, these peripheral settlement areas became seats of Methodism and, as Thomas points out, the chapel, often itself an isolated building, became the focus of social life; in this way 'Bethesda', 'Zion' and even 'Nazareth' became part of the Welsh scene. These small-holdings do serve to emphasize the problems of studying rural settlement from a purely morphological viewpoint; they are often entirely isolated, set within a tangle of haphazard small closes, but a closer examination reveals a logical relationship to rights of way, and a hill-slope of squatting cottages may have an underlying unity that is in a sense greater than the sum of the parts. This is merely to reiterate that 'no material and no activity may be studied in isolation', particulary the isolated dwelling of the humble cottager.[18]

7

Postscript

THE MAN-CREATED landscapes of rural settlement present a complex and ever-changing scene. In part, however, this scene is a product of stability or inertia, with each generation accepting and utilizing what has been inherited from the past, perhaps even valuing it because of the links it provides with earlier centuries, although this perception is one found more commonly today: in former times the past has usually been viewed with the tolerance of indifference. On the other hand, past landscapes are constantly subjected to a continuous process of change, and centuries of adaptive change have brought to the landscape new buildings, new fields and new roads, all superimposed upon the discarded structures of former centuries. The pace of this change can vary from a slow process of gradual adaptation to rapid, even cataclysmic upheavals. What is present within the landscape of any region or any local area is the end-product of many centuries of such stability and change. Nevertheless, to recognize this dichotomy is not to explain it, and some understanding of the complexity of temporal explanations can be achieved when it is understood that the landscapes of rural settlement occupy an interface between two contact zones: the zone where the land meets man, involving the varied terrain contrasts and the multitude of slight differences in relief, soil quality and micro-climate, and the zone where man meets the land, an invisible web of property rights in land.

Terrain, soil and climate, although not immutable, constitute the framework within which human societies of former centuries made their living, for, in G. C. Homans' words cited in Chapter 4, men lived on and off the land as the first condition of their survival. They still do. The skills at their disposal, their agrarian and industrial technologies, their ability to cull a succession of harvests from farm and fell, sea and sea-cliffs, woodlands and marshlands, quarry and mine, inseparably welded to the character of their social orderings and their numbers, have conditioned the extent to which a surplus was possible, and made the difference between scraping a bare existence and living well, with the ability to extend creature comforts and invest in improvements which contemporary opinion considered would make the uncertain future more safe. This surplus, however, was never evenly distributed, for men are not only fortunate and unfortunate: they are also wise and witless, cautious and feckless, ruthless and gentle, powerful and weak, while the four horsemen — death, disease, famine and war — have long been part of the human condition. If a 'golden age' has ever existed, it was surely in the Mesolithic period, the Middle Stone Age, when small numbers of skilled hunters had before them the unculled game and woodland resources of the whole of Britain, indeed of Europe, while the uncertainty of a grain harvest for which man, bird and beast competed lay in the future.

The emergence of territoriality as numbers increased presaged the importance in human affairs of land rights and the control over this basic means of production, for, important as capital is, land, except when in a completely virgin state, has always been the source of economic and political power. It still is. Rights over land, forming a complex sequence of layers superimposed upon the soil beneath, are as important as the nature of that soil in affecting, or even controlling, settlement. Rural settlement occupies a complex transition zone between the rights of the mass of the population, however restricted, shared and defined, and the rights of the more powerful landholders, lords of vast acres. Land ownership constitutes the framework within which positive decisions concerning land are taken, for while governments sometimes attempt to enforce their will by enacting that something shall be done, it is in general easier for them to forbid a course of action and impose penalties for those who ignore their edict. Within this broad framework of law, individual landowners take their own decisions concerning rebuilding or destruction, enclosure or improvement, and it is these decisions which have often had the most direct impact upon the lives of ordinary folk.

In practice, terrain variations and land-ownership contrasts operate in different ways at different scales. In general it is true to say that the larger the area being considered the more evident will be the impact of purely physical considerations, and the more likely will those appear to offer a reasonably satisfactory explanation of the patterns observed, for all men are at the mercy of inhospitable climates and poor soils. Turn, however, to a region at the scale of a 1:50,000 Ordnance Survey map sheet, and all the factors of land ownership loom large; the presence of great estates and small estates, good lords and weak lords, freehold and copyhold, even the decisions taken by individual personalities, can no longer be ignored, for the capabilities or inefficiencies of one steward or one landowner can create a pattern visible for generations. This is most clearly manifest in the great mansions and landscaped county estates of this prosperous realm, but it is more often subtly evident in the characteristics of local rural settlement.

Finally, the evidence of the landscape is as vital to a clear understanding of the past as is a room full of documents or the careful excavation of an individual archaeological site. It cannot be sufficiently emphasized that we live at a time when our power to destroy earlier landscapes is greater than ever before. In their recent volume on *Deserted Villages* Maurice Beresford and John Hurst emphasize the need to study shrunken villages, i.e. surviving settlements which show visible signs of shrinkage in the form of earthwork remains; in many parts of the country this call is already too late, yet it is this evidence, garnered painstakingly, village by village, which will ultimately provide us with an understanding of the extent to which the settlement systems with which we are familiar have responded to the economic and demographic pressures throughout the changing centuries; if we cannot do this, then, to borrow Denman's words, our understanding of reality will be short by a whole dimension. Landscape is evidence, and as such it must be collected, classified, analysed and then incorporated, in its proper place, within the wider framework of knowledge.

Notes and References

Chapter 1 *Man, Land and Time in Britain*

1   E. Estyn Evans, 'Sod and Turf Houses in Ireland', in G. Jenkins, *Studies in Folk Life* (1969), pp. 79–90.

2   C. Renfrew (1974), introduction.

3   C. Renfrew (1974); J. G. D. Clarke, 'The Invasion Hypothesis in British Prehistory', *Antiquity*, 40 (1966), 172–89.

4   The volumes of *Antiquity* contain a regular series of reports concerning the discoveries of Professor J. K. S. St Joseph of Cambridge University.

5   P. J. Fowler (1972), ch. IV.

6   I. G. Simmons, 'Evidence for Vegetation Changes associated with Mesolithic Man in Britain', P. J. Ucko and G. W. Dimbleby (eds) *The Domestication and Exploitation of Plants and Animals* (1969), pp. 113–22.

7   J. Turner, 'A Contribution to the History of Forest Clearance', *Proc. Royal Soc.* B161 (1965), 343–54. See also Pennington (1969).

8   B. K. Roberts, J. Turner and P. F. Ward, 'Recent Forest History and Land Use in Weardale, Northern England', in H. J. B. Birks and R. G. West, *Quaternary Plant Ecology* (1973), pp. 207–21. The author is indebted to Mrs A. Donaldson for allowing him to use the as yet unpublished material from Holiwell Moss.

Chapter 2 *Problems of Prehistoric and Roman Settlement*

1   A stimulating review of some of the practical problems involved in the initial sea-crossings is to be found in a paper by H. Case, 'Neolithic Explanations', *Antiquity*, XLIII (1969), 176–86. See also *Antiquity*, XLIV (1970), 105–14 for a discussion of the questions raised in the initial paper; B. Soudsky and I. Paulu, 'The Linear Pottery Culture settlement Patterns of Central Europe', in P. J. Ucko, R. Tringham and G. W. Dimbleby, *Man, Settlement and Urbanism* (1972), pp. 317–28.

2   S. Piggott, *The West Kennet Long Barrow: Excavations 1955–56* (H.M.S.O. 1962) and R. J. C. Atkinson 'Old Mortality: Some aspects of burial and population in Neolithic England', in J. M. Coles and D. D. A. Simpson (eds), *Studies in Ancient Europe* (1968), pp. 83–93. See also R. J. C. Atkinson 'Burial and Population in the British Bronze Age' in F. Lynch and C. Burgess (eds), *Prehistoric Man in Wales and the West* (Bath, 1972), pp. 107–16. This last volume also contains a paper by J. X. W. P. Corcoran 'Multiperiod Construction and the Origins of the Chambered Long Cairn in Western Britain and Ireland', 31–63, which discusses the question of the multi-stage construction of the great funerary monuments.

3   A critical re-evaluation of 'causewayed camps' by I. Smith is to be

found in her chapter 'Causewayed Enclosures', in D. D. A. Simpson (1971), pp. 89–112, where the literature of the field is listed. This volume is a vital source of specialist studies concerning the impact of man on his environment in the third and early second millennia BC. A wide-ranging series of essays, of very variable quality, can be found in P. J. Ucko, R. Tringham and G. W. Dimbleby, *Man, Settlement and Urbanism* (1972). The question of the precise function of the great sacred sites of the second and third millennia BC is a troubled one; R. J. C. Atkinson's volume *Stonehenge* (1956) remains a classic, while a vigorous debate concerning their astronomical significance is to be found in *Antiquity*, XL (1966), 212–6, 262–76 and XLI (1967), 91–8, 174–80, where Jaquetta Hawkes concludes that many of the theories impose modern astronomical knowledge upon a structure which can be adequately explained in simpler terms; furthermore many of the measurements are taken from plans of dubious accuracy.

4   C. Renfrew (1974), ch. 5 by C. Burgess; C. Burgess, 'Chronology and Terminology in the British Bronze Age', *Antiquaries Journal*, 49 (1969), 22–9; C. Musson, 'House Plans and Prehistory', *Current Archaeology*, 21 (July 1970), 267–75.

5   Two recent discussions of Iron Age settlement are to be found in B. Cunliffe, *Iron Age Communities of Britain* (1974) and D. W. Harding, *The Iron Age in Lowland Britain* (1974).

6   A. L. F. Rivet (1958), ch. 2; H. C. Bowen, 'The Celtic Background' in Rivet (1969), pp. 1–48; Jones's arguments are distilled into his paper 'The Multiple Estate as a Model Framework for Tracing Early Stages in the Evolution of Rural Settlement' in *L'Habitat et les Paysages Ruraux d' Europe* (Université de Liège, 1971), 251–67, but see also his 'Early Territorial Organisation in England and Wales', *Geografiska Annaler* 63, parts 1–2 (1961), 174–81, and his essay 'Post-Roman Wales' in H. P. R. Finberg (Cambridge, 1972), pp. 281–382.

7   Rivet (1969), Fig 5.4. The report, a model of its kind, of the excavation of Little Woodbury by Dr. G. Bersu is to be found in the *Proc. Prehistoric Soc.,* 6 (1940), 30–111.

8   P. J. Fowler and H. C. Bowen 'Romano-British Rural Settlements in Dorset and Wiltshire' in Thomas (1966), pp. 43–67. Important primary evidence is to be found in the volumes of the *Royal Commission on Historical Monuments*, England, Dorset, 2, pts 1–2 and 3, pts 1–2.

9   Important references for this section are Rivet (1958), Thomas (1966), Collingwood and Richmond (1969) and Rivet (1966) and (1969). The *Ordnance Survey Map of Roman Britain* (1969) and I. A. Richmond, *Roman Britain*, Pelican History of England, 1 (1955) are invaluable, while an important recent discussion is to be found in H. P. R. Finberg (Cambridge, 1972) by S. Applebaum, entitled 'Roman Britain', pp. 3–265.

10   Mrs Hallam's arguments are to be found in C. W. Phillips (ed.) *The Fenland in Roman Times*, Royal Geographical Society Research Series, no. 5 (1970), pp. 22–113; V. B. Proudfoot in 'Clachans in Ireland' *Gwerin*, 2, no. 3 (1959), 110–22 discussses the fluctuating sizes of small Irish cluster settlements, *clachans*.

11   *Field Archaeology: Some Notes for Beginners* issued by the Ordnance Survey (H.M.S.O. 4th ed. 1963) is an excellent summary by C. W. Phillips,

A. L. F. Rivet and R. W. Feacham of landscape survivals and field monuments, ranging from Paleolithic sites to Industrial Archaeological structures.

12 Essays by Jobey concerning Romano-British settlement north of the Wall in Northumberland can be found in Rivet (1966) and Thomas (1966); see also *Current Archaeology*, 15 (July 1969) for a summary of the northern situation.

Chapter 3 *Domesday Book and Beyond*

1 The literature of Domesday Book is large, but a good basic account is to be found in Welldon Finn (1963). Maitland (1897) and Lennard (1959) are two studies particularly concerned with analysing the significance of the documents and what they can tell us; Darby (1952, 1954, 1962a, 1962b, 1967) treats the material from a geographical viewpoint, while Loyn (1962 and 1965) synthesizes many of the problems.

2 A very readable translation of the Chronicle is to be found in G. N. Garmonsway's edition published in Everyman's Library (no. 624, 1953).

3 Darby (1954), p. 277.

4 Maitland (1897), pp. 41–3. A clear discussion of some of the problems of handling and interpreting Domesday figures is to be found in Sir P. Vinogradoff, *English Society in the Eleventh Century* (Oxford 1908), pp. 261–9, where he identifies single farms, hamlets (2–5 homesteads), small villages (6–11 homesteads), villages, medium and large (12 homesteads or more).

5 One of the clearest references to a Saxon plough takes the form of a riddle found in the *Exeter Book*, one of the subsidiary volumes of the Domesday series; it is printed in J. B. Passmore, *The English Plough* (*Reading University Studies*, 1930), pp. 3–4.

6 R. Welldon Finn in *The Norman Conquest and its Effects on the Economy 1066–1086* (1971) discusses the impact of the invasion upon economic life, attempting to trace the routes followed by various contingents of the Norman army.

7 G. T. Lapsley in *Victoria County History of England*, Durham, I (1905), pp. 259–422; J. E. A. Jolliffe, 'Northumbrian Institutions' *English Historical Review*, 161 (Jan. 1926), 1–42. See also G. W. S. Barrow, 'Northern English Society in the Twelfth and Thirteenth Centuries,' *Northern History*, IV (1969), 1–28. *Cornage* is a render which, sometimes under other names — *Beltancu, commorth, horngeld, neatgeld* — is found throughout the four northern counties and Wales; probably originally a trienical render of cows, it appears in the records in the guise of a cash render. *Metreth* appears to mean 'cow-tribute'.

8 Darby (1954), pp. 53–5; F. Seebohm (1887), ch. 6; G. R. J. Jones (1964), 19–36; G. C. Homans (1941), pp. 26–8. A full discussion of 'Post-Roman Wales' by G. R. J. Jones is to be found in Finberg (1972), pp. 281–2, and Welsh field systems are examined by the same author in Baker and Butlin (1973), pp. 430–79. Jones Pierce (1972) is a further important corpus of work on medieval Wales.

9 V. B. Proudfoot, 'Clachans in Ireland', *Gwerin*, 2, no. 3 (1959),

110–22; J. H. Johnson, 'The Development of the Rural Settlement Pattern in Ireland', *Geografiska Annaler* 43, nos 1–2 (1961), 165–73. See also Morris (1973), pp. 445–65.

10   F. Fraser Darling, *West Highland Survey* (Oxford 1955), p. 282.

11   Sir Cyril Fox (1955). This essay is a classic, and although large amounts of new information are now available and many re-interpretations and changes in emphasis are now necessary, *The Personality of Britain* remains a magnificent synthesis of the 'invasion hypothesis'. Morris (1973) provides an up-to-date view of the arrival of the Anglo-Saxons in Britain in an important volume concerning the history of the British Isles from 350 to 650.

12   R. L. S. Bruce Mitford, *The Sutton Hoo Ship-Burial*, British Museum (1968).

13   Bede, *Historia Ecclesiastica,* I, ch. 34. H. P. R. Finberg, *Lucerna* (1964).

14   Discussions of the arrival of the Saxons are to be found in Blair (1960) and Loyn (1962), but the recent volume by Morris (1973) is particularly detailed and closely referenced. A key paper is to be found in J. M. Dodgson's discussion 'The Significance of the Distribution of the English Place-Name in *-ingas, -inga* — in South-east England', *Medieval Archaeology*, 10 (1966), 1–29.

15   Morris (1973) contains a very full account of the British states between AD 350 and AD 650. See also M. Dillon and N. K. Chadwick, *The Celtic Realms* (1967), N. H. Chadwick, *Celtic Britain* (1964), and L. Alcock, *Arthur's Britain* (1971).

16   Beresford and St Joseph (Cambridge, 1958), pp. 83–91.

17   A recent summary of Professor P. Sawyer's arguments is to be found in Sawyer (1971), ch. 7; see also K. Cameron, *Scandinavian Settlement in the Territory of the Five Boroughs: The Place-name Evidence* (Nottingham, 1965), Inaugural Lecture.

18   A. Small 'The Historical Geography of the Norse Viking Colonisation of the Scottish Highlands', *Norsk Geografisk Tidsskrift*, 22 (1968), 1–16.

19   T. H. Aston, 'The Origins of the Manor in England', *Trans, Roy. Hist. Soc.,* 5th ser. 8 (1958), 59–83; G. R. J. Jones, 'Early Territorial Organisation in England and Wales', *Geografiska Annaler*, 63, nos 1–2 (1961), 174–81.

20   See Darby (1954), pp. 270–308; H. Thorpe, 'The Growth of Settlement before the Norman Conquest' in *Birmingham and its Regional Setting* (British Association for the Advancement of Science, Birmingham 1950), pp. 87–112; R. H. Kinvig, 'The Birmingham District in Domesday Times', *Ibid*, pp. 113–34; J. B. Harley, 'The Settlement Geography of Early Mediaeval Warwickshire' *Trans. Inst. Brit. Geographers* 34 (1964), 115–30. The author is indebted to Mr D. J. Pannett for the map of Warwickshire parishes and townships.

21   The quotations are derived from H. P. R. Finberg's essay 'Continuity and Cataclysm' in *Lucerna* (1964), 1–20, and this volume is an important source for many of the points made in the remainder of the chapter.

22   A. L. F. Rivet, *Town and Country in Roman Britain* (1958), p. 76; Sir C. Fox, *The Archaeology of the Cambridge Region* (Cambridge, 1923), maps 2, 4, and 5.

23 P. V. Addyman, 'A Dark Age Settlement at Maxey, Northants',
Mediaeval Archaeology, 8 (1964), 20–73.
24 S. Piggott, *Ancient Europe* (Edinburgh, 1965), pp. 140–1, 226–9; G.
Clark and S. Piggott, *Prehistoric Societies* (1965), pp. 308–10.

Chapter 4 *Patterns of Village Settlement*

1 G. C. Homans (1941), p. 12; F. Fraser Darling, *West Highland Survey*,
(Oxford, 1955), p. 282ff.; J. C. Grant, *Plough and Coble* (1967), 'Spring
Plough' pp. 30–3.
2 H. Thorpe, 'Rural Settlement' in *The British Isles* eds. J. W. Watson
and J. B. Sissons (1964), pp. 358–79; J. M. Houston (1963), p. 80–1; C. T.
Smith (1967), pp. 260–96; one of the more practical solutions to the
problems of definition has been offered by Mrs S. Hallam in C. W. Phillips
The Fenland in Roman Times, Royal Geographical Society Research
Series, no. 6 (1970), p. 52ff. where she very carefully defines single farms,
small hamlets, large hamlets and small villages. Significantly, as Haggett
(1965) demonstrates (Chapter 4), geographical studies concerning population clusters and the size continuum, and those concerning the size and
spacing of clusters have tended to ignore the small settlements at the lower
ranges of the hierarchy; this is no accident, as generalization becomes
increasingly difficult at this end of the settlement spectrum. Douglas
Fraser's small volume *Village Planning in the Primitive World* (s.d. Studio
Vista SBN 289 79567 2) provides many beautiful illustrations of primitive
'villages'.
3 The author is indebted to his colleague Ian Evans for permission to
base a portion of Fig 2 on his seminar paper entitled 'The properties of
Patterns of Points, Measured by Space Filling Angular Relationships'
Geographical Articles no. 8 (Cambridge March 1967), 63–77. Such classifications assist in the accurate definition of settlement patterns but they go
no way towards explaining them: indeed it may be necessary to distinguish
carefully between settlement geography and settlement geometry. Fig 2
above may, for example, be compared with Fig 17 in Houston (1963).
Houston's conclusion (p. 107) still remains valid, however: 'Specific data
for each environment and for each historical period are required before any
generalisation of types and patterns can be accepted as valid.'
4 The scheme used here is a modification of von Thunen's model,
discussed by Chisholm (1962); G. Duby's view is to be found in *Rural
Economy and Country Life in the Medieval West*, trans. C. Postan (1962),
pp. 5–27, in particular p. 11.
5 H. C. Darby (1951), Figs 18 and 19; J. A. Steers, *Field Studies in the
British Isles* (1964), ch. 15; J. Palmer, 'Landforms, Drainage and Settlement in the Vale of York' in S. R. Eyre and G. R. J. Jones, *Geography as
Human Ecology* (1966), pp. 91–121; M. W. Beresford and G. R. J. Jones,
Leeds and its Region (1967), ch. 10, especially Figs 25–6; Beresford &
Hurst (1971), pp. 121–2.
6 Some very useful comments on hazard perception are to be found in
M. A. Genthe, 'Valley Towns of Connecticut', *Bull. American Geog. Soc.*

39 (1907), 513–44; some of the practical problems of pioneering a 'new' environment are examined by C. Sauer in 'Conditions of Pioneer Life in the Upper Illinois Valley' (1963), 11–22.

7   Chisholm (1972), ch. 6; J. C. D. Clark (1952), p. 104; M. Alexander, *The Ealiest English Poems* (Penguin 1966), 'The Ruin', p. 30. The text of this chapter was written before the report on the Saxon village of Chalton, Hampshire, appeared in *Current Archaeology*, 37 (March, 1973), 55–61; Chalton appears to have been a large village of hall houses, belonging to the latter part of the early Saxon period, the sixth or seventh century AD. By the late Saxon period the site was deserted, being replaced by three other settlements. In this case, Chalton was placed on virgin soil, on a windy, waterless hill-top.

8   P. Haggett (1965) ch. 4, Fig 4.5; A. R. H. Baker (1969), pp. 123–32 , Fig 11.

9   Martha Genthe (note 6 above) illustrates her article with maps which show this process occurring in the Connecticut valley; see also H. Thorpe, 'The Lord and the Landscape' *Trans. Birmingham Arch. Soc.* 80 (1965), 62ff.; J. E. B. Gover, A. Mawer and F. M. Stenton, *The Place-names of Warwickshire*, English Place Name Society, 13 (1936), pp. 133–5, 144–5, 275; H. P. R. Finberg, *Early Charters of the West Midlands* (Leicester, 1961); M. W. Beresford and J. K. S. St Joseph (Cambridge, 1958), 146–7.

10   See C. T. Smith (1967), ch. 4; B. H. Slicher van Bath (1963), introduction and ch. 3; climatic change is discussed in H. H. Lamb, *The Changing Climate* (1966).

11   The literature of field systems is large: H. L. Gray *English Field Systems* (Harvard 1915, reprint London 1959), remains a classic, but see Baker and Butlin (1973) for recent discussions and extensive bibliographies; C. T. Smith (1967) contains important generalizations while J. M. Houston (1963) is a crisp summary of the problems.

12   The account of 'Measures and Fields' by F. W. Maitland in *Domesday Book and Beyond* (Fontana 1960), pp. 422–62, has yet to be satisfactorily replaced, although D. R. Denman (1958) contains a clear distillation of many of the complexities. Seebohm (1883) remains a classic study of the detailed links between field structures and fiscal tenements. See also Sir Paul Vinogradoff *Villainage in England* (1892), pp. 257–6.

13   The work of B. H. Slicher van Bath (1963) forms a vital background to this section; the statements concerning the carrying capacity of a peasant holding are interpolated from Fig 2.2 in 'De oogstopbrengsten van Verschillende Gewassen, Voornamelijk Granen, in Verhouding tot het Zaaizaad, ca. 810–1820', in *Afdeling Agrarische Geschiedenis Bijdragen,* 9 Landbouwhogeschool, (Wageningen, 1963), 29–125; in volume 10 of the same series is to be found a full discussion of 'Yield Ratios', and an English summary of the arguments presented in Dutch in volume 9. The figures cited in the text are very generalized, as the Taunton example demonstrates; see J. S. Titow 'Some Differences between Manors and their Effects on the Condition of the Peasant in the Thirteenth Century', *Agricultural Hist. Rev.* 10, pt 1 (1962), 1–13.

14   Chisholm (1962), pp. 144–7; the author is indebted to Ms D. J. Pannett for supplying him with a map of open-field land in Warwickshire in *circa* 1700 from which the following measurements have been taken:-

I. Median maximum distance from named village to parish or township boundary, in kilometres (where possible including deserted village sites);

II. Median maximum distance from named village to perimeter of the open subdivided fields;

Rural District	Distance I	Distance II
Rugby	2·3	2·2
Shipston on Stowe	2·6	2·6
Southam	2·5	2·4
Stratford Upon Avon	2·5	2·3
Tamworth	2·6	2·2
Warwick	2·4	2·1
Meriden	2·9	1·6
Alcester	2·3	1·8
Atherstone	2·5	—
County	*2·6*	*2·2*

Warwickshire lacks the great strip parishes of Lincolnshire and where open-subdivided fields occurred in the early eighteenth century, they tended to occupy a very large proportion of each township, normally extending almost to the most distant point on the boundary. Very few townships or parishes possessed boundaries whose furthest point was less than 1 km from the village, and over 80 per cent of the parishes have this same point between 1·8 and 3·3 kms from the village, the inter-quartile range for the whole county falling between 2·1 and 3·3 kms. One point seems very clear, in over 40 per cent of the cases recorded, the open-subdivided fields extended more than 2·5 kms from the village and in barely 20 per cent of the recorded cases was this less than 1·8 kms. If Chisholm's figure of 0·8 to 1·6 kms can be accepted, and these figures for Warwickshire do not necessarily disprove his point, then we are faced with the fascinating problem of why folk were prepared to undertake the arduous journeys in Warwickshire. More comparative data is badly needed.

15 The processes of appropriation are summarized by W. G. Hoskins in the 'History of Common Land and Common Rights', appendix II of the report of the *Royal Commission on Common Land 1955–1958,* Cmnd. 462 (H.M.S.O., 1958).
16 B. K. Roberts 'Village Plans in County Durham: a Preliminary Statement', *Medieval Archaeology,* 67 (1973), 33–56.
17 This discussion is based upon A. H. Smith, *English Place Name Elements* (Cambridge, 1956).
18 C. T. Smith (1961), pp. 234–6; B. K. Roberts 'A Study of Medieval Colonisation in the Forest of Arden, Warwickshire' *Agricultural Hist. Rev.* 16, pt 2 (1968), 101–13; S. Erixon 'Swedish Villages without Systematic Regulations', *Geografiska Annaler,* 43, nos 1–2 (1961), 57–74; S. Erixon, 'The Age of Enclosures and its Older Traditions' *Folk Life,* 4 (1966) 56–63.
19 M. W. Beresford and J. Hurst (1971), p. 147, Table 1 and pp. 117–31; H. Loyn, *Anglo-Saxon England and the Norman Conquest* (1962), pp. 164–5; H. L. Gray (1915), p. 60; H. P. R. Finberg (1972), pp. 490–1; T. H. Ashton 'The Origins of the Manor in England', *Trans. Royal Hist.*

Soc., 5th ser, 8 (1958), 59–83; W. G. Hoskins, 'The English Landscape' in A. L. Poole (ed.), *Medieval England,* 1 (Oxford, 1958), p.12.

20   M. W. Beresford (1954) and M. W. Beresford and J. Hurst (1971) are the key references for any consideration of 'lost' or deserted medieval villages.

21   There is a splendid map in the *Royal Commission on Historical Monuments for England* volume on central Dorset (3, part 1, 1970), xlv, showing surviving and deserted settlements in the upper Winterbourne valley; three existing villages and a scatter of farms are the survivors of nine separate settlements in the Middle Ages! A generalized model of the evolution of a settlement pattern is to be found in the paper by B. W. Blouet 'Factors Influencing the Evolution of Settlement Patterns' in P. J. Ucko, R. Tringham and G. W. Dimbleby (eds.) *Man, Settlement and Urbanism* (1972). The processes at work are considered by J. C. Hudson in 'A Location Theory for Rural Settlement', *Annals of the Association of American Geographers,* 59, pt 2 (1969), 365–81.

Chapter 5 *Village Forms*

1   John West in his book *Village Records* (1962) provides a remarkably painless introduction to the basic historical sources for village studies. Two studies by J. B. Harley, *The Historian's Guide to Ordnance Survey Maps* (National Council for Social Service, 1966) and J. B. Harley, *Maps for the Local Historian: a Guide to the British Sources* (National Council for Social Service, 1972) provide basic knowledge of key map sources.

2   M. R. G. Conzen, 'Modern Settlement', *Scientific Survey of North-Eastern England* (Newcastle 1949), pp. 75–83; W. G. Hoskins (1967); C. O. Sauer, 'Foreword to Historical Geography', in *Land and Life,* ed. J. Leighley (Berkeley and Los Angeles, 1963), pp. 351–79.

3   J. Houston (1963), pp. 109–34; R. W. Brunskill (1971); M. W. Beresford and J. G. Hurst (1971), pp. 100–17, Fig. 27.

4   P. V. Addyman, 'A Dark-Age Settlement at Maxey, Northants.', *Medieval Archaeology,* 8 (1964), 20–73; S. E. West, 'The Anglo-Saxon Village of West Stow', *Medieval Archaeology,* 13 (1969), 1–20; 'The Mucking, Essex, Crop. Mark Sites', *Essex Journal,* 7, no. 3 (Autumn 1972); H. Parker, 'Feddersen Wierde and Vallhagar: a contrast in Settlements', *Medieval Archaeology,* 9 (1965), 1–10; 'Feddersen Wierde' *Current Archaeology,* 13 (March 1969), 56–61; 'Chalton. The Excavation of an Anglo-Saxon Village', *Current Archaeology,* 37 (March 1973), 55–61.

5   W. G. Hoskins 'The Rebuilding of Rural England 1570–1640', in *Provincial England* (1963), pp. 131–48; M. W. Barley (1961); see also I. C. Peate (Liverpool, 1944).

6   Moated homesteads are discussed in ch. 7; I. F. Grant, *Highland Folk Ways* (1961), pp. 141–66.

7   C. T. Smith (1971), p. 260ff.; a useful review of work on rural settlement in Germany is to be found in A. Mayhew, *Rural Settlement and Farming in Germany* (1973); see also H. Thorpe, 'The Green Village in its European Setting' in *The Fourth Viking Congress* (Aberdeen, 1965), 85–111.

8   The terminology suggested in this paragraph follows discussions between the author and Dr June Sheppard, Queen Mary College, London. For a classification of the varied types of green villages see Thorpe (1965), note 7 *supra*, and D. R. Denman, *Commons and Village Greens* (1967), pp. 207–8. Professor H. Uhlig emphasises the problems of analysing forms in his paper 'Old Hamlets with Infield and Outfield Systems in Western and Central Europe', *Geografiska Annaler*, 43 nos 1–2 (1961), 285.

9   To anticipate a general conclusion, there are no facets of settlement geography about which it is more difficult to generalise than the impact of land ownership and inheritance practices. Paradoxically, the literature is large, but it is not directed towards the field of settlement studies. Thirsk (1967), Ch. 1 contains important comment, as does Homans (1960). The study by J. A. Raftis, *Tenure and Mobility* (Toronto, 1964), based on the court rolls of Ramsey abbey, is a model of its kind.

10   B. H. Slicher van Bath (1963), pp. 77–97 provides a concise summary of the European picture; Sir John Clapham, *A Concise Economic History of Britain, from the earliest Times to 1750* (Cambridge, reprint 1963), pp. 77–8, 185–6. The table in the text is derived from van Bath.

11   W. G. Hoskins, 'The Population of an English Village 1086–1801' in *Provincial England* (1963), pp. 181–208.

12   M. M. Postan and J. Titow, 'Heriots and Prices on Winchester Manors' *Econ. Hist. Rev.,* 2nd ser. 11 (1958–9), 392–417.

13   H. Thorpe 'The Green Villages of County Durham' *Trans. Institute of British Geographers*, 15 (1951), 155–80. Dr Thomas Sharpe in his small book *The Anatomy of the Village* (Penguin 1946) prints a splendid series of plans recognizing *roadside* villages, *squared* villages, *seaside* villages and *planned* villages.

14   J. R. C. Hamilton, *Excavations at Jarlshof, Shetland*, Ministry of Public Buildings and Works, Archaeological Reports no.1 (London 1956). I am indebted to Dr Alan Small's paper 'The Historical Geography of the Norse Viking Colonisation of the Scottish Highlands', *Norsk Geografisk Tidsskrift* 22 (1968), 1–16, Fig 4, for the idea of Fig 25. The lines 'At Lanyon Quoit' by Arthur Caddick appear in *Cornish Archaeology* 7 (1968), 14.

15   J. A. Sheppard, 'Pre-Enclosure Field and Settlement Patterns in an English Township', *Geografiska Annaler,* 48 Ser. B (1966), 59–77.

16   The most accessible material concerning Wharram Percy is to be found in Beresford and Hurst (1971), where the material from this important site is woven into the fabric of the entire volume, which is the source of many of the points made in the remainder of this chapter. Detailed reports and brief notices concerning village excavations currently in progress appear in the volumes of *Medieval Archaeology*.

17   D. R. Denman, *Land Use and The Constitution of Property* (Cambridge, 1969), p. 13; P. Wade Martins, 'The Origins of Rural Settlement in East Anglia', unpublished seminar paper based upon his Ph.D thesis 'The Development of the Landscape and Human Settlement in West Norfolk from 350–1650 AD with particular reference to the Launditch Hundred' (Leicester, 1971).

18   The author is deeply indebted to Dr June Sheppard for discussions concerning the problems of terminology. Accurate description is the basis

for all comparative work and it is hoped that the terminology used in this chapter may represent a meaningful step on the road towards a measure of standardization. The next step is accurate *measurement* of settlement compactness — perhaps best achieved by means of an index derived from dividing the actual area of the toft-lands of a village by the area of a circle circumscribing the greatest width of the toftlands; thus a perfectly clustered settlement, with perfectly circular toftlands (for instance, *moshav* Nahalal comes very close to such an ideal — G. H. Blake, 'The Origins and Evolution of Israel's Moshav' *Kulturgeografi* 109 (Århus 1969), 293–311.) would have an index of 1.0 but the more linear and extended a settlement, the lower would be the index. The *value* of such an index would be to assist in precise description and precise definition, a necessary part of such work.

19   See note 19 of Chapter 4 *supra*; G. White, *The Natural History of Selbourne* (1789), Letter 1.

20   B. K. Roberts, 'Village Plans in County Durham: A Preliminary Statement' *Medieval Archaeology*, 16 (1972), 33–56; Mayhew op.cit. note 7 *supra*; B. K. Roberts, 'Rural Settlement' in J. C. Dewdney (ed.) *Durham City and County with Teesside* (Durham, 1970), pp. 235–250; J. A. Sheppard, 'Metrological Analysis of Regular Village Plans in Yorkshire', *Agricultural History Review*, 22 pt ii (1974), 118–35.

21   Village regulation is discussed by G. C. Homans, (1960), pp. 83–106; see also S. Göransson, 'Field and Village on the Island of Öland: a Study of the Genetic Compound of an East Swedish Rural Landscape', *Geografiska Annaler*, 40 (1958), 101–58, and S. Göransson, 'Regular Open-field Pattern in England and Scandinavian Solskifte', *Geografiska Annaler*, 43 (1961), 80–104. An illuminating note is to be found in Sir Paul Vinogradoff's work *The Growth of the Manor* (2nd edition 1911), pp. 263–7.

22   Sir Frank Stenton in 'Documents Illustrative of the Social and Economic History of the Danelaw', *British Academy, Records of Social and Economic History*, 5 (1920), pp. xxxvff. discussed the 'intimate association of the recognised shares in the fields with the tofts in the village'. The temporal changes in 'share units' in Northumberland are examined by the Earl Percy in 'The Ancient Farms of Northumberland', *Archaeologia Aeliana* 17 (1895), 1–39.

23   Dr Gabrielle Schwarz, *Allgemeine Siedlungsgeographie* (Berlin, 1966), 147, fig 22.

24   H. Thorpe (1951), note 13 *supra*; a distribution map of villages with greens is to be found in D. Stamp, 'Common Lands and Village Greens of England and Wales', *Geographical Journal*, 130, pt 4 (1964), but although thought-provoking this map is demonstrably incomplete and it will be some time before the national distribution of these settlements can be pictured with any clarity, if indeed a map of 'village greens' in the country could be meaningful at all, for the sprawling, irregular greens of East Anglian villages are very different from the formal, rectangular ordered greens of the north country.

25   One of the more important publications throwing light on the structural components of the medieval landscape is the volume by M. W. Beresford and J. K. S. St Joseph (1958) and the chapter on 'Village Plans' repays

repeated study. Bede in *The Ecclesiastical History of the English Nation*, Book 1, ch. 30 gives the text of Pope Gregory's letter.

26 J. G. Hurst, 'The Changing Medieval Village in England', in P. J. Ucko, R. Tringham and G. W. Dimbleby (eds) *Man, Settlement and Urbanism* (1972), pp. 531–40, Fig 3; M. R. G. Conzen 'The Use of Town Plans in the Study of History' in H. J. Dyos (ed.), *The Study of Urban History* (1968), pp. 113–30. There may be a simple archaeological problem involved — it is easier to detect change rather than continuity on a site.

27 B. K. Roberts (1970, 1973), note 20 *supra*.

28 D. Stamp (1964), note 24 *supra*; D. Stamp and W. G. Hoskins, *The Common Lands of England and Wales* (1963).

29 C. and R. Bell, *City Fathers* (Pelican, 1972), 215ff.; *The North East of Scotland* (British Association for the Advancement of Science 1963), pp. 87–99. It is perhaps worth appending to this section Ralf Brown's description of Sunderland, Mass., founded in 1714: 'The proprietors surveyed a wide main street along which house lots 14 rods wide were regularly spaced. The result was a closely knit community fronting onto its boulevard-like street', *Historical Geography of the United States* (New York, 1948), p. 56. This is a 'green' village, a regular street-green-village, translated to a new environment.

30 M. W. Beresford, *New Towns of the Middle Ages* (1967), pp. 142–163; O. A. W. Dilke *The Roman Land Surveyors* (Newton Abbot, 1971), particularly pp. 188–200.

Additional note: a paper in *Medieval Archaeology* 16 (1972), 1–12, by Professor Barry Cunliffe entitled 'Saxon and Medieval Settlement-Pattern in the Region of Chalton, Hampshire' is an important contribution to the problems outlined in Chapters 4 and 5 of this volume.

Chapter 6 *Farms and Hamlets*

1 The quotation from Marshall is derived from J. C. Loudon, *An Encyclopaedia of Agriculture* (4th ed. 1839), para. 2950. This splendid volume involves the 'Theory and Practice of the Valuation, Transfer, Laying Out, Improvement and Management of Landed Property; and the Cultivation and Economy of The Animal and Vegetable Productions of Agriculture, including All the Latest Improvements; A General History of Agriculture in all Countries and a Statistical View of its present State with suggestions for its future Progress in the British Isles'. In spite of this, the Preface of 1831 warns us that 'the main comfort of all those engaged in agriculture as a profession, from the labourer to the gentleman farmer, will ever consist more in *the possession within themselves of the essential means of comfortable existence,* than in the power of accumulating fortunes, such as manufacturers and commercial men frequently acquire.' R. W. Bunskill's volume entitled *Illustrated Handbook of Vernacular Architecture* (1971) is invaluable, and incorporates (pp. 170–82) a fascinating series of maps dealing with building materials. Studies of 'farm groups' are to be found in the volumes of the *Royal Commission on Historical Monuments*, for example *Dorset*, vol. 2, South-East, part 1 (1970), plates 50 and 51.

2 A. W. B. Simpson's book *An Introduction to the History of Land Law* (1961) is a clear modern summary of this difficult topic, while for the earlier

periods D. R. Denman's *Origins of Ownership* (1958) is exceptionally readable. It is worth citing two comments which appear in D. R. Denman's inaugural lecture *Land Use and The Constitution of Property* (University of Cambridge, 1969) when he says, 'If we fail to recognise that land use is a function of property rights in land our cognisance of the truth is deficient by a whole dimension of reality' and later, 'Recognition of the proprietary land unit, its characteristics and function, can lead to a fuller understanding of the criteria by which land-use patterns are determined and to a deeper planning intelligence and profundity of analysis.' (p.13). Roger Millman's study of 'The Marches of the Highland Estates', *Scottish Geog. Mag.*, 85, no. 3 (Dec. 1969) 172–81 is an interesting statement, and the final paragraph on page 177 says much concerning the problems.

3   See T. A. M. Bishop, 'Assarting and the Growth of the Open Field' *Econ. Hist. Rev.*, 6, no. 13 (1935), 13–29; H. E. Hallam, *Settlement and Society* (1965).

4   The discussion of Tanworth is based on the author's Ph.D. thesis *Settlement, Land Use and Population in the Western Portion of the Forest of Arden, Warwickshire, between 1086 and 1350*, University of Birmingham (1965); see also B. K. Roberts 'A Study of Medieval Colonisation in the Forest of Arden, Warwickshire'. *Ag. Hist. Rev.*, 16, pt. 2 (1968), 110–13. Studies of land-reclamation in the Middle Ages are widely scattered, but the following items are of particular importance — T. A. M. Bishop, 'Assarting and the Growth of the Open-fields', note 3 *supra*; E. M. Yates 'History in a Map' *Geog. Jnl.* 126, part 1 (1960), 32–51; E. M. Yates, 'Dark Age and Medieval Settlement on the Edge of Wastes and Forests', *Field Studies*, 2, no. 2 (1965), 133–53; J. Z. Titow, 'Some differences between Manors and their Effects upon the Condition of the Peasant in the Thirteenth Century' *Agric. Hist. Rev.* 10, part 1 (1962), 1–13; W. G. Hoskins, *Devon* (1954), chs. 3, 4 and 5; H. E. Hallam, *Settlement and Society — a Study of the Early Agrarian History of South Lincolnshire* (Cambridge, 1965).

5   Jean le Patourel's article 'Moated Sites of Yorkshire' in *Chateau Gaillard* (Caen, 1972) discusses the implication of moated sites. See also C. C. Taylor, 'Medieval Moats in Cambridgeshire', in P. J. Fowler (ed.). *Archaeology and Landscape* (1972), pp. 237–49. W. G. Hoskins, *Devon* (1954), ch. 5; W. G. Hoskins and H. P. R. Finberg, *Devonshire Studies*.

6   Royal forests are very clearly discussed in A. L. Poole, *From Domesday Book to Magna Carta 1087–1216*, Oxford History of England (2nd ed., 1955), pp. 28–35; H. C. Darby's chapter 'The Economic Geography of England AD 1000–1250' in H. C. Darby (ed.) *An Historical Geography of England before 1800* (1936) is still essential background to colonization.

7   R. I. Hodgson, 'Medieval Colonisation in Northern Ryedale, Yorkshire', *Geog. Jnl.*, 135, pt 1 (March 1969), 44–54.

8   See J. Turner, B. K. Roberts, and P. F. Ward, 'Recent Forest History and Land Use in Weardale, Northern England' in H. J. Birks and R. C. West (eds), *Quatenary Plant Ecology* (Oxford, 1973), pp. 207–21 for a discussion of the palynological data. Fig 4 is derived from a study made of the two small bogs financed by the Natural Environment Research Council. See also S. R. Eyre 'The Upward Limit of Enclosure on the East Moor of

North Derbyshire', *Trans. Institute of British Geographers*, 23 (1957), 61–74.

9   G. R. J. Jones 'Some Medieval Rural Settlements in North Wales' *Trans. Inst. Brit. Geogrs.*, 19 (1953), 51–72; *Ibid.* 'The Pattern of Rural Settlement on the Welsh Border', *Agric. Hist. Rev.* 8, 6 (1960), 66–81; *Ibid.*, 'The Distribution of Bond Settlement in North-West Wales', *Welsh Hist. Rev.* 2 no. 1 (1964), 19–36; T. Jones Pierce, 'Pastoral and Agricultural Settlements in Early Wales', *Geografiska Annaler*, 43, nos 1–2 (1961), 182–9; J. Thirsk, 'The Farming Regions of England', *The Agrarian History of England and Wales*, 1500–1640, 4 (1967), pp. 1–15, G. C. Homans, *English Villagers of the Thirteenth Century* (1960), book 2.

10   A summary of Cistercian activity, with an important bibliography, is to be found in a paper by R. A. Donkin, 'The Cistercian Order in England: Some Conclusions', *Trans. Institute of British Geographers* 33 (1963), 181–98.

11   H. Fairhurst, 'The Rural Settlement Pattern of Scotland, with special Reference to the West and North' in R. W. Steel and R. Lawton, *Liverpool Essays in Geography* (1967), pp. 195–209; A. R. B. Haldane, *The Drove Roads of Scotland* (1952); I. F. Grant, *Highland Folk Ways* (1961); an important overview of the points raised in this section is to be found in a paper by E. Estyn Evans, 'The Ecology of Peasant Life in Western Europe', in W. L. Thomas (ed.), *Man's Role in Changing the Face of the Earth* (Chicago, 1956), pp. 217–39.

12   The transition from cattle-station to farm was documented by G. H. Tupling in his volume 'The Economic History of Rossendale' *Chetham Soc.*, New Ser. 86 (Manchester, 1927); see also H. Ramm, *Shielings and Bastles* (H.M.S.O., 1970).

13   A general review of enclosure is to be found in W. E. Tate's volume (1967), from which the table is taken. See also J. D. Chambers and G. Mingay (1966); W. E. Minchinton (ed.) *Essays in Agrarian History* (2 vols., Newton Abbot, 1968) contains twenty-four important essays covering the era from the appearance of the manor to the present century; E. L. Jones (ed.) *Agriculture and Economic Growth in England 1650–1815* (1967) contains valuable papers and introductory comments concerning the period in question. Enclosure looms large in A. R. H. Baker and R. A. Butlin's (eds) volume *Studies of Field Systems in the British Isles* (Cambridge, 1973).

14   The literature of specific studies of the impact of enclosure upon the landscape is very large; of particular importance is the volume by Alan Harris, *The Rural Landscape of the East Riding of Yorkshire 1700–1850* (Oxford, 1961). A brief review of the literature is to be found in W. E. Tate (1967), 179–82.

15   D. Mills, *English Rural Communities* (1973); R. C. Russell, 'The Enclosures of Burton upon Stather, Thealby and Coleby 1803–1806 and Winterton 1770–1772', *Journal of the Scunthorpe Museum Society*, Series 1 (Local History), no. 2 (1970). This is one of a series of careful studies of Lincolnshire enclosures published by R. C. Russell. The quotation from the work of J. A. Clarke is derived from the *Jnl. of the Royal Agric. Soc. of England* 12, parts 1 and 2.

16   P. Wade-Martins, 'The Origins of Rural Settlement in East Anglia', a seminar paper delivered in Leeds, February, 1972, note 17, Chapter 5,

supra. Ph.D. thesis *The Development of the Landscape and Human Settlement in West Norfolk from 350–1650 AD with particular reference to the Launditch Hundred*, Leicester University (1971); *Royal Commission on Historical Monuments, England, Dorset* 3, Central part 1, introduction 44–6.

17 W. G. Hoskins, *The Midland Peasant* (1965).

18 A. Everitt, 'Farm Labourers', in Thirsk (1967), pp. 396–465; J. Gareth Thomas, 'Settlement Patterns — Rural and Urban', Part 1, in E. G. Bowen, *Wales* (1957), pp. 141–57; F. A. Barnes 'Settlement and Landscape Changes in Caernarvonshire Slate Quarrying Parish' in *Geographical Essays in Honour of Professor K. C. Edwards*, eds R. H. Osborne, F. A. Barnes and J. C. Doornkamp, Dept. of Geography, University of Nottingham (1970).

Bibliography

The following bibliography is not exhaustive. It draws together some of the more important references consulted during the writing of this volume. The reader is referred to the notes and references at the end of each chapter for more specific material.

Baker, A. R. H. 'The Geography of Rural Settlements' in Cooke, R. U. and Johnson, J. H. (eds), *Trends in Geography* (1969), pp. 123–32

Baker, A. R. H. *Progress in Historical Geography* (Newton Abbot, 1972)

Baker, A. R. H. and Harley, J. B. (eds) *Man Made the Land* (Newton Abbot, 1973)

Baker, A. R. H. and Butlin, R. A. (eds) *Studies of Field Systems in the British Isles* (Cambridge, 1973)

Barley, M. W. *The English Farmhouse and Cottage* (1961)

Barley, M. W. 'Rural Housing in England' in Thirsk (Cambridge, 1967)

Beresford, M. W. *The Lost Villages of England* (1954)

Beresford, M. W. and Hurst, J. G. *Deserted Medieval Villages* (1971)

Beresford, M. W. and St Joseph, J. K. S. *Medieval England: an Aerial Survey* (Cambridge, 1958)

Blair, P. H. *An Introduction to Anglo-Saxon England* (Cambridge, 1960)

Bowen, H. C. *Ancient Fields*, British Association for the Advancement of Science, n.d.

Briggs, M. S. *The English Farmhouse* (1953)

Brunskill, R. W. *Illustrated Handbook of Vernacular Architecture* (1971)

Butzer, K. W. *Environment and Archaeology* (1964)

Childe, V. G. *The Prehistoric Communities of the British Isles* (Edinburgh, 1947)

Chisholm, M. *Rural Settlement and Land Use* (1962)

Clark, J. G. D. *Prehistoric Europe: the Economic Basis* (1952)

Cole, S. *The Neolithic Revolution* (1961)

Collingwood, R. G. and Richmond, I. *The Archaeology of Roman Britain* (1969)

Conzen, M. R. G. 'The Use of Town Plans in the Study of Urban Geography' in Dyos, H. J. (ed.), *The Study of Urban History* (1968)

Darby, H. C. *An Historical Geography of England before 1800* (Cambridge, 1936)

Darby, H. C. *et al. The Domesday Geography of Eastern England* (Cambridge, 1952)

Darby, H. C. *et al. The Domesday Geography of Midland England* (Cambridge, 1954)

Darby, H. C. *et al. The Domesday Geography of Northern England* Cambridge, 1962)

Darby, H. C. *et al. The Domesday Geography of South East England* (Cambridge, 1962)

Darby, H. C. *et al. The Domesday Geography of South West England* (Cambridge, 1967)

Darby, H. C. *The New Historical Geography of England* (Cambridge, 1973)

Denman, D. R. *The Origins of Ownership* (1958)

Finberg, H. P. R. *The Agrarian History of England and Wales*, I–ii, AD 43–1042 (Cambridge, 1972)

Fowler, P. J. *Archaeology and Landscape* (1972)

Fox, Sir C. *The Personality of Britain* (Cardiff, 1952)

Frere, S. *Problems of the Iron Age in Southern Britain*, University of London, Institute of Archaeology, Occasional Paper no. 11 (1961)

Frere, S. *Britannia — a History of Roman Britain* (1967)

Gabel, C. *Analysis of Prehistoric Economic Patterns* (New York, 1967)

Gray, H. L. *English Field Systems* (Harvard, 1915; reprint London, 1959)

Haggett, P. *Locational Analysis in Human Geography* (1965)

Harvey, N. *A History of Farm Buildings in England and Wales* (Newton Abbot, 1970)

Homans, G. C. *English Villagers of the Thirteenth Century* (New York, 1960)

Hoskins, W. G. 'The Domesday Book in the Highland Zone' in *Provincial England* (1963)

Hoskins, W. G. *Fieldwork in Local History* (1967)

Hoskins, W. G. *History from the Farm* (1970)

Hoskins, W. G. *The Making of the English Landscape* (Harmondsworth, 1970)

Houston, J. M. *A Social Geography of Europe* (1963)

Jones, G. R. J. 'The Distribution of Bond Settlements in North-West Wales' *Welsh History Review*, 2, no. 1 (1964), 19–36

Jones, G. R. J. 'The Multiple Estate as a Model Framework for Tracing the Early Stages in the Evolution of Settlement' in *L'Habitat et les Paysages Ruraux d'Europe* (Liège, 1971), pp. 251–67

Jones, G. R. J. 'The Earliest Settlement in Britain' in Baker, A. R. H. and Harley, J. B. (Newton Abbot, 1973), pp. 22–36

Jones Pierce, T. *Mediaeval Welsh Society* — selected essays, ed. J. Beverley Smith (Cardiff, 1972)

Lennard, R. *Rural England, 1086–1135* (Oxford, 1959)

Loyn, H. *Anglo-Saxon England and the Norman Conquest* (1962)

Loyn, H. *The Norman Conquest* (1965)

Maitland, F. W. *Domesday Book and Beyond* (1897, reprint, 1960)

Morris, J. *The Age of Arthur* (1973)

Ordnance Survey, *Map of Roman Britain* (1956)

Ordnance Survey, *Map of Southern Britain in the Iron Age* (1962)

Peate, I. C. *The Welsh House* (Liverpool, 1944)

Pennington, W. *The History of British Vegetation* (1969)

Piggott, S. *The Neolithic Cultures of the British Isles* (Cambridge, 1954)

Piggott, S. *Approach to Archaeology* (1966)

Prince, H. C. 'Real, Imagined and Abstract Worlds of the Past' in Board C. *et al. Progress in Geography* (1970), 3, pp. 1–86

Renfrew, C. *British Prehistory* (1974)

Rivet, A. L. F. *Town and Country in Roman Britain* (1958)

Rivet, A. L. F. *The Iron Age in North Britain* (Edinburgh, 1966)

Rivet, A. L. F. (ed.) *The Roman Villa in Britain* (1969)

Sauer, C. O. *Land and Life*, a selection from the writings of C. O. Sauer, ed. J. Leighley (Berkeley and Los Angeles, 1963)

Sawyer, P. H. *The Age of the Vikings* (1971)

Seebohm. F. *The English Village Community* (1883)

Sheppard, J. 'Pre-Enclosure Field and Settlement Patterns in an English Township', *Geografiska Annaler*, vol. 48, Ser. B. (1966) pt 2, 59–77

Simpson, D. D. A. (ed.) *Economy and Settlement in Neolithic and Early Bronze Age Britain and Europe* (Leicester, 1971)

Slicher van Bath, B. H. *The Agrarian History of Western Europe* AD 500–1850, trans. O. Ordish (1963)

Smith, C. T. *An Historical Geography of Western Europe before 1800* (1967)

Thirsk, J. *The Agrarian History of England and Wales* IV, AD 1500–1640 (Cambridge, 1967)

Thomas, C. (ed.) *Rural Settlement in Roman Britain*, Council for British Archaeology, Research Report no. 7 (1966)

Wainright, F. T. *Archaeology and Place-Names and History* (1962)

Watson, J. W. and Sissons, J. B. (eds) *The British Isles* (1964)

Welldon-Finn, R. *An Introduction to Domesday Book* (1963)

Wood, E. S. *Collins Field Guide to Archaeology in Britain* (1968)

Acknowledgements

A volume such as this necessarily draws heavily upon the work of others and I wish to acknowledge the great debt I owe many colleagues for so freely giving me permission to use their material. Some of the drawings and all of the typing were done in the Geography Department at Durham and I am indebted to both Professor W. B. Fisher for the use of these facilities and to Gerry Donnini, Peter Howe, Derek Hudspeth, Ian Middlemass and Mrs. Suzanne Eckford for their practical assistance. I am grateful for permission to use the following items; to Professor Harry Thorpe for Fig 1; to John Hurst for material used in Figs 2, 25 and 31; to Frank Emery and Mrs Joan Thirsk and Cambridge University Press for material used in Fig 2; to B. K. S. Surveys Ltd. and Durham County Council for Fig 4; to the National Coal Board for Fig 5; to Mrs Pamela Ward and Mrs Alison Donaldson for material in Fig 6; to Aerofilms Ltd. for Figs 7, 35, 37, 38, 39, 40, 44 and 47; to Mr. R. W. Feacham and Edinburgh University Press for material used in Fig 8; to Professor A. L. F. Rivet and Routledge & Kegan Paul for Fig 9. Crown Copyright material is included in Figs 8, 9, 10, 11, 12, and 29; I am grateful to Professor H. C. Darby and Cambridge University Press for material in Figs 13, 14 and 18; Professor G. R. Jones for Fig 15; to Cambridge University Press for Fig 23; to Norman McCord and University of Newcastle for Fig 26; to John Hunt for material used in Figs 2, 25 and 31; to June Sheppard for Fig 30; to the Geographical Magazine for permission to use their drawing in Fig 32; to His Grace the Duke of Northumberland, the Northumberland County Archivist, the Durham County Archivist, the Nottinghamshire County Archivist and Mr J. Fagg of the Department of Palaeography and Diplomatic, Durham University, Dr M. Jarrett and the Editor of *Archaeologia Aeliana* for material incorporated in Fig 34; to Cleveland County Council and Meridian Airmaps Ltd for Fig 36; to R. W. Brunskill for Fig 41; to the Moated Sites Research Group for Fig 43; to Rob Hodgson for Figs 45 and 46; and to the Natural Environment Research Council for support for the work involved in producing Fig 48 as part of a study of pollen diagrams in Weardale. To these and many others I offer my thanks. Finally I must thank Brian Harley and Alan Baker for their patience as editors.

216

Index

Included in this index are all textual references to specific place-names, persons and systematic discussions; excluded are references to counties and other localities, except where these are discussed specifically. Figures in *italics* refer to an illustration on the specified page.

217